Emily Jenkins has a Ph.D in English Literature from Columbia University. She is the co-author of a novel for children, *The Secret Life of Billy's Uncle Myron*, and author of a forthcoming picture book. Her writing has appeared in *The Village Voice*, *Nerve*, *Swing*, *Feed*, *Mademoiselle* and *Glamour*, the anthology *Surface Tension* (Touchstone), and the forthcoming *Letters of Intent* (Free Press). She lives in New York City.

D1151707

tongue first

adventures

in physical

culture

emily jenkins

For my dad, Len Jenkin,
without whose inspiration I would not be a writer

A *Virago* Book

Published by Virago Press 2000
First published by Virago Press 1999

First published in the USA by Henry Holt and Company, Inc.,
New York 1998

A CIP catalogue record for this book is available from the British Library

ISBN 1 86049 755 1

Typeset in Sabon by M Rules
Printed and bound in Great Britain by
Clays Ltd, St Ives plc

Virago Press
A Division of
Little Brown and Company (UK)
Brettenham House
Lancaster Place
London WC2E 7EN

contents

acknowledgments

Darcy Tromanhauser helped me make a proper book out of a collection of essays, laughed at all my jokes, and edited with amazing clear-sightedness. Alessandra Bocco saw me through publication with enthusiasm, creativity, and hot pink fishnets. Everyone at Holt has taken tremendous trouble—thanks. I am hugely indebted to my agent, Lydia Wills, for her canny representation of this project (and for some gorgeous bras), and to the people at Artists Agency for their help. Clifford Harris critiqued my first draft with patience and insight. Hilary Liftin has been a wonderfully consistent advocate and critic. Ned Block, Susan Carey, Meg Daly, Ian Kerner, Kate Meyer, Rob Moss, and Amy Schlegel lent critical eyes at various stages. Jason Schmidt took foxy pictures of me on a bad hair day, which is a hard thing to do.

Mona Fafarman, Kate Hildebrandt, Steven Johnson, and Matthew Payne helped me in more ways than one. Thanks to Marjorie Abrams, Jason Bagdade, Jonathan Bing, Sarah Benolken, Aaron Bernstein, Jason Blum, Raoul and Phyllis Bott, Matt Buckley, Jim Cain, Tom Comet, Ariella Evanzehev, Christine Fasano, Evelyn Frank Friedman, Little Gloria, Miriam and Marcy

Goldsmith, John Goulian, Kathryn Haber, Erik Hahn, Helen Houlder, Josiah, Neil Levi, Eric Liftin, Catherine Martinez, Mary Martinez, Laura Stempel Mumford, Harriet Nadler, Polly Noonan, Denise Parker, Alexander Ruas, Betsey Schmidt, Richie Scoffier, Martin Simon, ThEnigma, Sonya Tillson, Wendy Todaro, Alexa Robinson, Lily Wang, Josh Warner, Edith Wool, Dick Zigun and his staff at Coney Island USA, my aerobics students and fellow staff, the members of my internet newsgroups, my curious and clever writing students, and the wonderfully chic, late Elizabeth Engdahl. Elizabeth Wurtzel shared her contacts with me most generously. Charlotte Sheedy, Neeti Madan, and Regula Noetzli got me started and worked hard on my behalf. My professors at Columbia were very supportive, in particular Martin Meisel, Franco Moretti, and George Stade. Daniel Aukin loved me when I was bald and sleep deprived. He has been utterly great and supportive, willing to read and comment at very short notice, very many times, and I can not thank him enough. Thanks especially to my family: Johanna Jenkins (who lent her stories), Len Jenkin, Joan Carey, Ramona Vitkevich, Beatrice Jenkin (who provided so many introductions), and Zoe Jenkin.

tongue first

stick out your tongue

my first kiss, sex kiss, the kiss that felt like a first kiss, was donated to me at a pitifully late age by a tall boy named Ace. He was wearing nothing but a toga made out of the American flag. We frenched each other in a yard littered with beer cans, the sounds of frat rock thumping from the party inside. The red, white, and blue draped over his skinny white arms, his spiky punk-rock haircut, his near-naked body shivering in the moonlight—that Marlboro-tasting kiss has lasted me for years.

Truth is, it was a pretty bad performance all around. I had almost no idea what I was doing, and Ace went about the whole procedure tongue first. Too much drool, too dizzy drunk. But it marked in me a liberation, a reevaluation of my body and how it functioned in the world. I began to think of myself as a girl who kissed boys. I had a body with desires that might get fulfilled. That's cool, I thought. Who else can I kiss?

Your body is the vehicle for your wildest adventures. It will speed you through fondlings in the backseat, jumps off the high dive, orgasms, and tequila shots, hurtle you through three-point baskets, chocolate mousse cakes, and surges of adrenaline. Stick out your tongue and taste the wind as it goes past.

Of course, you can't get out if the motion starts to sicken you. You can't even brake. None of us can, because the body is also a prison in which we are forced to live out our days. You are captive forever in your skin. It will wrinkle, scar, blemish, and bleed. It will rebel against you and defy your attempts to control it. When your mind is still buzzing with kinetic restlessness, your body will be sagging with age or disease. You are trapped by your sex, trapped by your pain, trapped by your physical limitations.

There are many books about the prison of the body—books about child abuse and eating disorders and drug addiction and AIDS—and they have been extremely valuable and interesting to me, but this is not one of them. I am too interested in dressing up, getting off, and getting high to rattle my chains for long. Nor is this a book of personal growth. I am not here to tell you what I've learned, how accepting and understanding I've become now that I've had some new experiences and abandoned all my preconceptions about body and mind. And soul. I haven't abandoned them at all. What I *am* doing is identifying those preconceptions, interrogating them, and situating them in a cultural context.

What fascinates me is the contradiction—how the body is both a prison *and* a vehicle for adventure. That contradiction shapes our culture and our behavior. Think of the weirdest bodily practices, but also of the most ordinary daily physical rituals. Both are worth investigating. I want to understand nudist colonies. Bald women. Women who are really men. Sensory deprivation. Heroin addicts. Leather underwear. Also plucked eyebrows. Afternoon naps. Boxer shorts. Good-bye kisses. Happy hour. Aerobics class. Here we are, squeezing blobs of congealed oil from our pores and reading Dr. Ruth, or tying our lovers to the bedposts and shooting up, but never looking any closer at what we're doing unless it's with the help of a twelve-step program. What is really going on?

Our sense of our bodies is shaped by various social institutions. In school, we learn sex education and sportsmanship. In the family, we learn about toilet training, table manners, and taboos. In hospitals, we learn a very particular way of analyzing and treating illness. Reading magazines and watching movies, we learn what appearances are socially acceptable. But that doesn't mean we swallow our lessons without protest, and it doesn't mean there aren't many smaller institutions that might offer alternatives. What it does mean is that we are taught to live by a lot of invisible institutional rules, and whether we rebel against them or adhere to them rigidly, we are defining ourselves in relation to them.

Everyone is living in and negotiating through a network of these rules. My aim is to identify some of them, and the functions they serve in our society. We walk a twisted middle road between extremes that both frighten and fascinate us. In a way, we are building defenses, protecting ourselves from exposure, illness, sexual rejection, rape, failure, or simply from difference in ourselves or in others. Fear can be a major factor in creating culture. But with one turn in the road we find ourselves flirting with those same risks from which we used to protect ourselves. Thrills, conquests, achievement, and enlightenment beckon. A tattoo, for example, can be either a violation or a reclaiming of the body. The same cosmetics that bring a woman in line with social norms of beauty can also catapult her into an extreme glamour that borders on parody. An altered state of consciousness can lead to psychotic delusions or to spiritual understanding.

Working on this project, I went into things *tongue first*. To see how they tasted. So the title doesn't refer only to an inept brand of kissing practiced by Ace and various other make-out artists I've encountered—it tells you my approach to writing about culture. I confronted many of my own fears, and did more than flirt with the beckoning thrills. I explored a range of physical experiences, as you can see from the table of contents. From "Flying" through altered states to "Decorating" my body and "Fucking" as much as possible, from "Revealing" myself in public to trying alternative "Healing" practices and finally to investigating people's fear of their bodies "Rebelling," I paid microscopic attention to my sensations and my environments. I was Rolfed. I went to strip shows. I went to freak shows. I got a tattoo. I tried out techniques I read about in sex manuals, and I shaved my head. I also pushed myself up against others whose relationships to their bodies fascinated me: octogenarians, an out-of-body healer, heroin users, drag queens, a blue man. Inevitably, their attitudes about physicality taught me something about my own.

My body and its experiences are probably pretty average. I'm not a drug addict or an anorexic or a prostitute, and I never have been. My vices are of the beer and Oreo variety. My traumas have been limited to a broken thumb, some boring sex, and a distressing quantity of orthodontic work involving headgear and rubber bands. I bite my fingernails. I teach aerobics, but not so often as I used to now that I'm nearing thirty. I am white. My hair is blond (but it wasn't always). I don't floss. I say I do, but I don't. My medicine cabinet has four different smelly lotions for muscle aches in it. I sleep with men, when I can find a nice one with high cheekbones and an IQ to match.

But as I write this, trying to define my body to an outsider, I know it is much more complicated than that. I haven't explained or admitted what elements my behavior shares with drug addiction, anorexia, and prostitution—how walking along the borders of those experiences holds a fascination and repulsion for me. I haven't told you what I mean by "sleep with men" or how often it happens. I haven't told you why those lotions are in my medicine cabinet, why their eucalyptus smell makes me feel safe, why I put them on when I do. I haven't told you why I prance around in aerobics class when Olympian Jackie Joyner-Kersee is my hero. So when I say I sleep with men, or I drink too much beer, I have not yet explained what is really going on with my body. There is so much more to say.

Magazines are always talking about how each person has a body image, but they don't make sense to me. They say anorexics see cellulite at ninety-eight pounds. Bodybuilders who were scrawny as children never get over feeling like weaklings. Perfectly normal men are sure their penises are smaller than everyone else's. I understand the distorted images these people are talking about. I just don't see why they limit themselves to one.

Some days my body is matronly, shelter to a housewife in slacks who spends her afternoons making Jell-O molds in Far Rockaway. My belly rounds out in expectation of childbirth and my shoulders curve forward with years of scrubbing. Other days it is frail: I can see the bones in my hands and feet; my shins are sharp; my back aches; blue veins ooze across my skin like a grandmother's. Still others find me feeling like a superhero: thighs bulging with muscles, shoulders spread broad, the swollen veins becoming part of my athlete's physique.

My body is not the same from day to day. Not even from minute to minute. I look at myself in the mirror and think, "This lump of flesh and fluids, this is where I live." Sometimes it seems like home, sometimes more like a cheap motel near Pittsburgh.

The body is the single place no one can ever leave. It is permanent, yet fragile and mercurial. Its distortions, anxieties, ecstasies, and discomforts all influence a person's interaction with the people who service it. Contact with my dentist is markedly different from contact with a manicurist, masseuse, acupuncturist, drug dealer, prostitute, or exercise instructor. The substances and products we put into our bodies also reveal our attitudes toward our corporeal selves. Beer says one thing, mai-tais another, smack something else entirely. The clothes and cosmetics we wear—lipstick, wigs, old clothes, the fake breasts of a female impersonator—can shift our perceptions of ourselves. Bodily rites reveal our hidden assumptions about ourselves and our physiques: Why do we walk with our arms around our lovers? Why do we fuck in the missionary position? Are all those people taking up yoga reliving their childhoods? Why do men like striptease more than women? And what happens if we take everything off and run around naked?

Oscar Wilde once said, "Those who see any difference between soul and body have neither." Although I've used several metaphors here to talk about the way the soul inhabits the body, in essence I agree with Wilde. Body and soul *are* one, but it's more like the slippery union of oil and vinegar than any ultimate fusion. Certain experiences I've had while writing this book made me feel I could pour the vinegar off the top and into a different jar. Others shook the ingredients together so hard it felt like they couldn't possibly separate.

When I was small I used to draw all over my face with colored markers. My mother let me, because, really, there was nothing she could do. I could not be stopped. I would do it after preschool until she'd plunk me into a hot bath before dinner. Drawing on my cheeks in the mirror was very difficult, and the pictures never came out quite how I meant them to, but somehow I was getting what was in my head onto my body. I was trying to make myself look the way I felt inside, reconciling the physical with the mental, and vice versa. *Tongue First* is an extension of those ink-stained afternoons.

flying

craving oblivion
....

Sleep is my archenemy. My Uriah Heep. It calls me, pulls me in, embraces me, and will not let me go. It wastes my time and casts its soporific thrall over my groggy mornings and woozy afternoons. My need for it slows my work, dampens my sex drive, and drags me home from lunch meetings to fall into its arms. "I'll nourish you," it whispers to me, "rejuvenate you, heal you." My two warm cats, my four fat pillows, and that old patch-work next to an open window, curtains floating on a cool breeze: "Come here!" they hiss together, voices carrying softly to my kitchen. "Come to bed with us. Come, come. You've worn your-self out. You might have the flu. Doesn't your throat feel sore and swollen? Didn't you write two pages today? You deserve some rest. You do, you do."

My head feels heavy and my breathing is shallow and thick. It's two in the afternoon. I succumb under protest, turn off the phone, and bring my work to bed: book, glasses, pencil, Post-it notes, and paper clips.

"At last!" cries my body as it sinks into the downy pile: cozy, stress-free. I'm asleep in minutes, I stay so for hours. A liquid state, sweet and soft, feet tangled in the covers, clothes crushed. Then I stagger awake, dizzy, sorry. Time wasted. Stumble about, smoky brain. Lie down again for a minute. Roll over and look out the window. It's getting dark.

I fumble for my glasses, bent out of shape under the pillow. Propped up in front of my computer in sleep-rumpled clothing, I dig for buried thoughts. When I find them, they are sticky, thickly coated by an oily, oozing residue left behind by my nap. I stumble to the kitchen and stare into the fridge, then the cupboard. Not hungry. I curl up on the couch.

"Come back!" calls my comforter, agent of my nemesis. "Isn't it cold out there in the living room? Lie down for just a little longer."

"Back off!" I cry from my fetal position on the love seat, but my brain aches to shut down again, to sink back into the comfort tempting me from the bedroom.

I fear the seductive, time-sucker sleep and I fear my sleeping self, the alter ego created by the pleasures of rest. I become slothful, unproductive, antisocial. It is a daily fight, and the enemy is winning. My standard weapons are feeble: caffeine, exercise, a well-rounded diet. They fail me again and again. Three cups of coffee and the nap still calls me. Cold air and activity only make me happier to sink into the haven of my bed when I finally get home. Yesterday, I got up at eight, went back to bed at ten; woke at noon, went back to bed for another hour at one-thirty; was asleep again by eleven and slept through the alarm this morning.

People across the country swallow daily melatonin to combat insomnia, but there's no legal drug that will keep me awake. I test negative for everything: anemia, hepatitis, mononucleosis. This is not chronic fatigue syndrome. It is not depression. I don't have a diagnosis. And I'm not alone. Forty percent of healthy young adults in one survey met the criteria for "excessive daytime sleepiness." They performed poorly on tests designed to measure alertness, and the cause was thought to be chronic sleep deprivation. But why must that be the case? Perhaps those healthy young adults, like me, have a craving that doesn't go away even when they get their eight hours right on schedule. Perhaps some of them, too, have a nemesis and no medicine with which to poison him.

If conscious perception is the norm, sleep certainly qualifies as an altered state. J. G. Ballard calls it "an eight-hour peep show of infantile erotica." Like booze or drugs, sleep offers relief from the tyranny of consciousness and the boredom of reality. Like cigarettes and caffeine, its pleasures are part of our daily routine. And like most altered states, it exerts an insidious pull on the susceptible among us. It is easy to abuse. Going up against sleep is a fight against temptation, against an addictive activity that I cannot live without, even if I kick the habit. The lure of the nap is like the call of the binge for the bulimic; she cannot quit altogether because she has to eat to live. Once she tastes, she cannot stop.

I set out to stay awake for two nights or more. Cold turkey. I'll weaken sleep's hold on me by eluding it completely, though temporarily, and replace the altered state I crave with its opposite—the high of sleep deprivation. I outfit myself: one pound of Ethiopian coffee, a borrowed CD collection, three videos, a pile of work, my tax forms, and a computer game. Also a sex partner, my beloved younger man, who insists on leaving at 2:00 A.M. although I beg him to stay.

The night is speedy. I'm eating candy and drinking the coffee and building simulated cities that are under attack by giant spider-monsters and hurricanes. I'm ignoring my taxes. I've got some rock music, and a little television in the background, and I'll get to my work pretty soon, but first I just want to build a marina and see if that improves citizen satisfaction. It doesn't. I shower three or four times, starting the day repeatedly. "I've got it now!" cries my internal clock each time. "It's morning!"

Almost before I know it, and certainly before my citizens vote to give a parade in my honor, a hazy blue creeps into the sky, turns orange, and I realize I am seeing the sun rise. How zippy. I go outside for a minute to watch, but I'm too edgy to pay attention. All I can think about is whether there are any chocolate-espresso cordials left, whether the residents of my city will object to my recent tax increase, whether there's anything on TV at this hour, whether my skin will dry out from so many washings. I feel dirty, sort of clammy and sour, even though I know I'm clean.

It is pretty amazing to me how easily I have replaced my regular vice, sleep, with others. It is not so hard to forgo the indulgence I usually crave when I'm allowing so many others I usually deny myself. In a single night, I've acquired a ton of bad habits. I particularly favor the cheap stimulations that keep America running all week: chocolate, pastry, coffee, video games, movies featuring naked blondes. My usual pursuits seem boring, soporific. The idea of vegetables repulses me, reading would only send me to sleep, drawing or writing requires too much effort. Even highbrow indulgences have lost their appeal: I don't want lobster, or the ballet, or fine wine, much as these things usually tempt me. It is a fast-paced, shallow entertainment I seek, one that mimics my caffeine high. The programming on MTV suddenly meets my innermost needs, as does the food at McDonalds. My eyes may ache, my skin break out, my teeth rot, and my stomach churn, but I am fulfilled.

Going without sleep has brought me in sync with the products disseminated for mass America. Normally, I like these things in a mild sort of way—they're pleasant, but consuming a lot of them doesn't much interest me. Today, awake for forty hours, they jolt me with a pleasure that is partly the shock of recognition: somehow this food, these images, are just what I want. No longer will I wonder why the night watchman doesn't read a book, why the mother of a wakeful infant watches such trash on TV, why the sex workers in my neighborhood are always eating candy. The body on overdrive does not know what's best for it, and the mind attached cannot be probed too deeply or it will collapse upon itself like a punctured ball. Are we a nation that just needs a good nap? Would we return to reading *David Copperfield* aloud in the evenings and eating good nutritious food if only we got a proper night's sleep? Perhaps a nationwide afternoon siesta would solve the problem of our country's cultural bankruptcy.

By midafternoon the next day I become weirdly conscious that I cannot look anyone in the eye. The world seems out of focus and I have to force myself to concentrate and respond to what people are saying to me. I am unable to make decisions. Do I want to have dinner with my beloved younger man and his parents, who are in town only this weekend of all weekends from across the Atlantic Ocean? I don't know. It's cold outside. But I want to see him. But I'm not exactly up to it. But I want to get out of the house. But I'm so tired. What should I do? What should I do? What should I wear?

No, really, what should I wear? I can't get dressed. One unexpected side effect of sleep deprivation is a dissociation with and even hostility toward my body. I have made a decision—not to sleep—that defines my body's needs as forbidden. Not only its needs (because, after all, I probably *need* only six or seven hours a night) but also its comforts (the other five hours I usually take) are to be denied. What surprises me is how big a difference even a temporary commitment to such a hostile attitude makes in my feelings about myself. I feel removed from any other needs I would usually have: I am barely hungry, I don't want to have sex, I'm thirsty and let myself get dehydrated. And for the first time, probably since high school, I am horrified when I look in the mirror. Not responding to my body's needs has made me hate my physical self. I see flaws everywhere: fat legs, bad haircut, saggy boobs, bony shoulders, patchy cheeks. I am distinctly unhappy in this skin.

So I go to the dinner, where everyone is very nice to me, only my artichoke comes with this disgusting egg sauce and I can't eat it and I quiz the younger man's friend about a catastrophe in his love life that happened only yesterday and then I drink some wine and show the poison ivy on my legs to some nice computer programmer man who is a friend of their family's and Oh God I hope he didn't see my underwear and then I think I better have some espresso and I tell this girl who works for *Ms.* that I don't ever read it even though I really sometimes do but I just can't concentrate on feminism now and the younger man looks strained and I wonder if I'm misbehaving and I'm certain I wore the wrong dress entirely. Then I kiss everyone good-bye and thank those nice parents oh so much and skitter off to a birthday party for my ex-boyfriend, which is full of crazy literati and people who went to Harvard.

The party is a crush, but it fits my mood. My whole body has a hum, like a stereo left on with no music. I talk to a notorious musician and her agent for a while, until the musician says loudly that she has loads of personal things to tell the agent but she can't do it in present company. I shove off. It is entirely unclear to me whether they were rude or whether I was being ludicrously boring. A poet in an angora sweater calls me by the name of my ex-boyfriend's new girlfriend, but I don't care. Or rather, I hate her forever and put a hex on her. I cheerfully attack a woman I know, demanding to meet the significant other I've heard so much about, but it turns out she's just decided to leave him. Instead of recognizing my faux pas and atoning properly, I become hypnotized by a flat-chested stripper who has miraculously appeared to gyrate in front of my ex, birthday boy, who is sitting rather shamefacedly in an armchair. When she is down to her leopard-print underwear, she stops and stands there as if not sure what to do next. He gets up and the two of them dance a stilted two-step, his arm around her gingerly as if she might crack. It is so surreal that I wonder if I am having a kind of NC-17 vision that reveals something profound about the nature of our past relationship. Now the musician is making out in the kitchen with a man who is not her main squeeze, and I ogle them blatantly, nudging my friend Jeff to see if he's shocked. That Uriah Heep, my exhaustion, is at me again from a new angle. I think I'm awake, but I've lost all sense of decorum.

Being sleep deprived is not just like being drunk, although it's certainly a cheap way to lose your inhibitions. It's more like having the floor crumble beneath you; your tastes teeter off balance, your body seems soiled and displaced, the principles on which social behavior is grounded slip out of grasp. Around midnight, my vision begins to blur. Everything fuses into blobs of color. I catch a cab home and install myself in front of the computer. I struggle with my taxes, fiddle around with my city (still no parade), make coffee, and dance around to some disco. I take another shower.

And now, I have to confess, the next fourteen hours (4:00 A.M. to 6:00 P.M.) are a total blank. I should have taken notes. I've got no idea whatsoever what happened next. I swear I swear I swear I didn't go to sleep. I know at some point I saw John Travolta on an old *American Bandstand* episode and he wore a red turtleneck sweater and a gold chain and lip-synched a love song called "I'm Gonna Let Her In." I know I thought of a number of dirty interpretations for the lyrics. I know I didn't once go out of doors because I couldn't bear seeing all those happy, perky people doing errands and things. I know I ate leftover Chinese food and that I was unsure whether my head was properly attached to my body. I probably took a few more showers. The rest is a mystery.

At six, I am wakeful again, the stupor shaken off. The younger man comes over wearing a suit. He's been at a family reunion. I tell him I feel absolutely fine, and how was his day? I am operating on a sort of synthetic energy, a manic cheer that has its roots in self-denial. I don't ask him to rub my shoulders and make me another pot of espresso, nor do I complain to him about sleep licking at my heels every moment. I cannot kick it away; its fawning threat is always lapping at me with lascivious enthusiasm. I just ask the younger man about himself and give evasive, happy answers to his inquiries. I have no needs and no thoughts that I am aware of, only trivialities: John Travolta and leftover chocolate. We cook some noodles and watch part of a movie on TV, but I stare at the screen like one of the undead. I think I am even drooling.

Eventually the younger man notices, and gently reminds me

that he wants to sleep at his house because he's got to be at work early in the morning. Maybe I could get my things together and we'll go across town before I get too tired? I say all right, and begin to set the kitchen in order, but before long I burst out crying. How can I possibly go to his house when I've been awake for fifty-eight hours? How can I get the dishes washed and put pajamas and pills and things in a backpack and turn out the lights and go down the stairs and find a cab and get in the cab and then climb five flights to his apartment where I'll have to talk to his roommates and actually speak in sentences? And then use a bathroom where I don't have my favorite soap and brush my teeth with the wrong kind of toothpaste and have to look at his clock radio glowing in the dark? What about my needs, huh? Why can't he be more sensitive? All he thinks about is what he wants and all I do is give give give and I just can't possibly accommodate him anymore and he just needs to grow around and smell the coffee that's been right under his nose all along only he was up on a high horse that wouldn't drink any! Copious tears follow.

Of course the younger man offers to sleep right here, right now, says it doesn't really matter if he goes home at all. Is a good sport, a kind darling of a younger man who I just don't appreciate enough and who puts up with all my insane projects and is simply ridiculously handsome and has the cutest little accent and wouldn't he like some chocolate because someday I'll make it up to him, really I will, it's just that Heep is after me and I'm losing ground.

I stumble to the bed and fall into the arms of my addiction with abandon. It draws me in heavily, smothering me with obsequious love and coating my frayed nerves with strokes of its oily tongue. I've been up for nearly sixty hours: the best of all excuses to sleep late.

I know a guy named Grant who once stayed awake for five days. Grant is a Grateful Dead fan and reformed acidhead. He is also an excellent photographer. He's only eighteen, and he kept awake with his friends when he was at summer camp. There was nothing else to do there, he says. He'd heard from his older brother that extreme sleep deprivation results in hallucination, so he convinced his friends they should all stay up together—telling stories, looking at the sky, comparing their sensations.

For Grant, staying up was not a fight against the potent addictiveness of sleep; it was almost the opposite—an attempt to replicate the psychedelic highs he enjoyed. I think he managed this superhuman feat of endurance because he wasn't escaping oblivion. He was chasing it. His manic cheer did not have the roots in self-denial that mine did: Grant was running *after* an altered state, whereas I was running *away* from one that tempted me. Therefore he had the drive to push his body harder than I did mine. But it also occurs to me that Grant managed to stay awake so long because he had the company of his fellow campers, since an altered state in solitude is very much different from sharing one with your friends.

Grant and I talked a lot about contexts for mood alteration. He was studying the scientific uses of LSD, particularly what therapists did with it in the early years. They would go out to cabins in the woods and trip with their patients, using the acid as a kind of shortcut to the unconscious that would speed up therapy. Supposedly, seven years worth of analysis could be accomplished in something like seven days. It's very interesting to me that a legitimate social institution such as psychotherapy once approved acid trips; later, the therapeutic context would be succeeded by the countercultural rainbow of dancers at Dead concerts and the mysticism of Timothy Leary.

Grant's group of friends provided the same kind of support for his altered state that a therapist or a Woodstock festival would for an acid tripper—a social sanction. That sanction reduces the fear an altered reality might induce. Grant's friends could validate his experience, either directly (Whoa, man. Look at those clouds moving around. See that?) or indirectly, by sitting next to him and staying awake. On the other hand, I propelled my sleep-deprived self into social situations where it was not only abnormal to do what I was doing, but in which I was particularly invested in behaving well—dinner with my boyfriend's parents and a party for my ex. I wasn't really willing to go all the way: when I saw myself deviating further and further from social norms—from good manners, from the ability to concentrate, from a friendly familiarity with my body—I succumbed to my chosen oblivion. Sleep is an unusual altered state in that way. It supports, rather than disrupts, so-called normal behavior. Get enough sleep and you'll be a happy, functioning person.

Very often you do something to your body—stay up all night, drink a martini, snort a line, float in an isolation tank—and something tangible and dramatic happens to your sense of self and your vision of the world. The average person experiences this modified vision at a few points in her life. Some people experience it every day. For recreational indulgents, an altered state involves a flirtation with extremes of consciousness. Social institutions allow this kind of flirtation by establishing behavioral norms for the experience and situating it in a community: the ritual of a bong hit before dinner in the dorm room, the congregation of bitter exiles smoking cigarettes in the cold outside the office, the Bloody Mary buzz of the brunch crowd, or the club culture that sanctions crystal meth and Special K. There is pleasure and pain in these flirtations, and we toy with the idea of losing control, with the possibility of succumbing to addiction or madness.

the cocktail hour
• •

the party I went to in my sleep-deprived state was not quite a cocktail party. People drank cocktails, but they mixed them by squinting their eyes at plastic cups to see if the right amount of gin was in there before adding tonic. They sloshed them about with inordinate amounts of ice and switched to beer halfway through the evening. There was what my grandmother calls "cocktail chow," but it might also have been mistaken for snack food—cookies and taco chips. There were cigarettes laid out in candy dishes.

Parties like that are the sort of parties you have when you're on the verge of admitting you're an adult, only you haven't yet. Adulthood might mean descent into the staid, quiet consumption of a glass of wine as the only indulgence in a life where bedtime is at ten-thirty and the diet is limited to lettuce and poached chicken breasts; or it might mean descent into the formalized decadence of the cocktail hour, which made glorious the alcoholism of our forefathers. Either way, it means descent.

What I'm saying isn't really true in a practical way so much as it is in an ideological one. There's certainly more to adulthood than sober dietary asceticism or ritualized inebriation. Lots of people, old and young, don't like cocktail parties, and will certainly never adapt themselves to the 6:00 P.M. onset of the cocktail hour. Even more people never had ancestors attached to such an expensive, middle-class habit. But as *ideas* about alcohol consumption, both sobriety and cocktail drinking have enduring social power, and the party I went to was in dialogue with them.

Nick Charles embodies the idea of cocktail drinking. He chugs martinis like sweet lemonade. He gets up in the middle of the night for a whiskey and soda. He hints publicly that he is unfaithful to his wife, Nora, younger and better looking than he by half. In the movies based on Dashiell Hammett's *The Thin Man*, William Powell plays Nick, cocktail drinker incomparable. We are meant to find him devastatingly attractive, dashing, and suave. Objectively, though, he is rather skinny and wrinkled, besides which he has no chin to speak of. The charm he exudes is somehow linked to his hollow leg. We are meant to love him for his daring party spirit, his disregard for convention, his penchant for embracing beautiful young women—in short, for his alcoholism.

Thirties audiences first met Nick as he shook cocktails to dance rhythms. A dry martini must always be sloshed to the beat of a

waltz, a Manhattan to the fox-trot, a Bronx to two-step time.
Drinking a glass of milk nearly kills him: he must immediately follow it with an alcoholic "antidote." A day without a drink is so rare
it's worth reporting: in *After the Thin Man,* Nora quips to a relative
on the phone, "We had a lovely trip. Nick was sober in Kansas
City!" And at the sound of a cocktail shaker, he comes like a dog.

These days, the idea of the unrepentant alcoholic is a nostalgic
one. Alcohol dependence is not something to joke about. It is a subject for sensitive, artistic dramas about suicide or recovery. Dean
Martin, famous as an incorrigible, adorable lush ("You are not
drunk if you can lie on the floor without holding on"), has no contemporary counterpart in these days of Betty Ford centers and
celebrity confessions. Nick Charles has been bested as a cheerful,
heroic addict only by Cheech and Chong. No happy-go-lucky crack
user has sprung up to replace them in the comedies of the nineties.
No cocaine addict ever gets the girl. Devotion to the ultimate buzz
ceased to be amusing sometime during the Reagan administration.

But while Cheech and Chong exist solely for the pleasures
involved in the importation and inhalation of marijuana, swallowing martinis is only a sideline for Nick. He is, after all, a detec-
tive. Although he's the best drinker there ever was, it's just a
hobby, which tells us something about the way cocktail drinking
functions in our culture as opposed to other kinds of drug consumption. Nick never has to admit how badly he needs a drink,
because he's never without one. Alcohol is legal, so he needn't
devote his life to pursuing his drug. He might dream of the perfect
martini, but a decent one is available nearly anywhere he goes.

The primary institution upholding alcohol use is the bar. After
that is the cocktail hour. Whether it be done with the grown-up
purity of the martini, or the childish finesse of brandy Alexanders
and piña coladas with miniature parasols, cocktail hour is a ritual
of consumption unlike any other in our culture. The ornate
process of concocting a cocktail differentiates before-dinner drinking from other kinds of alcohol use, and from the rituals
surrounding other drugs. The psychic energy involved in creating

and consuming a Park Lane (gin, lemon juice, grenadine, orange juice, and apricot brandy) distinguishes the unspoken alcoholism of a dashing young Wooster from the sordid lurching of some old geezer who's forgotten himself. Cocktail mixing relieves drinking of its cares and worries, of its bad reputation and its sordid past. The process remains somehow untainted by the intoxicating nature of the product: Nick Charles has his philosophy of dance rhythms, and even a child can be taught to make a good martini. Auntie Mame, in the film of that name, is another embodiment of the ideal cocktail drinker, and she uses her young nephew Patrick to mix her drinks. Mame's idea of breakfast is black coffee and a sidecar, and Patrick's martinis are so dry he pours the vermouth out after sloshing it around in the glass. "Would you care for an olive?" he asks a guest. "Auntie Mame says olives take up too much room in such a little glass."

Patrick's skill affirms the innocent fun of mixing drinks. Mame has simply shown him the adult version of the chemistry set. When the guest questions the wisdom of teaching a child to make martinis, Mame replies, "Knowledge is power!" In the world of the cocktail, drinking is an art, or it is a folly—anything but a problem. Park Lane drinkers in their patio chairs are blocks away from the drunk on the street corner with his bottle of cheap gin. Far enough to feel safe.

Mixing cocktails is investing creative energy in something you are actually planning on putting inside your body, or which you expect your friends to put inside theirs. But unlike cooking dinner, it has the added thrill of potential toxicity. You are dealing with strong potions, even flammable ones. It's possible you will poison yourself and your guests, or you might make everyone ecstatically tipsy on your clever new version of the Zombie. You can then hand this recipe down to your children and your children's children, along with Grandma Pinkie's special eggnog mixture and Uncle Bonzo's buttered rum. There is also a pleasure in customizing drinks. One person prefers his Kamikaze strong and iced, another likes hers neat with extra triple sec. No other drug or drinking ritual is so much about catering to each consumer's individual preferences, and doing so in the comfort of home.

In 1951, *Harper's* columnist Bernard DeVoto published *The Hour,* a book that celebrated the cocktail hour while contemptuously denigrating many of its most enthusiastic participants. Rum drinkers, eggnog drinkers, even gimlet drinkers are subjects of his scorn, as are those who indulge in clever cocktail napkins or venture to make their drinks from recipes. The Manhattan, he says, is an offense against piety. "There are only two cocktails," writes DeVoto: a slug of whiskey and a dry martini. DeVoto blames the degeneration of drinking on the corruptive influence of the Bronx, fashionable favorite of the gay nineties Park Row set. The Bronx is a sort of baby's martini—gin and vermouth sweetened by a considerable amount of orange juice. "It spawned the still more regrettable Orange Blossom," DeVoto complains. "Infection spread and there were worse compounds on the same base . . . then, swiftly came the Plague and the rush of the barbarians in its wake, and all the juices of the orchard went into cocktails . . . it was not bathtub gin that came close to destroying the American stomach, nervous system, and aspiration toward a subtler life. Not the gin but the fruit juices so basely mixed with it: all pestilential, all gangrenous, and all vile."

Sweet liquors, says DeVoto, are drunk in a regressive fantasy, "a sad hope of regaining childhood's joy at the soda fountain . . . An ice-cream soda can set a child's feet in the path that ends in grenadine, and when you see someone drinking Drambuie, crème de menthe, Old Tom gin, or all three stirred together and topped off with a maraschino cherry, you must remember that he got that way from pineapple milkshakes long ago. Pity him if you like but treat him as you would a carrier of typhoid. For if the republic ever comes crashing down, the ruin will have been wrought by this lust for sweet drinks."

He is not entirely joking about the decline of the republic resulting from whimsical cocktails. Though he does not say so explicitly, DeVoto implies that the subtle combination of cold gin and vermouth create a short-lived paradise of taste that embodies the fleeting artistic impulses that separate the civilized from the barbarians. The delicate merger of elements (martinis deteriorate if premixed and kept in the fridge) symbolizes a harmonious marriage that would collapse if subjected to the intrusion of a bumbling third party such as olives or orange juice.

Forty-five years after DeVoto wrote his treatise, the tradition by which we trip downstairs in evening clothes for a snozzle of something about sixish is almost gone, though its specter haunts us. Our parties still define themselves in relation to that age of boozy chic, but they never re-create it. Abandoned after the sixties gave birth to dry martini candy and the push-button Cocktailmatic, forlorn despite the valiant efforts of Tanqueray's Mr. Jenkins ads to breathe life into the rites of upper-class sousing, cocktail hour has been replaced (or nearly so) by what is probably an older ritual: happy hour, or the after-work drink. Same hour, same drug. Different class, different poison. At happy hour, no one drinks so much as a whiskey sour. Forget Grasshoppers (crème de menthe, white crème de cacao, heavy cream) and Copacabanas (too frightening to describe—I can only tell you they involve pineapple juice and chocolate syrup). It's all wine and beer, vodka tonics and Screwdrivers, scotch on the rocks.

It's possible that the preference for the basic bar is a move toward purity. The death of the ladies' cocktail does imply a return to simplicity, the loss of the whimsy DeVoto could never manage to squash in that golden age of mixed drinks. But as Peter Mayle observes, the discriminating alcoholic's palate is also disappearing: "Beers are lighter, spirits are paler and drier, wine is being contaminated with soda water, and sales of taste-free vodka are booming. Ice is used with such reckless abandon that . . . the serious drinker now risks frostbite of the tongue more than cirrhosis of the liver." Thanks to AA and other sobriety movements of the late twentieth century, cocktail hour—a social institution that encourages excess—gives way to happy hour, a forum for the public demonstration of self-discipline.

DeVoto and his cronies drank in their living rooms. Their bar-tending guides recommend assuming guests will drink four cocktails apiece, and if dinner is served, two cocktails, two glasses of wine, and one liqueur and two highballs after. These days we drink in public. At 6:00 P.M. people I know are more likely to have a beer after work with the guy from marketing than to drink vodka at home with friends. The public forum means we have to ask a stranger for what we want, and we have to pay for it—both good ways of keeping a lust for liquor under control. We ask for simple drinks, drinks in which we taste the alcohol, so the sweet-ness of a Singapore Sling won't fool us into having more than is proper. Anyone who drank four Long Island iced teas before seven-thirty in the manner of Nick Charles would be rushed by his caring friends to the next meeting of Alcoholics Anonymous.

Why defend the pretentious perambulations of a bunch of highly paid, overeducated boozers who are edging around their addictions by means of fancy recipes and expensive liqueurs? What good are frivolous pink cocktails reeking of maraschino cherries? Or, for that matter, what use is the self-aware purity of a dry martini? Cocktail hour, some will say, is nothing but a snobby and pointless justification of numbing the senses, a social institution we are better off without. We should all just stick to an honest glass of beer or whiskey sometime after dinner when we've got a little food in our stomachs. This shift toward moder-ation—public consumption, the basic bar—is a healthy one. Alcohol doesn't need the shrine of the cocktail hour deifying its risky pleasures.

True enough. But I've still got a yen for a liquor cabinet of my own, for a rack of martini glasses and champagne glasses and highball glasses, for sticky jars of bright red cherries. There is a feeling of bounty in the square bottles jammed together, anisettes and crèmes and syrups and gin. Each one costs so much, and their precious contents sometimes last for decades. Beer and wine don't keep once opened, but a liquor cabinet seems like it could live for centuries. Shiny bottles with overwhelming aromas clink with the chime of Christmas bells. Miniature dishes hold salty jewels: oily green olives, toasted nuts, crackers in amusing shapes.

There is a peaceful gaiety to the cocktail hour that is unlike any happy-hour bustle or late-night jaunt. Drinking in bars and clubs feels busy, a push through crowds, a walk home through city streets on tired, tipsy legs. The 6:00 P.M. cocktail is like a liquid oasis. It makes each evening a celebration, warranting the careful shaving of lemon rind and crushing of ice, even if everyone will be spending the rest of the night watching television and paying bills. It suggests a luxury to which we rarely treat ourselves in other aspects of our lives: when else do we actually set aside time for an activity that isn't good for us? When else do we make one another miniature presents, little works of art served up with a twist? When else do we stop and watch the sky darken?

The luxury of the cocktail and its ritualized consumption create an altered reality that is safe because it's shared, unremarkable because it's so accepted. There is an hour of the evening when it's appropriate to enter the transformative state of tipsy. It is also legal. Illegal drugs have more covert rituals, and less charming paraphernalia. More important, they don't have the classy history of the cocktail hour casting a sophisticated glow over their recreational use. Very often they have the dark shadow of street use hanging over them instead.

heroin

I know three people who snort heroin regularly. Or have done so until recently. I probably know more, but it isn't cocktail party chat. Even when everyone is full of alcohol and antidepressants, and most of them are getting a little snort of something more scandalous in the privacy of the powder room, heroin use is kept under wraps. All three of my friends live in big cities and hold arty jobs that get them invited to parties given by struggling mag-azines and famous raconteurs. None of them fits my idea of a user, which is probably why they don't talk about it much. There's a taboo attached to heroin that doesn't apply to other drugs.

When I first found out these friends of mine used, I was a lit-tle shocked. Still, I figured they did what I did when I tried drugs in college—I'd see what it was like, feel rebellious and cool, sleep it off. Been there, done that. Why do it again? But soon it became clear that a woman I've known since I first moved to New York has capped every day with heroin for a period of nearly half a year. And my friend Jeff is telling me he's been off for three months now, but he'd been doing a bag every single night.

Jeff and his girlfriend, Rachel, would use regularly for about a month, take a month off, start again. The first few days back would feel great, but then he'd almost stop noticing it, would sit around and watch TV, drink beers with friends, even work at his computer. He wouldn't let himself up his dosage—many addicts do ten bags a day—so after a few weeks the effects became barely perceptible. Still, he says he definitely has a dependence, and suf-fered withdrawal each time he stopped. Pain in his fingers. Now that he's clean, he sleeps better, his skin isn't so dry, his weight is up. He's even started jogging.

Jeff's vision of heroin addiction is almost a tempting one. It seems to stem from a hunger for grand experience, an illicit, expanded understanding. Talking to him, I forget the history of lives cut short by overdose, sour rock stars and runaway teenagers lying choking and bloated on countless bathroom floors. I forget the junkie kid lolling on a corner in the East Village, hair spiked like Johnny Rotten, patting a sad-looking dog and holding a cup full of change. Instead, I think of heroin's other history. I think of Sherlock Holmes, alter-nating cocaine and heroin's chemical cousin, morphine. Holmes injects in pursuit of the life of the mind: "Give me the most abstruse cryptogram, or the most intricate analysis, and I am in my own proper atmosphere," he tells Watson. "I can dispense then with artificial stimulants. But I abhor the dull routine of existence. I crave for mental exaltation." I think, too, of Thomas De Quincey, the five-foot-tall author of *Confessions of an English Opium-Eater,* whose narcotic hallucinations fueled the most interesting autobiography of the nineteenth century. "I do not readily believe," he wrote, "that any man, having once tasted the divine luxuries of opium, will afterwards descend to the gross and mortal enjoyments of alcohol . . ." I think of opium user Samuel Taylor Coleridge and the sick power of his lyrical vision: the albatross hung about the Ancient Mariner's neck is an image of unshakable weight, such as that of addiction. I even think of William Burroughs, whose hollow eyes earned him Nike ad spots. Coke may be the drug for the Bret Easton Ellises of the world, and acid for those who deify Jerry Garcia; but heroin is the drug of literary immortality.

That siren calls. Jeff phones to tell me he's gotten me some to try. I tell him I'll pick it up on Monday, but he says no—he'll do it with me. He can do it casually, he swears. It won't be a problem.

"What about me? What if I barf on your floor?" I ask. Heroin makes you nauseated.

"That's okay with me," he says cheerfully. "Don't be nervous." I hang up, and am overwhelmed with fear.

What exactly am I afraid of?

Last fall, I was sitting in my apartment drinking beer and reading, ironically enough, some poems by Coleridge, when the dark shadow of heroin's ugly self fell over the safe little haven of my living room. A woman was screaming in my hallway.

Crowding down the steps into the fluorescent-lit passage with two guys from across the way and an old man or two from the top floor, I realized I was the only person who had any idea what to do. A gorgeous, WASPy boy was lying on the hall tiles. He lived in the building. I had said hello to him and his girlfriend on the stairway. He sometimes played guitar out on the fire escape. His face was deadly blue.

The girlfriend, a white-trash redhead, was screaming breathlessly, trying to get him to sit up. "No, honey," I said to her. "You

want the oxygen to go to his brain. We have to lie him down."
He slid to the floor, his head banging lightly, and I commenced
mouth-to-mouth resuscitation.

"Is he on any drugs or something?" asked a heavyset, mustached man whose dogs were trying to run out into the hall.

"Yeah," she answered, as I put my mouth on his and heard the
air rasp painfully into his lungs, "he's on heroin." No time to
look for track marks, no time to look for open sores. The little
hairs from his five o'clock shadow bit into my lips. His pulse was
slowing. The redhead kept saying it must be his asthma. There
was nothing to do but keep on breathing into him and wait for
the singing of the ambulance.

Scott the Junkie died, shortly after the EMS people took over
from me.

Seconds later, he was shot back to life with a needle full of
adrenaline. "Welcome back from hell, Scott," barked a pink-
faced policeman who had followed the ambulance worker up the
stairs. His adolescent-looking partner quizzed the redhead about
her dosage.

"I don't have heroin in my system," she answered. "I got into
a methadone program last week. They took me because I'm a girl,
but he"—she pointed to the ashen body on the floor—"he got put
on the waiting list."

"Who is he?" asked the cop.

"My husband," she answered.

"I got asthma," muttered Scott, as soon as his eyes fluttered
open.

"We didn't give you for asthma," a uniformed woman wearing
rubber gloves scolded him. "We gave you for heroin, and that's
what worked, Scott. How much did you take?"

"Not that much. Just a bag," the redhead answered for him.
"There musta been something in it. I came home and he was
passed out on the couch." There had been stories in the news that
week about China Cat, some superpure heroin that was causing
a lot of junkies to miscalculate their dosage.

As soon as Scott sat up, I ran back into my apartment and spat in the sink. Over and over, I rinsed my mouth out, as if I could wash the taint of death and drugs off my lips. I brushed my teeth and threw the toothbrush in the garbage.

In the months after, I would pass Scott and his girl on the street and in the stairwell. They never seemed to see me. Then, one day, she was moving things—garbage bags, stacks of LPs—out into the hallway. Three cats and a ratty little dog wound around her feet. She stopped working and called to me. "Hey! Are you the one who . . . ?"

"Yes," I told her. "I am."

"Thanks," she smiled. "He's not here anymore. His dad and his brother kidnapped him into rehab. They just drove up one day and threw him in the car. They don't care that I'm pregnant. They don't want him to see me at all, even with the baby coming, but I know he loves me."

"Are you moving out?" I asked her.

"Getting kicked out is more like it." She pointed down at the cats. "I've got friends to take these two, 'cause they're pure-bred Abyssinians, but nobody wants Babydoll. The people I'm staying with won't let me bring her. Do you know anyone who will take her?" Babydoll, a black-and-white longhair, gazed up at me sadly.

"I have two already," I said, which is true. But really I was afraid of her in a way, didn't want to take care of her any more than I already had, didn't want to nurse her cat for her and tell her my name and number. Her addiction and the problems it created were so overwhelming to me that even having her downstairs was too close for comfort—knowing that behind closed doors she and Scott had been sniffing down their rent money, drooling on the couch cushions, festering in their rancid trap of an apartment like ancient invalids when they were barely legal drinkers. I suggested she see how long the ASPCA would hold Babydoll.

"Maybe I'll just sit with her on the street and hope someone comes along to take her," she said, looking at me with runny eyes. "Or maybe I should just leave her in the apartment when I go."

It seemed to me that the dingy sorrows of Scott and his girl were shadowing my life, making me responsible for Babydoll's suffering. I retreated, offering apologies, ashamed at my stinginess and resentful of her manipulation. Two days later, she was gone. I asked the super to check and see if the cat had been left in the apartment, and he told me she had taken it with her. I ached for her baby and her pets more than for her. Perhaps I have so ingested the "Just Say No" media slogan that I could have little sympathy with a girl who can't seem to say it at all, but I don't think that was it. I feared the way her drug dependency had created so many needs in her life. She had so many blank spaces, it seemed—no lover, no family, no home, no money; even her sense of responsibility to her beloved Babydoll was slipping away from her. I feared her cravings and her abandonment, her skinny little body, her distorted plea to a stranger in the hall.

Heroin is a drug that allays anxiety. Yet its image in our culture, or at least the image I have of it, is as a sort of monstrous gateway to an unquenchable need—once you've tried it, addiction can be startlingly quick, and once you succumb, you can't ever get enough. It is the return of anxiety that creates the need for more of the drug to stifle it. Confronted with the addict's raw need, I responded by trying to help, and also by refusing to try in the face of such a naked plea for comfort. It is frightening to see the addict failing to provide for herself what I perceive as the most basic necessities: food, shelter, health, safety. What a primal fear, being unprovided for. She is forever in this needy state, even when her veins are full of junk or methadone.

I am incredibly nervous all day before going to Jeff's. If I think about what I am afraid of, I am somewhat surprised at myself. Heroin and its fellow opiates were prescribed for years as analgesics before they were made illegal; if a doctor, warning me gently about the side effect of nausea, had given me this same drug as a powerful painkiller that would provide me with a sense of well-being, I would have no fear whatsoever. That official sanction would mean a great deal to me, because my fear is based in some way on heroin's illegality, its status—new this century—as a street substance, a drug for homeless kids and rock stars, the substance of choice for suicides. I do not fear I will like it too much. I do not fear becoming addicted. I am scared of the idea of it, and also of what heroin might make me in a more immediate sense: a quivering ball of chemically induced jelly, an infantile adult freaked out on a drug whose name is almost a dirty word.

I arrive as Jeff and Rachel are ordering food to be delivered from an Italian restaurant. They ask me if I want some, but Jeff advises me to eat conservatively, and as little as possible. Rachel puked the previous night, but happily orders minestrone. I have a piece of banana bread and some seltzer while they get out the drugs.

It comes in a tiny Ziploc bag, much smaller than I had imagined. Inside that is a paper bag which contains a microscopic amount of powder, barely enough to make two thin lines on the back of a coffee-table book. The dregs have to be scraped carefully off the paper with a credit card. We snort with a twenty-dollar bill, crispy from the ATM. "I've developed a Pavlovian response to the smell of money," Jeff says, laughing.

They buy their drugs on the street. "You tell them you want D, which is heroin," Rachel explains, "as opposed to C, which is cocaine." Tonight they have a brand called Paradise, but they used to do Fire, which you can't get anymore—all the dealers had been busted. Other brands are called things like Snake Eyes or Lethal Injection. I ask them why they don't use one of those delivery services (ahh, New York!), by which a clean-cut young man with a bicycle, a briefcase, and a cell phone will bring drugs to your door. They say those briefcase guys usually won't deal heroin.

We breathe the lines in gradually, the way you'd sip a drink rather than downing three glasses of scotch at the beginning of an evening. My friends have become eager conductors of my drug trip. "Do you feel anything?" they ask solicitously. "Maybe she should do a little more. Emily, your pupils are very small. That's a sign!"

I feel almost proud when my stomach begins to feel queasy, just in the sort of way that makes me feel like nesting on the couch with a cup of tea. Oh, delicious couch. These are the best cushions and this is my very own spot to sit in for as long as I want. It is very warm here. My hands are giving off heat. My eyes itch with a persistent buzz, like a mild pollen allergy on a hot summer day. I feel talkative without emotion, tell long stories that might be funny or sad but seem neither, relish my couch. I attack the little lump of beige powder offered me.

"Don't snort it quite so hard," Rachel recommends gently. "You can really just breathe softly in."

"Don't drag the bottom of the dollar bill on the book," says Jeff, walking by on his way to the kitchen. "You should snort harder." He stops to steal Rachel's minestrone away from her. "I'm not sure you should be having this," he says, slurping it down. She giggles and tries to make him give it back.

At their college, heroin was a recreational drug the way cocaine was at mine. Around graduation, some people, aspiring novelists with trust funds mostly, began to inject, and to combine heroin with coke. Rachel says the combo aids serious usage, because you feel energetic enough to go out; in a way, cocaine makes the heroin addict more functional. She has tried it only once, shooting up a speedball. She says it was the most intense drug experience she's ever had, a rush of powerful emotions, exhilaration. She and Jeff are wary of the combination, though; an ex-addict told them you can spend the rest of your life chasing the high you got from that first speedball, and never find it. They are also wary of injecting, and mark a division between those who shoot up and those who snort. One of the aspiring novelists died last February after spending most of his inheritance on heroin. He was "sort of in the process of cleaning up." Another went into rehab and doesn't even drink. Two nearly killed themselves. A number combine their heroin usage with serious alcoholism.

Jeff and Rachel are what hard users term "chippers," that is, dabblers. It's a derogatory name, said the way Manhattanites say "bridge and tunnel crowd" to describe the New Jersey revelers who line Bleecker Street on Saturday nights. What that means right now is that Jeff and Rachel form a heroin club of two. No social scene or institution supports their consumption. It's uncomfortable for them to be around heavy users, and no one they know uses lightly. So they do it together, at home. "But don't write that I'm a chipper!" cries Jeff, who by 10:00 P.M. is showing me pictures of himself in a bathing suit and lifting up his shirt to show how his stomach has bloated since the days of his youth. How wonderful, how funny. Stomachs are weird. I reciprocate and tell a long, inappropriate story about how my ex-boyfriend wouldn't sit next to me on airplanes, which Jeff and Rachel find more fascinating than it deserves.

"Is the ice cream store still open?" wonders Rachel, who has successfully digested the minestrone. We decide to venture out. As I get my coat on, something hits me. A wave of tainted energy swirls about and agitates a kind of magnetic silt that had settled within me as I nested on the couch. It vibrates through my limbs with a nearly sexual buzz, but more like an afterglow than like desire. We get in the elevator. Going down, I feel dizzy, sick. The overwhelming need to be still again. Once outside, the end of the block stretches away from me like the sidewalk's made of chewing gum. I cannot reach it. Jeff's building is very kind to me and holds me up when I ask it for support. I'll stay here, right now. Just for a bit. Rachel leaves to get ice cream by herself. Jeff keeps me company as I adhere myself to the bricks. Beloved wall. A lovely night. Drizzle. The cold air is the only thing preventing me from melting into a puddle on the sidewalk and oozing slowly into the gutter drains with a slurp.

Rachel returns and they finally convince me to venture back upstairs. It is pretty scary. My feet walk on solid ground, but the body above them is wiggly, tipping liquidly from side to side. I bend my knees to give my stomach a smooth ride. Once I'm back on the couch, though, life is groovy once more. What was I ever worried about? Sick? I don't feel sick. Who felt sick? Well, it wasn't me, and it wasn't Rachel. She is eating mango sorbet and talking to me about hair stylists. Jeff is jealous that I'm more interested in the merits of pomade than in looking at a stack of record albums he wants to show me, but I could not even crawl over to where the stereo lives, anyway. What does he expect? I have gone into hibernation on the couch. Oh, toasty. He makes an announcement. "We are making Emily talk too much. She's not getting the full experience. We all have to stop talking and lie down and try to nod off."

"Jeff!" Rachel purrs at him. "You are being such a drug fascist." But she goes over to the TV and starts playing video games while he and I sit with our heads leaning back on cushions.

Nodding off into a heroin stupor, Jeff tells me, is the best part. You see all sorts of pictures floating before you. "This is the point, Emily, where you close your eyes, have a little dream, and start to write 'Kubla Kahn.' Then a stranger comes along, interrupts you, and you can't finish writing it."

We lie there. Rachel talks. Jeff tells her to shhh. Then he talks. I tell him to shhh. We're eight years old at a slumber party. Be quiet. No, you be quiet. I nod a little. My thoughts are in Technicolor, but not particularly profound. Pretty things, done up in sailor suits, jangling shiny silver bells, rolling on the green grass. None last for more than a moment. They aren't graspable either. They skip away if I try to get close, dissolving into dust if I try to hold them.

Suddenly it's one-thirty. I am so tired my eyes are rolling back in my head as I speak. I yearn for home, my own bed. I wish it would just grow up around me as I sit here, but it is miles away. My things. I have to collect my things. I stand up for the first time in hours. Within seconds I am overwhelmed with the most startling nausea I have ever experienced. I retreat to the couch. Seconds after I sit down, the nausea subsides. I cannot go anywhere. I could not walk to the elevator, the bathroom, or the fridge, much less catch a cab across town.

Jeff and Rachel are so sorry; they should never have had me

come to their house, they should have come to mine. They want me to sleep over. It'll be fun. We can have breakfast in the morning. They've got a perfect sheet that fits the couch. I am silent, just thankful not to be puking banana bread across their coffee table.

Rachel makes the bed under me. Jeff offers pajamas, but I would rather sleep in my clothes than try to change. They make sure I have water to drink and promise to wake me up in time for my art class the next day. I have been transformed into the needy infant of my premonitory fears. I suck their generous help from them, unable to even tuck the covers in around myself. Not only do I want others to take care of my needs, I don't do even the most basic things for myself, prevented by nausea, but also by the simple desire to be still. I sink into the pillow and disappear.

Heroin is an immobilizer. The side effects keep the user from functioning, but the drug also makes that immobility seem pleasant, even something to be cultivated. What jerk would want to eat, dance, or have sex when we can all sit quietly? The body ceases to be a source of enjoyment, except as it relaxes in stagnation. The mind goes on as usual, a bit shinier and more colorful for its assumption of dominance in what used to be a mind/body dialectic. The body isn't numb, but kept so still in avoidance of discomfort that its needs and pleasures are forgotten. It's almost as if the mind is relishing its counterpart's reduction to an oozy puddle, taking advantage of a period free from the usual compulsions to move, urinate, or stretch. Therein lies the connection between the fantastic visions of Coleridge and the sad-looking teenager on the street, or the pale redhead with nowhere to house her cat. A body close to pain, and a mind that doesn't care.

sensory deprivation

I t seems to me that to escape the body would mean escaping *into* the mind, or maybe even into the soul. Trouble is, no matter how I alter my state of mind, I find myself brought back to my body in some way. Heroin offers a sense of removal from the body while at the same time enslaving the user to it through nausea and fatigue. Sleep deprivation does a similar thing: it alienated me from my physical needs, and plunged me into a hostile relationship with this body that was playing tricks on me. Cocktail drinking brings physical pleasure to the foreground: In the safe, sanctioned environment of a bar or living room, the tastes and smells and the tinkle of ice make one acutely aware of sensation. Is the body inescapable?

Sensory deprivation, also known as sensory reduction, aims to eliminate the stimulation the body usually receives. As removed as possible from the confines of the body, the mind shifts into a new dominance that veers out of control, glutted on power. People become especially responsive to suggestion, their sense of time is radically distorted, they exhibit unusual sleep patterns, and they often hallucinate. The reduction of sensory input can be effected in soundproof rooms using darkness, severely limited diets, light-diffusing glasses, restrictive gloves, or isolation tanks. This last involves the immersion of the body in a tank of skin-temperature, highly salinated water that allows flotation without effort. The sense of touch simply falls away. Floating in isolation tanks is also the only form of sensory deprivation that has inspired recreational use. There is a small community of users and a distinct social concept of the tank experience that is somewhat at odds with the actual thing.

Ken Russell's 1980 movie, *Altered States,* dominates the way people in America imagine isolation tanks, also called flotation tanks. The opening shot of the film shows us William Hurt's character, Jessup. His face is distorted, tinted blue by the light. Two layers of glass warp our vision: the window of the isolation tank and a heavy bubble helmet encasing Jessup's head. As the camera pulls back, we see the tank as a whole; it is vertical, and Jessup floats suspended in an upright position. He wears goggles, and wires crisscross his face. We hear the heavy rasp of his breathing and the sound of recording equipment tracking his physiological responses. A voice-over explains that a number of Jessup's students have undergone immersion and experienced hallucinations.

He himself is now trying the tank for the first time. Emerging, Jessup reports: "I hallucinated like a son of a bitch. A variety of dream states, mystical states, a lot of religious allegory, most out of Revelation." He has also relived his father's death. His immersion lasted five hours.

Later, Jessup injects himself with a mushroom solution brought back from Mexico and experiments with a different sort of tank. It sits, coffinlike and encrusted with salt crystals, in the basement of a Harvard University lab. Inside, Jessup returns to his most primal self. The tightly enclosed space fosters an inward journey through his mental and emotional history that eventually translates into the physical. He experiences a bodily regression toward a younger form of mankind, an earlier step on the evolutionary path. This primitive self is more compact than the WASPy, anemic-looking scientist played by Hurt; it is small and muscular, densely hairy. The tank has engendered a compression of the self it enclosed, reducing it to its essence.

Both isolation tanks in *Altered States* would foster claustrophobia and anxiety in any normal person. The first lies in the antiseptic environment of a hospital. The second can be reached only through a dungeon of slasher-movie hallways. Jessup is either enclosed in a heavy glass helmet, breathing filtered air, or shut into a virtual coffin. No wonder he shrinks, reduced to the smaller sinews of primitive man, and later balls up into a mangled-looking embryo during a sensory deprivation flashback. His tanks might be either substitute wombs or substitute graves. He *takes leave of his senses* in both meanings of the phrase—he is in sensory deprivation, and he is going mad.

An episode of the British television series *Absolutely Fabulous* puts pill-popping, neurotic starfucker Edina in the "iso" tank in her bathroom. Fearful of relaxation, or so it seems, she has brought her cellular phone and her best friend, bitch goddess Patsy. The episode, during which Edina adopts numerous Romanian babies and begs her daughter to invite her to a science presentation, turns out to be entirely a hallucination Edina has experienced while immersed in the tank. She has been in for only thirty seconds. The tank, white with surfer-style lettering on it, has been imported from L.A., and Edina floats wearing a brightly colored scuba suit. "No one here has one," she boasts.

"I heard Fergie had one," counters Patsy.

"No!" Edina is shocked. "Oh God! I have to get rid of it now!"

Absolutely Fabulous portrays the isolation tank as a ridiculously powerful hallucinogenic agent. Edina is so afraid of what might happen in there that she distracts herself from the experience with the telephone and insists that Patsy leave the door open when she exits. Edina's fashionable scuba suit and the surfer-style logo on the tank's plastic door both imply the stoned rush chased by California wave boys more than a new-age mellow meditation, and in the end, the hallucination is so powerful that Edina has trouble separating it from reality.

The media image of the iso tank stems from early research into sensory deprivation. Around 1954, a scientist named John Lilly did experiments with isolation tanks. Lilly, an M.D. who spent the first half of his career trying to communicate with dolphins, was originally trying to determine the resulting state of the brain when outside stimulation is reduced to a minimum. He devised the paradigm for the tanks we have today, particularly the use of skin-temperature, salinated water. Lilly was mainly interested in the effects of LSD combined with isolation in a tank, and experimented with floating while on acid beginning in 1964. These experiments were followed by flirtations with hypnosis, the dosage of some dolphins with acid, the teachings of a Chilean mystic, and a brief coma. Overall, he concluded that water immersion allows a person to separate mind from body (while on acid) and realize the existence of hundreds of other states of being, including dream travel to other worlds and contact with extraterrestrials.

Another set of early experiments in sensory deprivation and hallucination was conducted at McGill University in Montreal. These tests were, in part, designed to help scientists understand phenomena experienced by prisoners in solitary confinement, patients immobilized in hospital beds, and people who work in isolated, monotonous environments: polar weather stations, nuclear submarines, spacecraft. People in such situations sometimes have bizarre hallucinations and delusions. Early research was also directed toward an exploration of brainwashing techniques, although later scientists would claim there was almost no connection between reduced stimulation and mind control. The scientists at McGill tried an experiment involving a dimly lit, relatively soundproof room. The subjects wore goggles that allowed light in but prevented any patterned vision. Nearly all of them hallucinated like madmen, not just the floating geometric shapes and light flashes of a low-level visionary, but full-out alternative realities. In one such experiment the subject witnessed a miniature spaceship that shot pellets so real they caused pain on contact.

Reduced stimulation does not always result in illusions, however. For example, a bunch of scientists at Princeton locked over a hundred young men (one at a time) in a dark, soundproof room for four days. They were asked to lie still. The scientists made a variety of slight changes in the environment in hopes of inducing hallucinations similar to those achieved at McGill. They added white noise; they added occasional flashes of dim light. No luck. The Princeton students were not inclined to altered states of consciousness. It seems that extremely specific conditions were needed. Some scientists thought an important precondition for hallucination was anxiety, fostered by the conditions of isolation; others suggested that water immersion was more likely to induce hallucination than isolation in a chamber; a third factor might have been the length of time spent in sensory deprivation.

I am inclined to think the dominant factor is the amount of control the subject feels he has or doesn't have. Like sleep deprivation, the altered state created in an isolation tank can be made to disappear in an instant. To make it stop, you need only get out of the water. With altered states reached through rituals such as drinking cocktails, passing a joint, or eating acid at a concert, the social context creates a sense of safety and shared experience.

There is an external control (the established ritual, or the presence of others) that provides people the security to lose their self-control and succumb to the new mood.

Perhaps the medical environment of the isolation experiments provided not enough—and too much—of a good thing. That is, perhaps the subjects had too much control. They were made so cozy in their antiseptic wombs, given so many promises that they could get out whenever they needed and eat whenever they wanted, that no Jessup-like hallucination and compression of self could possibly occur. Kind, ethical experimenters told them they could escape on demand and all their comforts would be attended to—making them the opposite of the brainwashed POWs and lunatic lighthouse keepers who were the original impetus for the research. Or perhaps the subjects had not enough control. They were trapped in isolation and unable to track time, while powerful representatives of the medical world enforced and monitored their experience. A sense of being under surveillance might seriously impede hallucination: as anyone knows who has ever sobered up quickly when her parents came home, altered states can disappear pretty fast when confronted with authority figures.

For a person to hallucinate without artificial stimulants or brain chemical malfunction, I'd bet he needs a certain—but highly limited—amount of control over his body and the environment it's in. Even with artificial stimulants, the amount of control the environment exercises over a person makes a radical difference in the kind of response he has to a substance. Drinking alone is different from drinking in public, and the kind of public you're in makes a big difference too. So the question is, when undergoing sensory deprivation, what kind of environment will I be in? How will it affect me, and will it allow me to escape from my body the way no other altered state has done?

A beardless Santa in a Hawaiian print shirt greets me and shows me to a little room. In it, there's a shower, a tape player, a pile of towels, and a dish of disposable foam earplugs. In one wall of the shower stall is a door about four feet high. "Have you floated before, Emily?" he asks.

"Never."

Santa steps into the shower stall and pushes open the door. Steam pours forth, and a salty smell. Inside is a room about three feet wide and eight feet long, tall enough to stand up in. Foul-looking water covers the floor. Little bubbles dot the water's surface. It has a slimy appearance. "Eight inches of water . . ." reads the pamphlet, "1000 pounds of Epsom salts assure a sterile, bacteria-free solution . . ."

I am not so sure.

"The door is on a magnet catch, so you can open it easily," explains my host. He shows me two fat white buttons just above water level. One turns on the tape player and the other controls the lights. Pale purple bulbs glow in the ceiling. Santa explains that I should take a full shower both before and after floating, and turns the heat lamps on over the shower. We shine orange. "You'll be very buoyant in there," he says. "But often people don't trust that their heads will float. Their whole bodies will be at rest, but their neck muscles will be tense from trying to hold their heads up." He shows me how to put my hands behind my head until my neck relaxes, then move my arms back to my sides. "You'll want to reach out until you touch the sides of the tank, then move your arms back in a little," he says. "That way you'll be oriented." He will knock on the wall of the tank when my hour is up.

I get in. At first there is light through the crack in the door, but after a minute or two, the heat lamp clicks off and I am in total darkness. It is silent inside. I have left the music off. I want to be alone with my mind as I escape the confines of my body.

I float like Styrofoam in this water. My limbs are made of nothing but fluff and air pockets. But the earplugs itch; they seem to go into my ears at different angles from each other. And everywhere I've shaved that morning—lower legs, underarms—stings with toxic alarm at the salt water. The ominous bitterness of the Dead Sea and the claustrophobic Mormon morality of the Great Salt Lake are seeping into my open pores, ripping into my raw skin with stinging pain. As I lift my head to look for my feet in the darkness, the bitter water seeps from my hair into my eyes and the corners of my mouth. The eyes scream. I shut them tightly and let them tear. My breathing is loud, even to the point of distracting me. As my legs and arms disappear into a numb absence from my consciousness, my feet and hands remain oddly present. Every so often they bump up against the walls of the tank, reminding me that no, I am not soaring miles above the earth on a cloud one starless night, I am lying naked in a fiberglass box, somewhere in Manhattan. The confines of my body seem impossible to escape.

After what seems like twenty minutes, I become abruptly aware of noises in the building around me: footsteps treading up stairs, mysterious thumps and bumps from the massage room. No voices, just vague sounds through the thick water. Not much later, my rosy Santa knocks on the wall. The hour is up.

The flotation room I went to seemed designed to eliminate the mental compression and regression fostered by the sepulchral horrors of tanks such as Jessup's in *Altered States*. Nor did the environment promote the fashionable hallucinations indulged in by the tranquilizer-chewing drama queens of *AbFab*. In fact, it left me anxiety-free, in comfortable control of the experience. I did not close myself in; I could have easily stood in the space had I wanted to. I was given a range of options (lighting, music, earplugs) and instructions (relaxing the neck, positioning the arms) that allowed me to feel in charge of my environment and my position within it, rather than succumbing to the disoriented claustrophobia the old tanks would have produced. The spa float fostered relaxation and spiritual awareness.

In search of a bigger, better mindfuck than my gentle flotation, I asked Santa if there were any more traditional tanks in the New York area. He told me there used to be a number of places that housed several each, but that over the past decade they've all disappeared. There doesn't seem to be much interest anymore. I looked up flotation, isolation, and sensory in the Yellow Pages to no avail. Perhaps people in New York need no aid in taking leave of their senses.

My next step is to call up Samuel Brandon. Samuel is a millionaire salesman of automotive parts and an aspiring spiritual healer. He probably holds a world record for floating in isolation tanks; he's been doing it almost daily since 1978. The tank, he tells me, is the "best drug you could ever get addicted to." After growing up one of eight brothers and sisters in a one-bathroom house with a "crazy-ass" dad whose nickname was Hitler, Samuel fought in Vietnam. One of his brothers died from Agent Orange. After the war, Samuel drove west with $265 in his pocket and set to work making a new life for himself. He got a guru, got high, got colonics, fasted, and began to float.

The first tank Samuel bought was black polyurethane and looked like a coffin. He kept it in his garage, but it leaked and the pump would freeze in cold weather, so he later bought a newer one and converted the garage into a meditation cabin with cedar walls and cushions. At first, he tells me, he floated after a day in the office. He had to do it then because "it made me so much like a marshmallow that I couldn't do it and go to work. As time went on I've actually realized that it's better to do it in the morning. It coats my nervous system. . . . I find that if the shit starts flowing in the business world, I feel like I can handle it. It will burn, but just burn the coat and not my skin."

When he first started using the tank, it took Samuel about forty minutes to reach an altered state, but with time he could get there in about five minutes. At that point, he began to try having an out-of-body experience. He tried every single day for fifteen years without success. "I would call the ascended masters and angels and the light to protect me, and then ground my lower chakras in case I did go out of my body. . . . I tried all sorts of processes and finally it worked." He flew to the top of the tank and looked down on it. He floated through his garden and even above the city. He did it every day for about a year: "My goal was to fly to my mother's house in Dayton, or fly to Egypt."

Samuel then went to a retreat in Aspen where he heard a speaker who suggested that instead of striving for an out-of-body experience, people should focus their journeys inward. Samuel instantly abandoned his fifteen-year interest in getting out of his body and began to visualize his inner landscape, working intensively with a Brazilian mystic named Shoshana who channels a person called Dr. Q. Through Shoshana he began to develop an interest in sound. He went to a workshop where he entered a sound chamber built by a man who channels King Solomon. The chamber, Samuel tells me, "harks back to the rejuvenation center at Atlantis"—he assumes I am familiar with it—"which used a combination of gasses, Zion gas in particular, to heal all illnesses and help people live extended life spans." At the workshop, Samuel felt as if the people he met were all known to him from his former lives in Atlantis and ancient Egypt. They were coming together to be involved in "recreating the rejuvenation center on this planet." One guy he met there, a Jamaican man who had been floating in an isolation tank regularly for ten or twelve years, said he had acquired immense medical knowledge by listening to tapes in his tank, specifically a tape made by John Lilly.

Samuel's use of the tank has changed radically since he started incorporating sound. A near-illiterate who faked his way through school, he now uses the tank as a vehicle for learning. At age forty-five he's in the middle of reading his second novel. "It has helped me through my process of learning how to read. All these big words and I'm understanding what they're saying!" Not only is he listening to educational and inspirational tapes in his tank, he's also focusing inward by listening to music. His new orientation toward sound has resulted in massive spiritual breakthroughs over the past four months. He's working with Shoshana to become a healer and develop the rejuvenation center by the year 2000.

I doubt Samuel would call his experiences in the tank "hallu-

cinations," though many people might. But he's smoked his share
of pot, and he seems to find my secular interest in hallucination
and moving away from my body a valid one. He advises patience
and daily practice. He also strongly recommends I introduce
sound. "I've learned more about the tank in the last four months
with the tapes than I ever did before."

I search everywhere for the John Lilly tape but can't find it, so
I go back to the spa empty-handed. I am less than enthusiastic
about the new-age music Santa provides, which reminds me of
the elevators at the Marriott, but I give it a try anyway. As I lie in
the dark, sound penetrates the water with unexpected clarity,
trilling and whooshing and generally evoking a rain forest full of
angels, singing with cloying sincerity. I try to relax into it, and I
do gradually find myself oblivious to the minor stimulations of
touch, smell, and taste that so distracted me before. My attention
is entirely focused on my sense of hearing and my body falls
away, particularly because the sound of my own breathing is no
longer audible. I no longer feel like I'm floating. I no longer feel
myself at all. Still, the music is out of sync with my mind, a
smooth spoonful of frosting too sweet for my palate. My eyes are
open in the darkness, but they might as well be closed. I'm not
having any visions today. When the tape clicks off halfway
through my float, I feel relief.

I decide to try again and revisit the spa armed with the music
I deem most likely to induce hallucination. The decision is a difficult one: Pink Floyd? Nina Hagen? Beethoven? I've heard John
Lennon was into isolation tanks; maybe that record of him and
Yoko Ono having sex would be cool. I want something free of the
soothing chimes of spiritual space music; something pickled in the
sour juices of madness; something that will give me a trip. I settle
on *Use Your Illusion* by Guns N' Roses. That's the pair of albums
whose videos showed Axl Rose being psychoanalyzed naked and
having fantasies of floating around with dolphins in the ocean
and being buried alive—the perfect imagery to match my quest
for an altered state. John Lilly dolphins, weird womb graves, and

everything. There is a parental advisory sticker on the box, warning me about explicit lyrics.

Guns N' Roses does create a certain angry teenage atmosphere, banging my mind around like a Mod girl in a mosh pit as my body relaxes. But all that happens is I see some weird flashes of light when I open my eyes in the darkness. Isn't that pretty much what happens to anyone who presses on her eyelids, or to any eight-year-old looking up at the night sky in search of flying saucers? Also, the ceiling seems much lower than it was with the lights on, but that's not much different from being sure there's a brick wall in front of you if you walk for a moment with your eyes shut. At a certain point, Axl Rose becomes truly irritating and I have to turn him off. I just lie there, relaxed, a little bored. The flashes of light float lazily, doing nothing much of anything. Damn it. Is this all there is to a natural high?

I consider doing drugs, but decide not to. It would take away what is most fascinating to me about hallucinating in a tank. By using sound I've already partly disrupted the project as I see it— the idea that lack of stimulation can cause the sense organs to reel, to rouse themselves, in a sort of ocular or aural masturbation. I am chasing that moment of physical response to deprivation, that moment when my eyes begin to screw with my mind. Or my mind begins to screw with my eyes. The hallucinations sucked out of a tiny tab of blotter paper or breathed in through the thick smoke of the hookah don't seem as compelling to me. I know what's caused them: a chemical reaction inside me, a drug speeding through my veins. The experiments of a Jessup or a John Lilly appeal to me less than the studies in which people achieved altered states merely by being left to what is basically extreme boredom. It would be fascinating to tap the embryo of madness in my psyche, to watch as the link between body and mind becomes visible, to see firsthand the tricks the brain can play on itself without the aid of a controlled substance.

One book I read suggested that altered states of consciousness develop only gradually in sensory deprivation because the initial reaction to reduced stimulation is heightened alertness to bodily sensations and the features of the environment. And it did take Samuel fifteen years to have an out-of-body experience. I figure I shouldn't give up yet.

Next time, Santa isn't there. A girl with piled-up hair and crinkly skin is taking payment from a very tall woman who has obviously just had a high colonic. They discuss in detail what vegetable juices the woman should drink to keep her system clear. Having your rear flushed out like that is probably a bigger trip than sensory deprivation could ever be, but I think I'll pass on it just the same.

The crinkly girl sets me up with the tank. I am determined to be free of all the nagging little distractions that might impede my delusions. I smear Vaseline around my eyes to protect them, stick the earplugs in really far. I have remembered not to shave. I lie back in the tank and try to mellow out, but soon I notice that the violet lights are malfunctioning. A pale green luminance comes from one of the fixtures. I try to turn the light off, then on, then off, but nothing happens. When I stare at it, it moves slightly. Am I imagining things?

A short while later, my body begins to slumber. Not just to relax, but to twitch the way people do when they drift off, only I'm awake to notice it. After what I'd estimate is ten minutes, I make a noise. It is completely involuntary, the kind of sound people make when they're asleep and having a weird dream. Only I'm not asleep at all. I'm lying there worried about the green light and whether it's real and wondering what is going on when a person decides to give colon therapy a try, just for fun. My body, which is asleep, is separating from my brain, which is not. This seems to me to be something rather different from meditation, where the body relaxes and the mind becomes clear and peaceful; this is more of an enforced body shutdown, which doesn't necessarily relax the mind at all. It busies itself in something that is just a step closer to dreaming than everyday thought.

One thing my reading on isolation tanks has made me see is how

fine the line is between enlightenment and insanity; also the line
between boredom and meditation. The revelations Samuel experienced are nearly indistinguishable from benevolent madness, at
least as I see it. John Lilly's work linked acid trips with spiritual
growth; was he a druggie or a visionary? Possibly both. Lying sight-
less in a puddle of warm saline solution, I might be floating on the
border that separates the lonely trucker driving through the night
from the mystic sitting cross-legged in a mountain cave; the border
that separates the acid freak, tossing on her asylum cot, from the
deeply bored submarine pilot who sights the giant squid, or from
the Dalai Lama. What is the mind when it separates from the body
due to lack of stimulation? Will I ever find out?

O frabjous day. I actually do have a bit of a hallucination!
The problem is, it's an extremely stupid one. Here's what I would
like: a vision of skinny, naked old men cavorting on snow-capped
mountaintops, completely transcending the limits of their frail
physiques; a paranoid delusion, the hidden locations of thought-
police recording equipment suddenly revealed to me; the
monstrous, drooling figure of Carol Channing in white satin,
slobbering across a Las Vegas bar; a high-speed scooter chase,
neon zipping by, a time-lapse film of our techno culture; a parched
desert, aching limbs putrid with leprosy, a reminder of the
inevitable decay of the body.

Here is what I get: some sketches penciled through the air
above me; some houses, a sort of smiley face, some lines. All are
cheerful, like a commercial made to advertise public libraries or
family health care. This is what I've got for an unconscious? This
is my embryo of madness? If that's all that's in there, it's ludicrously insipid. It is horrifying to think that in the absence of
physical stimulation my brain responds by producing something
very close to *Schoolhouse Rock*. How come Samuel gets to fly
toward his mother in Dayton and some McGill University student
gets pelted with miniature bullets and John Lilly actually meets
God, but I just watch cartoons, and not very good ones at that?

Here is one possible answer: the meditative state achieved through sensory deprivation being nearly indistinguishable from extreme boredom, the visions the brain produces at that time are a needed stimulus. As everything is being withheld from the body—sound, sight, smell, touch—the brain must decide which need of many is most fundamental and try to supply it. Samuel connected with his home: his garden, his city, and his mother. Lilly connected with the divine. The poor McGill student was probably a secret self-flagellator whose deepest inner need was fulfilled by the pain of the bullets. If I returned to a childlike vision, sketching houses and faces with cheerful confidence, then perhaps that simplicity is what I need most.

Another possibility is that when I drifted away from the comfortable, familiar confines of my body, I returned instinctively to socially agreed-upon symbols of safety. Without the company of fellow users that makes the cocktail hour into a celebration and made my heroin usage a bonding experience, I found myself alone. The squeaky-clean cheer of the spa sanctioned my flotation in the same way a mainstream institution such as my local bar sanctions drinking and countercultural institutions such as head shops, Cheech and Chong movies, or the preppy coke dealer on his bicycle sanction drug use. But when I started to push past the boundaries the spa set up, and when I really started to lose connection to my body, the flotation no longer seemed safe: it seemed foreign and uncontrolled, like the spinning world of sleep deprivation. My mind may have provided me with the safety I wished for. Or perhaps a third possibility was true: the happy faces and gingerbread houses of my hallucination could have been products of the social institution of the spa, where everyone is clean and happy and no one meets either God or the Devil in the dark of the isolation tank.

decorating

ink marks
....

When I was nineteen, and still imagined my innocence would be a good thing to shed, I spent the summer working with a woman named Rebecca at a bead shop. She was a soft, generous spirit and at thirty-four or so seemed very old to me. She worked weekends as a masseuse, and spoke with the soothing affect of a new-age service provider. I used to lounge around reading Charlotte Brontë novels while she sorted beads and rang up sales. One morning, a man came into the store with his wife—he a burly dock-worker type, she a stout blonde holding a baby who was sucking hard on a pink rubber hedgehog. On the man's red, fleshy bicep was a tattoo, faded by years in the sun to a barely legible smudge of blue: SUSAN. They bought several sacks of beads and his wife paid with a check. Her name was Joan.

"That guy's tattoo was sickening," growled Rebecca as they walked out the door. I expected a speech on the sacrilege of permanent body modification. Thorny roses on the breasts of biker girls bared in naughty magazines, blurry anchors on the forearms of ancient sailors—the tattoos I had seen were all violations of the nurturing attitude Rebecca took toward her body. Even the process seemed angry to me—dark ink and sharp needles, a fat man with stained blue arms wiping blood off the pimply back of a frat boy, buzz-cut hair and friends drinking beer in the waiting room. What are the three traits common to serial killers? They are white, male, and possess a tattoo. Rebecca was the antithesis of what tattoos were about; she was all comfortable shoes, no meat, no caffeine, sweet-smelling massages.

But she surprised me: "A tattoo can bring your spirit to the surface." She spoke low so the customers wouldn't hear. "It should make your body reflect your mind."

"*You* have one?" I asked her. We ducked behind the canvas curtain that led to the storage area, and Rebecca lifted up her dress. Covering her torso was a blazing phoenix, red-orange and violet. Its head was in profile just under one breast, its wings soared up across her shoulder blades and down her belly. The tail feathers stretched through dumpy white underpants to trail along her thigh.

This phoenix transformed Rebecca from a meek woman living alone with a cat and six pairs of Birkenstocks into a mysterious person who underwent voluntary pain and indulged in secret moments of self-display. She had defined her body as a site for decoration, even celebration. It didn't make her pretty. Not at all. It made her visible in a way I had never imagined possible.

A few months later I was living in New York City on my own for the first time and I started drawing on myself. I was learning photography and earnestly reading all of Jane Austen. I didn't have many friends, and late at night I'd indulge in fantasies of a life more intensely lived. I had some idea about doing justice to Greenwich Village. There is a portrait I took of myself where my hands are covered in ballpoint pen. My fingers are crisscrossed with lines and sad-looking fish swim across my knuckles. I am wearing fake nails and smoking a cigarette. My face is the round moon of a nineteen-year-old who's barely outgrown *Little Women*, but my hands appear strangely savage and artificial. I would also draw false tattoos on my torso, blue lines coiling around my waist. A tattoo would give me depth, I thought, and I felt myself in need. It would be proof of something, of experience. There was a scary man with a tattooed face named Spider Webb whom I saw on public access television. You could find his phone number on the back page of *The Village Voice*. Maybe I'd have him do it.

It is ten years later and I still don't have a tattoo. What I have instead is lipstick. Lots of it, every day. My lipstick, in its little phallic tube, goes up when I want it to, down when I want it to, at my command. It can go with me anywhere; it's always in my pocket. Just like men who pat their pants to make sure their equipment is all in place, I pat my jeans to reassure myself my tube of Desire is there. Really, that's what it's called. If it's not in my pocket, I'm unprepared. Like a condom, it's a covering for one of my most sexual parts. I wouldn't go on a date without it. Carrying it is a sign of adulthood, but of course I don't take it out in public. I decorate myself with it in the privacy of the restaurant bathroom, and come out ready for action.

My favorite color before Desire was Media. It was practically black, very leather bar. Now it's out of fashion, and the names rolling around my top dresser drawer are less overt. Soft, cheerful titles like Cherries Jubilee or Spicy Rose make it seem like fruits and flowers are the images we think of when we draw attention to our lips. Hah. I say let's call 'em what they really mean: Postcoital Flush, Bloody Valentine, Costly Bordeaux, Vampire Sex Goddess, Adulterous Heat, Shark Bite. Names that imply the mouth is bloody with meat juice or murder, or that appetites for wine and sex have been recklessly indulged—because lipstick is about voracious consumption, in the marketplace and on the body. I always need another one, a matte, a gloss, a frost, a lighter or heavier, paler or darker version of my usual shade. I can never have just one. I need one for my purse and one for my jacket pocket and one for the bathroom and one at the office. At the very least. And when I carry them around so much, they get lost; Tawny Lust rolls out under the seat in the movie theater. Scarlet Indiscretion succumbs to a clumsy pickpocket. The dog eats most of Steak Tartare. My favorite, Manischewitz, got left in the bathroom of a dive bar in Lansing, Michigan. I have to buy more. The consumption process is in motion again.

My friend Roxy steals her lipsticks from the drugstore. She must have a hundred tubes. She says she read *The Beauty Myth* and decided that the true oppression of women by the patriarchy occurs when we pay too much for cosmetics.

Red lips require constant upkeep. Women eat lipstick off, kiss it off, dab it off with a napkin, talk it off. We reapply. We consume it literally, licking it from our lips. It has a chemical, waxy taste. As we age, lipstick bleeds into the wrinkles around our mouths, literalizing the blurred physicality that characterizes later life, when steps become more hesitant and the body shows signs of its tenure in the world. Ancient ladies with piles of half-used tubes in their bathrooms collect lipsticks like past loves, flavors they have tasted. Each color may have made only a temporary mark but still is not to be thrown out. Their present shades ooze into cracked old lips with something more like permanence.

I wander through the glitzed-out cosmetics floor of a major department store in search of the perfect lipstick. A clique of adolescent girls bounces from counter to counter. They try on lip gloss at the table next to me.

"I like this one, I like pale colors," says the ringleader. "I like, I like, I like." She puts two smears of color on one hand and shows them to her friend. "Which is better?"

"That one," the friend says pointing, "for your skin."

"Eeeew!" cries the leader. "That's disgusting. Am I that ugly? Ohmygod, you're so mean!"

Looking through a glistening rack of oily shades, I find myself sharing a mirror with a tall, freckled woman who has just had her lips injected with a prodigious amount of collagen. I can tell because they look like they're about to split open, especially the top one. She is very beautiful, and her dress shows a lot of tit. Her shoes are cheap.

"Are you buying *another* lipstick?" the saleswoman asks nasally, and walks away.

"Yeah," she says, a little challenge in her voice, as if to say, *so what if I am?* A California drawl. She leans in to me and whispers, "I hate shopping here. The people are so rude. They never help you at all."

"Not until you pull out your credit card," I say.

"They're always mean to you," she goes on, smearing her swollen mouth with a brownish color. "Last time I was here, one of them made me cry."

"What happened?"

"It was at Shiseido," she says. "And the lady was just so mean. I was all tired from jobbing and everything. I'll tell you, I am never shopping Shiseido again."

Two Indian women in cardigan sweaters have joined us, pushing in to reach the rack of lipsticks. They, like me, are in search of a phantom color, the red they picture and cannot find. One of them writes down notes on an index card, and complains to her companion about her Pekinese, who swallowed a lipstick she had just bought. "Now why would he do that?" the companion wonders.

"It smells nice," I offer, by way of explanation.

"Oh no," the Peke owner says. "I don't think it was the smell. I think the tube reminded him of the little canisters from the pharmacy that he likes."

"Look at this one!" cries the collagen woman. "It looks like I threw up." I wonder if she is a prostitute, and that is why the salesladies are so cruel.

Lipstick brings me, a grad student in a college sweatshirt, together with this possible call girl and the suburban Indian lady on prescription drugs. We share a miniature, frivolous passion. The Bonne Bell lipsmackers that shined on girls' lips at the roller rink in seventh grade have been replaced by dark slashes of adult color, but the special nature of the cosmetic remains the same. Women hide in the bathroom together at parties and share shades, confiding our secrets through lips heavy with the same pigment. Lipstick is an affirmation of sexual potency. It is a collector's item to be hoarded because it is perpetually in need of replenishing. Self-perpetuating material consumption and fleeting erotic appetites are fused in the moist moment of its application.

I think of lipstick as such a girlie decoration, such a badge of shared femininity, that I'm surprised to encounter two men shopping for themselves. A pale white European wearing a jeans outfit is pressing a series of tan lipsticks to his mouth without the usual American antigerm precaution of wiping the product with a tissue. He is being helped by a tiny Asian-American woman in angora. She has shaved off her eyebrows and her eye shadow is the color of egg yolks. The European man is rather uncertain, and she tries to make him buy a clear gloss. His English is not very good, but I can see he wants a color.

One counter over, a buff salesman wearing lots of eye makeup and a name tag that reads MONTANA is helping a tall, dapper man in a pinstripe suit. Montana is bustling about, confirming the sale of two sparkly eye shadows. The dapper man is round, with long fingernails and a sleek mustache. He asks for lipstick to match the shadows, and shows me a hand covered with purple streaks of cosmetic. "I'm not sure this doesn't look bruised," he chuckles, "like somebody has been in a bad accident." I smile at him. Is he a drag queen? Will he shave his mustache, then? Or is he decorating himself at home, alone? Or for someone in particular?

"I need it for tonight!" he calls to Montana, who has gone in search of a less violent color. When he comes back, the dapper man hands over his plastic.

I am coaxed toward another counter by a woman of terrifying drama whose devotion to cosmetics nearly obscures her humanity. Her weighted eyelashes are thickly fused together, much darker than her almost nonexistent brows, and she wears black lipstick interrupted by a blob of rust in the center of her bottom lip. She must be nearly seventy, and her dyed, red-brown hair is pulled tightly back from her face into an enormous bun that threatens to topple her backward. She wants to make me over. I offer excuses and escape with relief, as if the taint of her longing for a lost youth might rub off on me. The woman's face conveyed a kind of painful gullibility that's at the core of my worst fears about using makeup. She had, I suspect, a completely different image of herself than the one I saw. Her gullibility is the essence of mascara.

Mascara users have faith. They believe the lashes in the ads are real. They trust that the complex process of application looks natural, when heavy mascara is one of the most obvious cosmetics. That wide-open eye suggests youth and charming stupidity. When I was in junior high, a makeup expert told *Seventeen* magazine that of all cosmetics, black mascara (top and bottom lashes) was the most indispensable. I took this as gospel.

Mascara's trusting, unblinking gaze was Twiggy's great achievement, allowing her to embody an age when the nude beach and free love signaled people's wide-eyed faith in a universal oneness. The look has a true-believing, incorruptible optimism that was the ultimate goal behind Tammy Faye Bakker's weighted lashes. How could those open eyes be up to anything naughty? It is the "Oh, Mr. Grant!" face that Mary Tyler Moore can no longer sustain now that her years belie the girlish innocence her mascara tries to uphold. It is the face that Bette Davis as Baby Jane, angelic child star turned decaying alcoholic bat, was trying to hold on to.

Perhaps it is this apparent faith in what makeup can do for you that makes me uncomfortable around the nearly surreal excesses of ardent mascara users. They seem to have lost control over their looks, to be ashamed of their loss of innocence, to trust that they are creating an illusion even when they are making fools of themselves.

If mascara is about gullibility and lipstick is about the pleasures of consumption and self-decoration, then nail polish is about denial. And abjection. And power. And self-discipline. The person with long, beautifully polished nails says to the world, "I don't type. I don't do dishes. I don't finger-fuck. I don't garden. I don't change diapers. I don't pick my nose. Hell, I don't even dial my own phone." Even if she does do all these things with her two-inch red talons, it doesn't look like she can. If she did, her polish would chip or someone's soft flesh would get ruptured.

The perfect scarlet shine declares both a removal from traditional women's work such as typing and cleaning, and a dissociation from the grittier aspects of living in a human body filled with fluids and wastes. The woman with those perfect nails has transformed the hands that might get dirty with work and physical contact into decorative objects with little function—that is, traditional symbols of femininity. Nails are a contradiction. They emphasize femininity at the same time as they deny participation in the activities associated with women. The woman with perfectly groomed hands lives life on a pedestal—or else she's a CEO, so powerful she's never bothered with chores and diapers and letters to type. She's got a housekeeper, a nanny, and a secretary, or at least an obedient husband. Her hands declare her freedom from such low-paying, undervalued work. Barbra Streisand is famous for her nails. So is Imelda Marcos.

Four of the fourteen customers at my local nail salon last weekend were men. Two were tall and good-looking, brothers on their way to a family event. One was a corporate white guy in a suit, and one an enormous farmhand type (I swear to God) with a military haircut. Why were they there? Maybe their mommies never taught them how to trim their own cuticles. Maybe they, like the men at the lipstick counter, are pursuing the small pleasures of self-decoration that so many women indulge in every day. Or maybe they want access to the kind of strength conveyed by the manicured hand, a pristine power removed from the harsh reality of menial chores and the daily grime of physical existence.

The ladies who work in the salon know all about the meaning of nails, though their own are short and stained yellow with chemicals. They snicker at my chewed-on stubs and say gently, "Clear polish, right?" They can see I will never be one of the nail elite. I don't have denial nails at all. I have nails that confess all my sins—dirty, bitten, hangnailed. It's pathetic.

I ask for pink, just a pale one, but my manicurist will not let me have it. She makes me go with one that is all but clear, assuring me that my choice is no good. There are rules to nail beauty that I don't understand. I let her have her way. When I leave, my nails look fantastic, little pearly nuggets of cleanliness. Three days later, they are a cry for help. Color number 14 is bubbling up from the sides, loosened by several showers and a sink full of dishes. The hangnail on my thumb has come back from its temporary banishment, and I chewed one nail down several layers before I tasted polish and stopped myself. My denial isn't very effective, I guess. My bad habits and household chores will out.

By wearing makeup a person goes into dialogue with commonly held ideas about femininity. This is true of the thirteen-year-old with her mom's old blue eye shadow, of the executive applying blush behind the closed door of her office, of the man standing nervously at the cosmetics counter, of the ballerina lining her eyes for a performance as the dying swan. Makeup is a kind of self-decoration that's easy to be comfortable with because, unlike a tattoo, it accommodates a mind that isn't sure of itself. Its essence is to be temporary. It can be applied differently every day, and for all its claims to be long-lasting, can always be removed with the swipe of a tissue. Usually, makeup helps keep our social roles straight. Men don't wear it unless they're challenging convention. Women do. In painting my face, I actively bring myself more in line with the convention of what a woman is, here and now.

I paint my face only within certain unspoken limits, and only with the qualities it supposedly has from nature: rosy cheeks, red lips, shadowed lids, thick lashes. Lipstick is almost never blue. Eyebrows are almost never red. People in our culture rarely put representational drawings or even decorative designs on their faces. Socially acceptable makeup tries to be an enhancement, not a separate work of art with the body as its canvas.

This has been the easy thing to say about cosmetics. I think it is true, but something else is also going on when people wear makeup. Something about play that would begin to explain why I saw those two men at the lipstick counter. Something about sex that goes beyond just the way we construct our femininity or masculinity. Something about reinventing the self, about the freedom of having a changeable appearance. About products and purchases, the sensual pleasures of shining pots of gloss and sparkling powders. About artifice, and about art, about challenging the limitations of *beautification* in order to celebrate the body as a site for *decoration*. There is an intense pleasure in the reinvention of the self that makeup allows, and it is anything but trivial.

Makeup is a tool by which we shame, flaunt, and mold our inner landscapes along with our exteriors. It is full of meanings that can always be suspended or reimagined. It is sinful and deviant. It is normal, necessary for social acceptance. It is overt. It is secretive. The pleasure lies in the illusion that it isn't there, and isn't needed. The pleasure lies in its blatancy. It is sexually attractive because it is fake. It is sexually repulsive for the same reason. And because it is temporary, makeup triggers only fleetingly the shame or pride that more permanent or powerful tools might make more dramatically. Clothes. Haircuts. Surgeries.

clothes
••••••••••

at the Fan Club in New York City, I drift tremulously through racks of spangled gowns. The hangers sag with dresses donated from failed Broadway shows, glitter pantsuits and faded lingerie so fragile it would rip if one indulged in either sleep or sex while wearing it. A man with a red ribbon on his lapel has checked my coat. Most of the money here goes to charities for fighting AIDS. Clothes are donated by celebrities and theater producers. The only other customers right now are a gray-haired man in a wheelchair who is shopping with an aging fashion model. That is, she's around thirty. She seems to need a party dress.

I look for a dressing room, but can't see one. It doesn't matter much, though, since everything here is so fabulous I am too intimidated to take it off the rack. I don't think I'm ready for red feathers. And where would I ever wear that gold turtleneck stretch dress from 1976? Finally, as I hold up a high-necked Chinese gown, a voice behind me pipes, "Would you like to try that on?"

The saleslady is about seventy-five years old. She is four feet tall. Clutching the gown, I follow her to a corner of the store, marked off as an area for employees by the presence of a few ironing boards. Is this the elusive dressing room? It appears so. A man with a mustache is leaning against a rack of clothes, talking to a seamstress who is making alterations by hand. My saleslady conducts me around to an area between two other racks, and leaves me.

"Do you want me to help you with that?" the man asks, leaning his body around the rack that separates us. His voice is remarkably free of lascivious undertones. I tell him no and inch myself a bit farther away. He disappears, but I can still be easily seen by the seamstress and my fellow shoppers. The sense here seems to be that the clothes are what's valuable; they should be treated with care and viewed with pleasure, but the bodies they hang on are basically incidental. I pull off my sweater.

The dress doesn't quite fit. Well, actually, it's embarrassingly tight. I can't zip the side zipper, and the seams creak in protest as I squeeze them over my hips. Truthfully, I can't get it on at all. My saleslady comes to check on me. "Too small?" she asks sympathetically. "Those European sizes are always tiny."

China is not in Europe, but I don't say anything. She and I sit down among the heaps of clothing as she refastens the multiple buttons on the dress so it can go back on the hanger. "I used to be a hat model," she tells me. "I have the smallest size of head. And one season they sent hats over from Europe and—I don't know if they wore them like a pillbox, or just on one side of the head, or what—I couldn't get them on. They just sat up there. Tiny little things."

In this shop, an average-size woman like myself becomes a large-boned, well-fed American gal, conscious of her broad shoulders and fatty hips. She also becomes a consumer of another person's secondhand glamour—aware that she is costuming herself in someone else's life. A slinky fringed gown may have been the work uniform for some chorus girl, sweating out dance steps eight shows a week. A wool coat with a fur collar kept an opera star warm for several winter seasons at the Met. My Chinese dress could have been to cocktail parties on a society matron, indulging herself in the glamour of the Orient.

Old clothing, more than new, makes tangible the construction of identity that takes place whenever we get dressed. I began to understand this when my great aunt Lee mailed me the contents of her shoe closet. As a young woman, Auntie Lee wore tight little suits and piled her hair atop her head in a knot. She lived in Europe and in China, and—as greatly distorted family legend has it—her husband died falling down the grand stairway of a fancy hotel after only two months of marriage. After that, she smoked cartons of cigarettes, took painting lessons, and got fat. She had one of those deep, gritty voices that promises cancer. When she got old, she stayed in bed on the top floor of her Georgetown house and read mystery novels. I would see her on holidays, and one day when I was visiting, she asked me what size my feet were. Eight narrow.

She appeared to take my answer as an important revelation. A couple of weeks later, a large box arrived in the mail from Auntie Lee, addressed to me in her spidery handwriting. It was full of shoes: spectator pumps, silver spangled sandals, embroidered pink silk, alligator leather. About a dozen pairs, wrapped up in tissue paper. They all had four-inch heels. The size was scrawled inside: "8aaaa, custom-made."

When I put on the silver sandals, I became a seriously classy dame. Men took me to nightclubs and lit my cigarettes. My walk was different. I was tall, and glamorous, and sassy. I was also in total pain, but I didn't care. I put on my favorite black cocktail dress and danced around the house to Frank Sinatra records. I started wearing those shoes a little bit almost every day, feeling pampered by the luxury of custom-made footwear, even if it was made for somebody else.

I developed blisters just trotting about my apartment. I couldn't wear the shoes out of the house, because my feet hurt too much. I couldn't move quickly or take big steps, the heels were so high. Sometimes, I'd put them on just to sit on the couch and look at my feet as I gossiped over the phone.

Auntie Lee died recently, lying withered in a nursing home with no sense of where she was when she woke up every morning. She refused to get out of bed. Not for guests or meals or special occasions. Not to wheel out in a chair and see the spring flowers she used to cultivate in younger days. Although she was physically able, she would not even sit up. If she was to be trapped in this rotten body, with bad hips, bad knee, clogged lungs, tangled mind, she was not going to allow others to create an illusion that she took pleasure in life. Because she didn't anymore. I didn't see her before she went.

More of Auntie Lee's clothes are coming to me now. A winter coat with a real tiger-skin collar that my mother has been saving in her closet. Another coat, camel-colored, is given me by my grandmother. "I can't wear her clothes," Granny says to me. "They make me too sad. You take it." She sends me a strapless ballgown in the mail.

Aunt Sandy gives me a suit, a thousand buttons down the front of the jacket. "For your job interviews," she writes. But it's really because it was Lee's, and I am somehow the person in my family designated to receive these things, these relics of a life. They are worn and full of regrets in a way the jewelry she left to my mother is not. The suit fits. I never knew Lee when she was skinny, but once long ago she must have been. It's a sad suit, a reminder of a figure gone flabby and humped over with age, of a body once trim

and lively and fashionable, later a prison of discomfort and physical limitation.

Maybe Auntie Lee was sending me a two-sided message with
those custom-made heels. They were glamorous, sure, reminders
of a bygone era. Her need for so many pairs, a different one for
each outfit, brought home to me the difference between her life,
requiring clothes that were both sexual and formal, and mine, in
which a pair of sneakers is usually appropriate attire. The elegant
shoes awakened in me a sense of the life she lived before age and
illness swelled her feet and forced her to wear something more
practical. I imagine her trips to the racetrack, that little café in
Cannes, a tipsy evening dancing with navy officers, a series of formal dinner parties punctuated by cigarettes.

Life in her shoes was also uncomfortable. I think those pumps
gave me a sense of the limitations Auntie Lee had perceived or
imposed upon herself. In the four-inch heels I stood tall; only my
steps were tiny. My feet looked beautiful, but they were pinched
by the sharply pointed toes, even when the fit was perfect. She
had worn the shoes because she felt sexy, but also because she felt
short. The extravagance of having so many pairs made to order
reminds me of the pleasure she took in pampering herself. But she
also chose a luxury that hobbled her movement and spent most
of the time in a box at the back of a closet.

I've brought Auntie Lee's clothes to the Goodwill in my neighborhood. Most of them, anyway. Their history and the identity
they impose on my body is too weighty, too constricting. The
camel coat, the strapless dress, the spectator pumps—all are now
heaped in piles and draped on spindly hangers to be pawed by
bargain hunters under fluorescent lights. A sad man in a sweater
vest gives me a receipt for them. The shop smells rancid, like
canned pineapples. It is warm in here, and I can only squeeze
myself with effort between the loaded racks. Books are in a tumble in one corner. Prom dresses made of shiny acetate are col-
lected in another. They sell for about fifteen dollars each.

One fellow customer I pass, a respectable-looking woman in

black jeans and a heavy silver necklace, smells disconcertingly of shit. A couple in their forties looks through the winter coats. She tries one on. They speak Spanish to each other in low voices. The atmosphere here does not acknowledge the nostalgic interest of used clothes the way the gaudy feather boas of the Fan Club do. Nor, at first glance, do the clothes lend themselves to fantasy. This is mostly practical wear: sweatshirts and wool pants. These are clothes for going to the mall, fixing the plumbing, running errands. The wedding gowns hung high on the wall seem sad, their sparkle used up. I find a Coors Light sweatshirt, blue and faded, with a hood. It makes me think of a thirteen-year-old boy, scoping girls, feeling tough in a beer shirt, kicking a ball around a vacant lot. The arms are too short, but I buy it anyway. Two bucks.

I wear the sweatshirt all the time; it's old and soft. It's like some boyfriend's shirt from the days of middle school when other girls wrote notes to guys half their height and made jokes about locking braces, and I sat quietly in the back of the school bus, amazed at their intimacy with that frightening, blue-jeaned species. I loved Stone Gossard, now bouncing across TV screens in Pearl Jam videos, then king of the eighth grade when I was in seventh. He didn't know I existed. This sweatshirt is his, maybe. Or it belonged to that blond boy with the mole on his face who was nice to me in art class.

Other people's clothes carry their stories with them. They feel infused with history. Wearing them triggers imaginary memories of times I've never had, adventures belonging to the garment's original owner. They remind me that there is no single, simple way my body is, or looks—I can take on a new silhouette, a new identity, by wrapping my frame in Auntie Lee's many-buttoned suit, my grandpa's old crew neck, or the favorite jacket of my younger man.

An outdated shape, or color, or hemline feels almost threatening to me, so radically does it alter the image I am used to seeing in the mirror. This is easiest to see if you think of bustles or zoot suits, but it applies to the giant T-shirts and neon colors of the mid-eighties, or even to the peg-legged pants of my college days. Those clothes give me different thighs, a different skin tone. They have proportions that no longer fit the self I construct each morning.

O Mistress Mine is a small shop selling old clothes, jewelry, and other odds and ends. The mannequin in the window is missing some fingers. Inside, a heavyset white woman in a polyester shirt sits behind a glass case full of clip-on earrings. A sandy-haired, squinting man is selling her old watches, brooches, and necklaces. He has three boxes of costume jewels. The most enormous German shepherd I've ever seen comes charging up to greet me. "Basil!" shouts the woman. "Come back here. You'll make the customer nervous!" But Basil continues to sniff me as I shop.

I am in search of a knockout dress. I am going to a party being given by the most beautiful woman I know, a writer who manages to be friends with absolutely everyone in spite of her acid pen. I would like to look fabulous, since I can make better small talk if dressed like a film star. I get distracted by a coat of tapestry paisley with a goat-hair collar. "They don't kill the goats to get it," calls the woman, as I look in the mirror. "In case you're concerned about fur issues." Basil sniffs the coat with interest. I put it back.

I try on a pale yellow dress with a velvet waistband, circa 1958. It fits perfectly, shows a lot of skin about the shoulders, demure yet sexy. But I cannot bear myself in it. The hips I have with this dress are not hips that are appropriate in the nineties. Big, full, womanly hips, they are beautiful alone in the dressing room with my fantasies of proms and corsages, but they will not travel well. Not to a New York City publishing party. Not in yellow. Not in October, not at night, maybe not ever. This dress gives me a body—sexily curvy, and yet girlishly innocent—that does not feel my own. It makes me aware of how closely I follow the conventions of dress in my social world—dark, narrow, slinky clothes for evening— while pretending to myself that I am indulging my taste. In reality I am limited in the costumes I may choose without threatening my precarious acceptance of my body and my looks, and without risking judgment from my peers. I love the yellow dress, but I return it to the rack. I'll wear my favorite black cocktail dress to that party, a costume I'm familiar with.

That black dress structures my self-image just like Stone's sweatshirt or Auntie Lee's sandals—I just don't notice it, perhaps because I bought it new. It has no history other than my own. Still, it has a preconstructed meaning, like most new clothes. Like everything in my closet: my combat boots, my corduroy jeans, my favorite turtleneck sweater. Garments are designed to speak publicly about identity long before they have an owner. They are built to convey social class, occupation, financial status, sexual availability, and a host of more subtle meanings that both mask and shape the mind as they decorate the body. A pin-striped suit shouts power and conservative politics; a short, shiny skirt says she's on the make; a leather jacket is tough; penny loafers signal care-free wealth; and so on. Prefabricated meanings like these let me read the man in the mesh football jersey more easily than the daily news. It is a hot day, and his skin shines with sweat through the holes in the fabric. I can tell you about his body image: he likes his chest; he thinks big muscles on men are attractive; he is comfortable with self-display only in the context of a manly sport, yet it holds a certain appeal for him. I can also tell you about his character: he doesn't live in a big city; he lets the women do the cooking; his favorite drink is beer; he builds things alone in his basement; he lost his virginity in the backseat of a Chevy.

All these assumptions may very well be wrong. Or maybe only some of them. But the mesh jersey has a message, and the man's identity is interacting with it in some way. By wearing it he is in conversation with socially constructed ideas about masculinity, and about class. He is exhibiting a temptation both to hide and to display his body that is typical of our anxieties about self-revelation in this country.

"You're born naked and everything you put on after that is drag," says RuPaul, giving a name to these issues of dress and presentation. Her point is that drag happens when I choose my favorite old turtleneck the same as it does when I choose four-inch silver sandals. It happens when a man puts on a business suit or a mesh football jersey, just as much as when he puts on a dress. One may be more extreme than another, but getting dressed—like putting on makeup—involves creating a gender image no matter what. I am wearing a costume—loaded with imagined memories and the scent of bygone eras, or packed with the prefab connotations of some contemporary designer—even when I'm wearing only my pajamas. Hell, even when I'm wearing only my watch. And so are you.

drag

I am going to a garden party in the meat-packing district of Manhattan. The industrial doors of a food company building are open wide and flowers are bursting from its grimy metal floors. The loading dock sprouts a buffet and a DJ is blasting songs of the seventies interspersed with the pop divas of MTV. Donna Summer. Salt-n-Pepa. Yards from the privileged revelers, who are secure behind a wooden fence and a few parked trucks, the music is still loud and clear. As I walk toward the party across cobblestone streets, which on weekdays are soaked with blood and byproducts of the meat industry, the woman ahead of me begins to dance. She is wearing tight, electric yellow pants and an off-the-shoulder top. She is an African American, and stands maybe six feet tall in her heels. She moves with terrible confidence, arms carving sharp shapes in the spring twilight, butt swiveling on her flagpole legs. I suddenly realize she is a man.

A few minutes later, this amazonian queen and two of her friends boogie ferociously in the middle of a five-way intersection, moving like something between a many-armed Indian god and an old Supremes number. This is their last hurrah before they trek toward the river to sell sex in the dark beneath the overpass. The garden partyers burst into applause.

A drag queen invents her appearance in ways that most of us do not. Her clothes jettison the prefab meanings they once held on the rack. She takes shoes that say "hooker" and forces them to say "amazon." Her cosmetics don't make her look natural, but intensely, intentionally artificial. The queen's body may be out of line with her mind, but her outfits reflect it perfectly. And whereas I wear my cords and beloved turtleneck without even noticing, letting their influence wash over me like warm milk, the queen takes explicit, specific control. She *is* ready for red feathers, and for that gold stretch dress from 1976. She is a big plastic flower, where I am a shrinking violet.

A drag queen (at least by my definition) doesn't exist in everyday life at all. She exists onstage, in nightclubs, even working the streets; but when she does her laundry she is probably just Ralph. Many other types of men cross-dress, but they don't exhibit the extremes of artifice and self-display that make a queen a queen: transvestites who indulge in the privacy of their homes, pre-op transsexuals who live as women, transvestites like those documented in the film *Paris Is Burning,* for whom passing is the ultimate goal. A lot of men also wear women's clothes while somehow eluding the label of "transvestite" entirely. Monty Python, the Hasty Pudding theatricals at Harvard, the Kids in the Hall, and the Budweiser "Ladies' Night" ads—all feature men who dress in drag as a goof. Numerous straight men of my acquaintance will also leap at the chance to put on a dress. My ex-boyfriend dressed up as Courtney Love one Halloween. He wore a trashy blond wig and painted his fingernails black. My friend Marnie's boyfriend out-glammed her at Wigstock, an annual drag festival in New York. I have a photo of my high school sweetheart wearing a cute red prairie-style dress, and Roo the bongo player actually changed into a white prom dress one time when I went up to his apartment for a cup of tea. It was only our third date. He said he was showing me his Halloween costume, but I think really he enjoyed wearing those fifties flounces in a flirtatious environment.

Another sort of transvestism that doesn't really get labeled as such is the macho, celebrity drag worn by Howard Stern and Dennis Rodman for their book signings. They are glamorous, but always make it clear that they wear women's clothes for the shock value rather than for pleasure. It is a drag based on a masculine identity so established they can afford to show their peacock's feathers, even in a culture that considers such display effeminate. Their drag is not accompanied by any change of gait, voice, or gesture designed to impersonate a woman. I wouldn't call either Stern or Rodman a drag queen.

My point is: although none of these men get labeled as transvestites—indeed I think they'd vigorously dispute being called such—they are very likely getting pleasure out of their rare forays into artifice and self-decoration. Even when they do it for shock, or laughs, or holidays. The transformation has an appeal for them, or they would not instigate it.

In high school, I experimented with makeup a lot and got teased for it too. I'd wear sparkly green eye shadow, green mascara, and white lipstick that I made myself with cover-up stick and petroleum jelly. Later, I switched to blue—pale blue eye shadow, electric blue eyeliner, blue mascara, and harsh streaks of blush across my cheeks.

"You look so much better without it," coaxed that high school sweetheart, trying, I think, to be nice. He liked girls without makeup. But I liked girls with lots and lots of it, and I had one friend who shared my sentiments. Her name was Nicola, and she dyed her hair and wore pancake makeup and sang like a Broadway diva. A string of anemic-looking boyfriends in narrow ties drove her around on their motor scooters. They usually went to other high schools. She had this great, busy, nasal way of talking, and later went off to Europe to be an actor. Nicola had a big makeup mirror with lights around it. She'd sit in front of it, messing with potions and dishes of powder. She would pancake herself until she looked like Theda Bara. Then we'd dress ourselves up and traipse downtown on the bus to listen to punk rock and talk to boys in leather jackets.

I saw Nicola later, one summer near the end of college. Both our faces were scrubbed. Perhaps we'd grown out of what was only a teenage phase, but I think it's more accurate to say this: Now that we were actual women, we felt we could no longer play at being women. Our overt artifice had been replaced by subtlety. No Theda Bara, no green mascara, no makeup mirror. As an actress, Nicola had found a way to make theatricality her job, but it no longer seemed to infiltrate her life. I had simply learned to be natural, at some cost to what I think was really natural in me.

When I think back on those silly, extravagant nights downtown, it seems to me like the drag queens inside our scrawny teenage frames were trying to get out. Now that I'm nearly thirty I think mine has died of starvation and neglect. Nicola, wherever you are, I hope yours hasn't.

I admire the artificiality, the overtness of a drag queen's masquerade. It is not about subtlety or realness, but about a creative reinvention of the self, a vision of the body as a flexible core that can be molded to fit any number of theatrical realities. Women—most women—whose femininity is of the everyday, heels-at-the-office variety, keep our artifice covert. Sure, we wear lipstick, but our plucked eyebrows and highlighted hair are meant to look natural. Very often, elements of our everyday artifice— gesture, voice inflection, handwriting—are invisible even to ourselves.

In the Blake Edwards movie *Victor/Victoria,* Julie Andrews plays Victoria, a second-rate soprano who becomes the toast of Paris when she masquerades as a female impersonator. The first and best musical number Andrews sings in drag is "Le Jazz Hot." She wears full diva regalia: headdress, dramatic makeup, sequins, and shoulder pads. She shows a lot of leg, very little arm, and no cleavage, just as a man would do who was avoiding displaying a muscular, hirsute upper body. When Victoria removes her headdress to reveal her cropped hair, the audience goes wild. She really looks like a man who looks like a woman. In later musical numbers, Andrews's female sex characteristics are played up; in "The Shady Lady from Seville" she wears a low-cut floral dress with no back and short sleeves. In place of the headdress she has a simple, natural-looking wig. She is a less androgynous performer in this outfit, and a far less stylish one. When she removes her wig, she looks like a woman with short hair. It is after she performs this number that her love interest, King Marchand, is turned on enough to assure himself of her sex by spying on her in the bathtub. She may be a little frumpy in the floral dress, but he's pretty confident she's a woman, not a drag queen. A man dressing as a woman would have more flash.

I envy a drag queen her glamour, which is enormous, a glamour so huge and confident it signals strength along with femininity. Legendary lip-syncher Aphrodite has the body of Superman in a slip. The Lady Bunny, swishing in white stockings and a baby-doll dress, looks like she could beat up any thug who pinched her ass. Chicklet, nice Jewish boy turned Latina go-go girl, says that when a guy reached up her skirt, she ended up kicking one of his teeth out. In *Drag Diaries*, Joey Arias says of his alter-ego, Justine DeSade, "Women meet me and say 'I wish I was like Justine.' Because Justine has men coming up to her saying, 'Oh baby,' and she pushes them away, 'Get out of here!' Justine also becomes a heavy sex thing. Women are always touching the breasts. They touch you like you're a deity."

Few women would wear giant fake boobs, much as we might like to. Our lovers would be disappointed when we pulled off the falsies to reveal our own shrimpy mammaries, so we have silicone stashed under the skin or settle for a small cup size. The drag queen faces no such pressure to be natural, so she makes them as humongous as she wants.

The big breasts are matched by big attitude, an attitude that stems from a queen's acknowledged artifice. The new identity a man takes on when he goes in drag is fabulously different from Ralph who does his laundry, whereas if I dress up and put on fake boobs, red feathers, and a big red wig, I'm just Emily in a crazy outfit. The gestures of a drag queen are not feminine, but effeminate. That is, they are similar but not the same as what a biological woman would do. My own personality, complete with feminine gestures I've used since childhood, inhibits the development of a persona like Justine's. It is too close to my everyday drag.

"But you've got the real thing!" cries Josiah, formerly Miss Coffy. "I know a lot of drag queens feel that way." Josiah's drag was based on seventies blaxploitation movie heroine Pam Grier. Talking to him, my impression is that what he means by "the real thing" has to do with sexual possibility—something a drag queen is in some way closed off from. "It makes you less appealing if a gay man knows you do drag," he says. "Gay men want to live the fantasy of being with another man and all that that is: macho, sexy, ideally passable, male"—meaning he can pass as straight. "To be with a gay man in drag is strange for other gay men. But you knew that, didn't you?"

Honestly, I did not. I find drag queens sexy. This is partly because they display attributes I've learned to associate with sex. That is, I'm used to the trappings of female sexuality—cleavage and makeup and short skirts—standing for sexuality as a whole. I am responsive to it, even as a heterosexual. But more importantly, I can tell that drag queens are men. The soft fleshiness of Julie Andrews in her floral dress does nothing for me, but Wesley Snipes in spandex is another thing entirely.

My friend Stu lives in south Florida. His one foray into drag (he looked like a Bavarian countess) involved such a horrible hair removal trauma that he's never dressed up since—but he knows the scene. He takes me to Swirl, a lounge where drag queens run Betty Ford Bingo and dance till the early hours. There I see Miss Ash, an Asian-American queen in slinky black clothes. She has a body unmistakably male: very narrow hips, broad shoulders, strong jaw. She also wears a wet-looking shirt cut low at the neck and open at the bottom to expose her abdomen, platform shoes, streaked hair, and dramatic makeup.

God, men are so beautiful and they never show it off. Although Miss Ash is feminine, her maleness is unmistakable. It's even enhanced by her self-decoration. Femininity—the signal of sex in our culture—can be very attractive on a male body. In other words, I am attracted to a sex more than I am to a gender, and I've always assumed that most gay men felt the same.

Josiah says I'm wrong. "You kind of don't want people to know that you're a drag queen. There's a certain measure of shame in it with other gay men. . . . That's one of the reasons I stopped drag. It harks back to being called queer and faggot. It's a place gay men don't want to go." When he was working, lip-synching or go-go dancing as Miss Coffy at New York clubs, Josiah was a closeted drag queen: none of the men he dated knew he dressed up. In *The Drag Queens of New York,* Chicklet gives a reason for that kind of choice: "No muscle boy wants a queeny, faggy bitch roaming around the house in slippers."

Josiah also points out that some people are attracted to gender rather than to sex: "I was go-go dancing, three times a week in seventies drag, a big afro. It was the Pyramid club, and it was on a straight night. . . . This man came up and said, 'I want to spend the evening with you.' I was shaken, because I felt like a clown, very much like a clown, not sexual at all. I ignored him for a while and kept dancing, and he came back again and said, 'I want to spend the evening with you.'

"I said, 'I'm a man. You don't want to spend the evening with me. I'm a man!' He said (and I was floored), 'I don't care.' . . . It was only then, which was a few years ago, that I realized there were men, straight men, who wanted to have sex with men in women's clothes."

Straight men wanted Miss Coffy. Maybe I would have, too: Josiah is mighty fine. But she wouldn't want either of us, wouldn't even feel sexual. She doesn't have "the real thing," the sense of sexual possibility conferred by biological womanhood. Funny, though; I have it, and in a way I'd like to be rid of it. It carries with it such vulnerability, so many injunctions to modesty, natu-ralness, and self-control.

Stu takes me next to Amnesia, a nightclub in South Beach where there is a drag show every Sunday night. The club is open to the night air, the dance floor filled with topless men in jeans shorts and a few girls with too much hair spray. Somebody's mother is here. She dances with one hand waving above her head like the Statue of Liberty. Two hunky boys gyrating near us have Post-it notes stuck to their bare chests. One reads, "It's all about us"; the other, "Who's the fairest?"

The show starts. Our emcee is seven feet tall in open-back shoes much too small for her. She wears a purple fringe dress and has padded her ass as well as her chest. Her Afro is nearly a foot high, and her lips shine with glitter. "Tonight," she booms into the mike without the slightest attempt to disguise her voice, "is the Gloria Estefan look-alike contest."

The first contestant, Sugar Baby, is maybe four and a half feet tall. "Come over here, you little short boy," barks the emcee, straddling a railing on one side of the stage. Dressed in white, with a long platinum wig, Sugar Baby is a cream puff of a queen. She is a perfect angel of a child, so immaculately blond and neat I suspect her of torturing kittens when her nanny isn't looking. She does a rather stunted, latinate cha-cha and keeps her hands in fists.

The next entrant hits the stage to a round of applause. Stu tells me everyone knows her; Paloma is queen about town. She is, shall I say, of a certain age, but that doesn't stop her wearing a tight, tight yellow dress cut so low I'm sure her cleavage must be silicone-assisted. Her hair flies loose and she flirts a bright blue scarf through the air. Thick stripes of makeup highlight her cheekbones. Like Sugar Baby, Paloma jolts out sexuality despite a homely physique. Her arms are saggy and her beer belly squashed by a corset. Her masculine jawline prevents her from looking really female. Nevertheless, she exudes fantastic confidence in her assets, displaying them with as much pride as any Lolita whose breasts have just sprouted.

Paloma is followed by India, the most female-looking queen I've ever seen. A big-boned model-type with too much hair, she resembles Brooke Shields or Renee Russo. And the hair is her own, her chest looks implanted, her calves are not too muscular, her arms are soft and round. India looks real, but she could never pass. She's too decked out. She wears stage makeup and a floor-length purple sequined dress, slit up the front to nearly crotch height. She flips her hair around with unseemly pride. That is, she is a little ridiculous, and the combination of ridiculous and sexy is something a woman will rarely risk for fear the first will cancel out the second. Just as we wouldn't wear Joey Arias's giant fake breasts, most biological women (especially out of the media spotlight) wouldn't dare come so close to mocking feminine display as India does: we are too invested in it.

Watching the Gloria Estefan look-alike contest (which, by the way, nobody won; everyone just got a signed photo and a chance to meet Gloria at her recording studio) is like watching a bunch of little kids play dress-up. Before the boys learn that dresses signal weakness, and before the girls learn that natural beauty is more valuable in their culture than artificial and to be nonchalant and dignified about their femininity, little kids get off on the exaggerated. Wearing mommy's old bra and highest heels, lipstick on lips and cheeks and chin and eyebrows, wherever it seems fun to put it, they parade shamelessly, taking on sex characteristics that are not theirs yet, and might never be. Therein lies the fun in femininity—not in the Julie Andrews floral frump that signals true womanhood, but in the acknowledgment of artifice.

In the end, drag is about joy in being fake. I am unable to flaunt myself so overtly, much as I'd like to. I don't want to deal with the harassment I might encounter, although I'm sure drag queens suffer equally if not more on that count, since not everyone has mastered the brush-off like Chicklet or Justine. The more important reason is that I care too much about being "the real thing," as if naturalness is some sort of passport to lovability or success as a woman. I'm not willing to risk looking like a slut, verging on the ridiculous, or disappointing a lover who expects my fortified figure to be real. I would never want to be accused of trying too hard, of seeming desperate. That's the reason I stopped wearing the green eyeshadow and white lipstick; I'd guess it's why

Nicola stopped wearing the pancake makeup. Though stories like Josiah's attest that the shame of cross-dressing haunts many queens still—unsurprising in a culture in which a dress rebellion as minor as wearing a pink shirt to the office can still call a man's sexuality into question—drag queens hurdle the stigma attached to overt self-display and artifice, then grind it into the ground with the heel of one platform shoe.

body modification

To most people, the body is a subject of art, not a site for it, even when the line between the two is hard to discern. Paintings of naked bodies are okay. Paintings on naked bodies are not. Subtle artifice is good. Overt artifice is not. Beautification is appropriate. Decoration is not.

Many people see the body as sacred in some way, believing you should go out of the world in the same state you came in. Therefore, the less permanent something is, the more acceptable. Makeup lasts a day or less, so it's okay. Clothing can be changed quickly. Manicures last a week. Haircuts last two months. But piercing, tattooing, and scarification last something close to forever, and they are perceived by many people as a threat. Because body modifications involve making art *on* and *of* the body, not just enhancing its natural beauties (as most makeup and clothing might be said to do), and because of their relative permanence, they challenge our collectively held notions about self-decoration.

The rules are complicated. Not all permanent changes are taboo. Socially sanctioned, long-lasting body alterations such as waxing, perming, or straightening involve a certain level of commitment and even pain. For cascading curls and hairless legs we apply poisonous chemicals to the skin and expose intimate parts of the body to the trained hands of a beauty school graduate. These processes are not so different from getting a tattoo, but their results differ from what's called body modification in two major ways: the body will revert to its original state naturally, with no effort, and beauty salon processes are almost always employed to bring an individual's appearance in line with the social norm.

Hair removal cannot, in fact, be called decoration, or even beautification. It might enable body display, allowing the hirsute to parade the beach in confidence, but it is not the addition of something positive. It is removal of an attribute perceived as negative. It also pretends—if we don't look too closely at the plucked chicken skin and the unusually straight lines of hair growth beside it—to have never happened. Hair styling is also unmentionable. Is she a natural blonde? Of course not, but don't say anything. He wears a toupee, but we pretend not to notice. White women are often still vibrant redheads at age eighty-three. Asians have natural curls.

When hairstyles do announce their artificiality, as in graphic designs cut into short Afros or sixties bouffants rigid with hair spray, they are often at their most temporary. Hair will grow into the design within a week, and the bouffant can be washed out overnight. The more permanent a body alteration is, the more we want it to look natural, even if everyone knows it isn't.

Cosmetic surgery, the most permanent of beautifications, is socially acceptable because it does not announce itself as artificial. It is—at least, it is supposed to be—invisible. "My breasts were always this large and this perky," we say. "My nose came out naturally button-like. My lips have gotten fuller with age, my eyes wider, my skin tighter. Isn't it amazing what a healthy diet will do?" Although it's more permanent than piercings, many of which heal over when the jewelry is removed, and more permanent than tattoos, which can be removed with lasers, we are comfortable with surgery because it doesn't announce itself. Admitting we have gone through pain for beauty is something we are afraid to do. It marks a person as vain and in doing so reminds other people of their own vanity, highlighting the value we put on beauty and the suffering needed to achieve it. We hate to be reminded of that suffering, because it represents our self-loathing. Michael Jackson, his ever-changing face looking each day more like a Jack Russell terrier, and Cynthia Jackson, who has undergone nineteen plastic surgeries in an effort to look like Barbie, are disturbing because their surgical artifice is so easily visible. We cringe at how similar we are to them, how we hate and love ourselves enough to embrace the pain and risks required for the type of beauty we admire.

So our culture is uptight about decoration, which is overt, as opposed to beautification, which is covert. If we decorate at all, it should be temporary. And if we must decorate permanently, we should keep it to ourselves. A tattooed shoulder is one thing, but piercings and tattoos on public skin (face, neck, and hands) are guaranteed to make a gaggle of Americans—pumped up on collagen injections, earlobes pierced, smeared with Estée Lauder, and waxed from hip to ankle—decidedly uncomfortable. Earlobe piercing is the one form of permanent body decoration we accept in this country.

ThEnigma (pronounced The Enigma) has made choices that challenge almost everyone's ideas about self-decoration. Even those of a tattoo fan like myself. Formerly—according to Jim Rose of the Jim Rose Circus Sideshow—a "sweet-faced, wholesome-looking kid" named Paul, ThEnigma is now a puzzle. Literally. His entire body is tattooed as if he were a jigsaw, with pieces about an inch and a half in diameter. He's covered on public skin and private: face, neck, arms, palms, ass. His head is shaved, and marked likewise. He is gradually having the puzzle pieces filled in blue, some plain and some with patterns. He works in Rose's sideshow, comporting himself as a silent, nearly naked monster. He eats live bugs, swallows swords, and moons the audience. On an episode of *The X-Files,* he played The Conundrum, a circus freak who fishes with his hands and mouth like an animal.

ThEnigma seems barely human. More than human. In photos, only a few tiny details remind us of the man beneath the ink—a pinch of flab around his waist as he bends over, fingernails that look bitten to the quick, what is apparently a mosquito bite on his foot. The tattoo is the work of over a hundred artists, and he holds the world's record for being tattooed by the most people at one time: twenty-two. But, he says, it felt like only ten. All the work is done free, by artists who want to contribute to his self-creation. Although ThEnigma is a collector of work by some of the most famous tattooists alive, he is the one who graces the cover of *Savage* and *International Tattoo Art* while they go un-credited, too numerous to mention. He is not only the canvas, but the collector and the artist as well.

Sitting across a table from him in a crowded Chelsea restau-rant is one of the most intense physical experiences I have ever had: two hours with a blue man, a man whose history of pain is literally etched across his face, whose baby blue eyes match the color of his skin. His nose is bisected by a jigsaw line, half blue, half skin-tone. He is disturbingly sexy, exuding an incredible con-fidence in the power of his body to interest, shock, attract, repel. Next to him, no one else is worth looking at. He orders pasta.

ThEnigma's philosophy makes Rebecca's idea about the body reflecting the mind seem pretty limited. For him, self and art are completely merged. The young, white sword swallower of only a couple of years ago has completely disappeared. When I ask if anyone calls him Paul, he hides his face in his hands. "Oh please! Paul?! . . . When I go to Safeway I'm still ThEnigma."

Well, what does his mother call him?

"By my real name," he says, reluctant to pronounce it.

On one hand, it seems as if he is realizing a vision that is at the core of his wacked-out mind; on the other, his body is threatening to obliterate any shreds of his mind that are not commensurate with being blue. "The self is sacrificed for the art," he tells me with-out a trace of regret. "When you do this to your body you throw away everything that was. Or maybe you don't. Maybe you're already gone anyway. This isn't about me. All that matters is for some old housewife to see me, and maybe she'll let go a bit. Maybe she'll find some sort of freedom in herself that she didn't find before. . . . One person came up to me and told me that I'd never have to say another word in my entire life. It's all said. Right here."

He married the woman who tattooed the puzzle outline on his body. She is The Kat, and her skin is striped like a tiger. "Head to tail," ThEnigma says proudly. I ask him if getting the tattoo was a romantic gesture, like having her name etched on his arm. "It was kinda like a piece for a piece, you know?" he laughs, winking. "A tit for a tat. I always figure it's like a perfume commercial: ThEnigma—made by a woman for a woman."

I tell him about my tattoo fantasies, which have been proliferating at an incredible rate since we sat down to lunch. ThEnigma is very encouraging, but it is clear he views my interest as amateurish. He claims alternately that it's a good idea for everyone ("I think everybody should tattoo their entire face. What a colorful world it would be!") and that I should think it over with care: "You really have to know yourself. You have to really want this to get it, because of how painful it is."

ThEnigma's own commitment is written in the lines on his face—commitment to his wife, to his creative vision, to the tattoo community he represents every time he leaves the house, to his daughter. "Having kids is a bigger commitment than tattooing your body," he argues. "And people do that all the time. Most people don't know who they are. I know who I am, so it's safe to make this choice [to be tattooed]."

He is emphatic about the suffering he has undergone to become blue. "People are always asking me if it hurt. Well, the skin is full of nerves. Nerves, when you get hit by a needle, send signals to the brain. You're constantly explaining this to people and they're just fucking stupid. It's like, 'No, I'm completely numb from the head down.' Jesus Christ! Of course it fuckin' hurt." He shows me a little spot on the inside of his elbow that hasn't healed properly. He's got blue scabs.

I think the people asking don't realize ThEnigma's skin is ordinary—that if you prick him he will bleed, tickle him he will laugh. That his hair would grow back if he didn't shave it. It is easy to forget these things about him. As a representative of the tattoo community, ThEnigma always tries to be friendly, winking and smiling to remind others of his humanity. Yet it was hard for me, eating lunch with him, to remember that he has feelings, partly because he has chosen his strange identity, has deliberately made himself the ultimate other. I think that even for the most socially aware of us, tolerance and understanding of others in skins different from our own—whether because of color, illness, or disability—is based on the idea that people don't choose their bodies. They are born with them, or something happens to them, and remembering this fact allows us an empathy with a scarred face or another skin color. We have difficulty finding a similar empathy for a man who has turned himself blue, or for a man in a sequined dress and platform heels.

Being entirely blue is ThEnigma's ultimate goal, and he sees it as an escape from the dominant beliefs of mainstream white America. When he is all the way blue, he says, "I will have escaped that white man's guilt—being a colored person, a person of color."

As a teenager growing up outside Seattle, he watched *The Twilight Zone, Battlestar Galactica,* and *The Outer Limits* with intense fascination, only to be disappointed with reality as it was presented scientifically. "In chemistry class in high school you find out about the laws of equilibrium. You learn that you can't just make something appear from nowhere, and that dashes your dreams of being a biochemist or an alchemist. There are no hidden doorways to different dimensions. It's all just on TV. So then you have to do what's second-best and make impossibility as possible as you can. Yes, there are monsters in the world."

He didn't become a monster until 1993, but did develop a sense of personal agency and creativity in those *Battlestar Galactica* years. "In high school it all fell apart. My dad was in Vietnam. He had shrapnel in his brain, so he kinda went religious cuckoo. And then divorce and then depression. Explosion, you know? I think everybody kind of goes through that at some period. And then a sense of total freedom, craziness—like you can do anything and everything. Move things"—he waves his glass of

water and his spoon around—"woaah, there it goes! All of a sudden creation is everything. Art is everything. . . . Then you can
just be visionary. It has to do with the vision of 7-Eleven, and
a blue guy there. Or McDonalds, in Europe, and a blue guy
there. . . . I look at the stage and I say, I want to see a blue person. He's blue at first, and then as you get closer you see all these
images within it."

As the only blue person on the planet, ThEnigma can easily
manipulate people's perceptions of him. "If I don't want people
to notice me, then people won't, because they look to me for how
they should respond. As a blue person you can get away with a
lot more than you can as just a regular Joe. . . . People accept that
and expect it. They expect whatever you give them. I'm their first
experience with a completely tattooed blue guy. They don't know
how to judge a person like that. . . . Whatever I do is typical
behavior for me."

People proposition ThEnigma all the time. "Hey," he laughs,
"they all want to do a puzzle!" He writes their advances off as
interest in a novelty, evidence of the attraction people have for
performers, but I think he misses the real reasons. His sex appeal
goes beyond the standard erotic thrill of a tattooed guy with a
good build, or the politically suspect but nonetheless powerful
attraction of someone who is physically "other" to oneself. It is
more, too, than his superhuman confidence in the specialness of
his body. ThEnigma's particular tattoo invites a sort of voyeuristic interest because of his unfinished status. He is a work in
progress. While most people with heavy tattooing have large
areas of unmarked skin that await art, ThEnigma has created an
unusual scenario in that his whole body is covered in such a way
that its partially finished state is still always apparent. I want not
only to get under his shorts (is it blue, or is it pink?), but to get
under his tattoo. But I never can. I can only peek through the
holes of the puzzle to his skin beneath.

He is also sexy for the same reason Miss Ash in the Florida
dance club was sexy. Although ThEnigma's tattoos are hypermas-

culine, even frightening, and Miss Ash's drag is hyperfeminine, even silly—both are decorated men. They have the appeal of peacocks, strutting with tails extended around a barnyard full of lumpy gray beasts. Especially in the heterosexual circles I move in, men almost never show themselves off. If they do, it is almost always by removing their shirts, exposing what is (relatively speaking) naturally there, rather than enhancing it with cosmetics or decorating it with feathers, jewelry, or tattoo ink. A half-nude man is very nice—I'm not complaining—but he's not engaging with any of the subtle, overlapping, contradictory meanings that make self-decoration so interesting. He's too obedient to invisible rules about masculinity to be irresistible. Michael Stipe with his eyeliner and layers of clothes is much spicier than some cute boy with his polo shirt wrapped around his waist. And I don't think Stipe is androgynous, or in drag. He's just decorated.

I want to know what's going on under Miss Ash's wet shirt, under Miss Coffy's painted face, under ThEnigma's blue bathing suit. I am pleased that they have adorned themselves, turned on by the mystery of the reinvented self, intrigued by a male body unhampered by the usual restrictions on masculinity.

What does it say about our culture that we understand the scraping and sucking away of tissues we perceive as shameful (hair, dead skin, excess fat), but resist overt decoration of like permanence? Why is decoration acceptable only if it is removable or disguised as natural, and repulsive if it announces itself as permanent? ThEnigma forces everyone he comes in contact with to reevaluate their understanding of art and the body, of the possibilities for otherness. His status as a self-made, eroticized other forces us to revise our unacknowledged definitions of humanity. Looking at him, we have to admit our anxieties about blatant self-decoration and our investment in maintaining an illusion of impermanence with regard to our artifice, hiding our interest in self-display under a disguise of naturalism. Our standard preferences are unsettled by ThEnigma's presence, so obviously constructed and artificial, so obviously painful to achieve.

the tattoo
•••••••••••••••

I buy a lot of tattoo mags after lunch with ThEnigma. They are pretty trashy, most of them, and feature lots of mottled-looking flesh. An issue of *International Tattoo Art,* however, contains a story about Elizabeth Weinzirl, a heavily tattooed woman who died a couple years ago at ninety-one. Weinzirl was amazing. Her art covered her torso and thighs. Flowery vines encircled her breasts, butterflies flew up her back, a spider had made its web around her belly button. The article features twenty-seven photos of her, twenty of which show her naked, or wearing only her underwear. In several pictures she is in her late eighties, and in those that chronicle the progress of her tattoos, she is in her late forties. Nowhere else in my entire life have I seen a picture of a naked middle-aged or elderly woman that was presented as an image of beauty. And she was. Working nude at her desk, writing letters to tattooed pals, or standing demurely in front of the TV set in her living room, Weinzirl exhibited her body with pride, and we are meant to view it with admiration.

In her essay "The Carnivalesque Body," Margo DeMello writes that tattooed women reject middle-class assumptions about when the female body should be exhibited, what the boundaries of the body are, what aesthetic choices should shape it. She is basically saying that women who get tattoos are like men who are drag queens, decorating and defining themselves in a socially inappropriate way. Looking at Elizabeth Weinzirl, I realize that despite my anxieties, despite the pressure to be natural, I want to be like her.

The tattoo parlor is not hard to find. Although tattooing has been illegal in New York City since 1962, when there was a hepatitis epidemic, industry magazines print business cards of artists around the country, and the members of my internet newsgroup are happy to give recommendations. Inner City Ink is only a few blocks away. I ring an unmarked buzzer and walk upstairs past a piercing shop and a place that makes custom leather bondage wear. The shop door is painted with a grinning dragon.

A sign reads NO MINORS ALLOWED. A humming sound vibrates the air.

Inside, there are four cheap office desks, two tucked in a back room and two out front. On each is a tattoo machine, scraps of drawings, and candy jars full of rubber gloves, disposable razors, strips of gauze. Japanese screens shield clients from view if they prefer, but the atmosphere is more performative than private. Prospective customers lean over to see the work being done, and offer compliments. A shirtless young man, his overalls unpinned, looks in the mirror at the stencil that has been applied to his shoulder. It is a pair of wings, one reaching toward his collarbone, the other toward his spine. He is unhappy with its placement and asks the artist to wipe it off and put it on again. A tall, round-faced white boy with arms covered in tribal tattoos—some Native American, some African—answers the phone in a thick Brooklyn accent.

The shop is busy. On one wall are the "flash," standard drawings that people can choose from: skulls, flowers, cartoon animals, tribal designs. Below are large black books that show each artist's custom work. A young man with slicked-back hair and sideburns offers to help me. It turns out he is Jamie Worther, one of the artists. His book, which he shows me, is unlike the others. It has small, color snapshots in a suburban flip-through photo album with a floral cover. The tats in the book are fresh, arms slightly swollen, skin shaved bare. They are carefully detailed and free of the testosterone-pumped image vocabulary I see in the work of his colleagues. I am won over by a picture of an armband based on Edward Gorey's hilarious faux-Victorian cartoons. I show Jamie a picture of what I want and he tells me yes, he can do that. He'll draw it up for me by next week.

Even at first glance, the tattoo parlor sanctions totally different behavior than the other environments I've visited to explore the way we decorate ourselves. At the cosmetics counter, there is an emphasis on the beauty of the product—its colors, smells, textures—and on the ugliness of the customer. She is bathed in fluorescent light, reflected in magnifying mirrors, and generally exposed into buying something to cover her flaws. There are sanitary conventions for trying the products that create a slight sense of shame about the germs and spit and sweat we all carry around. At the Fan Club, the racks towered over me and clothes seemed more important than people. The strange lack of privacy made me think that bodies were nothing but shapely hangers there, hidden by the clothes, not decorated by them. At Goodwill, there was an atmosphere of practicality. Nothing there is beautiful, nothing is probably even laundered. You, the customer, need to cover up your sorry flab and protect it from exposure. Goodwill is where you can do that cheap. In these institutions there is always an undercurrent of shame or disregard for the body. It mitigates, though it doesn't erase, the pleasure of self-adornment. And it is absent at Inner City Ink.

No judgments are made about what kind of decoration is appropriate (although most studios won't do public skin unless a client has a lot of work already). If you want to have a fire engine put on your dick, that's cool. If you want Jimi Hendrix on your ass, that's cool, too. What matters is that the fire engine comes out a nice, bright shade of red, and the design fits the shape of your equipment. What matters is that Jimi's Afro arches in a curve that echoes your hip, and the shading on the face is carefully done. Tattoos are not for flattering the figure or accenting good features, so it doesn't matter if your butt is the size of a monster truck and your dick is the size of a paper clip. If the art looks good, you look good.

In fashion magazine photos, runway shows, cosmetics ads, and other displays of tools for self-adornment, clothes and makeup are shown on perfect bodies. At the tattoo parlor, people with recent work lift up their shirts to display it, offering themselves as living samples. The photographs in the portfolios are amateur snapshots of real people. Each body and each image is unique. This is very different from seeing the new line of cosmetics on a model's face, or a suit you want to buy photographed in a magazine. Then, the object is the exact object you will purchase, and its recommended use is being shown to you. You are seeing it in its perfect form. At

Inner City Ink, someone else's tattoo is never an example of how you should be. It is simply an example of what is.

"Look what I got last month," you can say. "Isn't it great-looking?" Your breast enhancement is supposed to be natural. Your foundation makeup is covering flaws. But because a tattoo is not about how well you fit in with social norms, because the invisible rules about beautification have already been broken, the rule about self-display can be broken, too. This is a safe context for exposure that I haven't seen in any other place that sells body adornments.

When I come back to see the drawing, Jamie is hard at work. It's lunchtime, and he is the only artist in the studio. A young Judy Garland in red corduroys lies on a padded table, her shirt hiked up and her pants eased down to expose black panties made of some synthetic fabric. Across her torso is a purple stencil of a tree, gnarled at the roots, stretching up across her breasts, which are covered by a T-shirt. A nocturnal rodent clutches the trunk, eyes bulging into the night. It has a cartoonish look that is at odds with the relative realism of the tree. I can see a star design already tattooed on her lower back. It seems intentionally ugly, a heavy black with orange and blue stripes inside. She chats casually to her friend, who is eating fried chicken on the couch about ten feet away. The work has clearly just started; only the roots of the tree are black and swollen at the edges, bearing the marks of Jamie's needle.

A short, pudgy man with a thick gold ring hanging from the middle of his nose runs into the room. He is from the leather bondage shop next door. He announces loudly that we no longer have to worry about the cops. Joe from downstairs at the (legal) piercing studio has a friend in the office of something-or-other who will make sure to let us know if anything is going down. Jamie and the boy with the tribal arms look relieved. They thank the leather man and he slams the door on his way out.*

After a few more minutes Jamie and Judy take a break and I see my drawing. Jamie's desk faces a bulletin board covered with

* Since these events transpired, tattooing has become legal in New York City. Shops are everywhere: it's hard to walk through the East Village without acquiring ink.

sketches—a winged dragon, designs for armbands, a buxom babe
in a space suit. There are also photographs of a baby ferret sleeping in various positions, displayed with all the pride of a new pet
owner. The drawing is great, though not completely finished. It's
on tracing paper, and there are a few alternative versions sketched
lightly on the side. We make an appointment: Wednesday at noon.
Jamie reminds me it's cash only.

The big day starts with Jamie making a stencil of my drawing. He
has to put it on me four times before I'm satisfied, and each time
my arm is covered with smudges of purple ink. He wipes it off
with paper towels and a green soap that smells like hospitals.
Finally, the image is in the right place. He shaves my bicep with a
blue ladies' razor.

I sit on a specially designed chair that supports my arm as the
ink goes in. It hurts. Hope, an aspiring painter with blue hair and
tragic skin, watches up close. She is Jamie's apprentice. She has just
done her first tattoo on herself and shows me her ankle. It is puffed
up around heavy red lines—an incomprehensible design. "I pushed
too hard," she explains. She has a Star of David on her abdomen,
a trendy seventies shirt tied up to expose it, soft flesh hanging over
velvet pants. I talk to her about painting and exercise and other
trivialities, but all the while I am conscious of Jamie's physical presence. He has rolled up his sleeves and his left hand pulls the skin of
my shoulder taut while his bare right arm rests on mine to do the
work. We sit like this for hours. It's like holding hands. There is no
visible blood, he tells me, because the ink is black.

A plain woman in sweatpants, blond with moist, red skin,
comes in with her boyfriend. He is black, with huge arms, wearing a clean white T-shirt. They kiss and fondle on the couch, run
outside to smoke cigarettes while they wait. When her turn comes,
she puts her hair in a ponytail and I can see her neck is tattooed:
a ghoulish face in black and gray, a vengeful spirit seeking release
from her body. She goes into the bathroom to change her clothes

and comes out wearing a man's tank top, cut low on the sides so the folds of her breasts are visible. She is getting her name, Tina, in ornate letters across her shoulders. "Take it easy on me, Will," she instructs, as she rests her head on a pillow before his machine. "I'm an exotic dancer, and I was out shakin' my fanny till four in the morning last night. Some days I'm just not in the mood for pain, and today is one of them."

A thuggish-looking man in a tank top is having a Jesus figure put on his shoulder by one of the other artists. "I won't do Jesus," says Jamie in a low voice as he leans close over my arm. "Or the Virgin Mary. People want them all the time, but it just creeps me out." Jamie, it turns out, is not just a tattoo artist. He is also a happy-go-lucky Satanist, friend to all ferrets, and design school dropout. He is in a punk rock swing band on his days off. They play songs about serial killers, mainly, and claim to worship the Devil. "But we don't really," he says. "It's just an act." He plays me the John Wayne Gacy song on their demo tape, but I can't understand the lyrics. After a while, he admits to having done one Jesus tattoo: Jesus was masturbating through the holes left in his hands by the crucifixion.

Despite these disturbing revelations, Jamie takes good care of me. He uses rubber gloves and disposable needles, both frequently changed. When we break for lunch, he offers me rice and beans. I run out to buy us sodas. He tells me I am a good sport, and takes an extra two hours doing detail work he doesn't charge for. "That's huge!" says the boy with the tribal arms, meaning that it's good work. "Jamie, you're sick! Look at that detail." I feel proud of it, because I am no longer the canvas. Its beauty has become mine, and the boy with the tribal arms is admiring a part of my body. The only part I chose. Jamie bandages me up and sends me home.

Ten years ago I imagined a tattoo would give me proof of experience, that it would bring out some latent toughness in my fragile soul. Perhaps it has. But it's also given me a left arm that I think is totally, permanently gorgeous. I have an unqualified pride in one part of my body. The beauty of the nineteenth-century literature I have loved since those days with Charlotte Brontë in the bead shop is part of me. On my arm forever is an antique scroll. It wraps around my bicep, and has a small tear on the upper edge. Its centerpiece is Tennyson's "Lady of Shalott," drawn by painter William Holman Hunt for a special 1857 edition of poems. The Lady lives up in a tower room on an isolated island. She weaves a tapestry as she looks into a mirror that reflects the road to Camelot, visible through the windows behind her. She watches reflections of the world and weaves them into the design of her web. A curse will strike her if she gazes down on Camelot directly. Then, the reflected beauty of Sir Lancelot tempts her. She looks at him through the window instead of the mirror: "Out flew the web and floated wide; / The mirror cracked from side to side; / 'The curse is come upon me,' cried / The Lady of Shalott."

This is the moment Hunt's picture portrays. The lady is a mammoth woman, heavy-jawed and dark in the Pre-Raphaelite tradition. She fills the tower in which she is trapped, dwarfing it. Her hair flies about the room and mingles with the threads from her sewing. She stands caught in the unraveling embroidery that is surging out the window. She knows she is doomed.

The Lady of Shalott mingles her body (her hair) with her art (the threads of her web). She has stopped looking in the mirror, which offers only pale reflections of the vibrant world outside the tower. She has chosen to pursue her physical desires, to live bodily in the world, even if it means her end.

The old books I love, the history, the art, the poetry, all are under my skin. Is my body reflecting my mind? Or is my mind changed by the change in my body? Both, I think. I am beginning to understand what ThEnigma meant: "This is only the back of the puzzle," he said, spreading his blue arms wide. "The art's on the inside." I roll up my sleeve in pride and pleasure.

fucking

strip shows
• • • • • • • • • • • • • • • •

The show at Chippendales is a case study in the weirdness of hetero sex in America today. A tuxedoed man with a ridiculously large chin greets me at the door. Seeing me glance around, he asks, "Are you here to meet another girl with hair like yours?"

He means short hair, but seems afraid to say it, as if to mention my pixie cut would be to question my sexual orientation or my femininity. With relief I see Jessica, fellow short-haired babe, waving to me from across the room. The crowd is Long Island bachelorette, most of them dressed with a rather synthetic kind of sexiness. They show great expanses of tan-stockinged leg, heavy lip liner, and hair spray. Giddy with celebratory anticipation, they take snapshots and trot from table to table. "How many are here for a bachelorette party?" asks the emcee.

The room erupts in screams. My friend Ruth, world traveler and marathon runner, fits in better than I do with her masses of curly hair and pink blouse, but she is a bit fatigued with the trauma of being the first to arrive. Sipping her plastic cup of beer and waiting for Jessica and me to make it through the snow, she was, for a moment, a lone wolf woman ogling the topless waiter, shelling out a thirty-five-dollar cover charge in exchange for a thrill. We commiserate with her. That wolfish consumption of sexual service is such a deeply unfamiliar role for a young woman. The three of us find relief in girlish camaraderie, very much like the bachelorettes.

There is something about going to a male strip show that calls the audience members' sexual legitimacy into question. We make various attempts to reaffirm it. The maître d's reticence about my hair, the bachelorette party's ritual celebration of one woman's success at landing a mate, the provocative evening wear of the people around us, Ruth's discomfort at being there alone—all these are symptoms of the precarious position that Chippendales' role reversal creates.

At first, that reversal seems extraordinarily simple. As Ken Siman points out in *The Beauty Trip,* the Chippendales waiters, shirtless with bow ties and white cuffs, are muscle-boy versions of the *Playboy* bunny. The stage boasts a classic stripper's pole. The emcee introduces the waiters to us by name and tells us they're there to serve our every little need. But things become more complicated once the show begins.

The lights dim, the music pumps, and a parade of dancers bops through a series of slightly dated moves, flashing chests but not much more. The bachelorettes squeal and hide their faces, wiggling in their seats when a stripper's G-stringed ass pokes out from beneath a trench coat. As the show gets going, I notice a hierarchy of dancers onstage. A number of average-looking men in tight black pants, headbands, and cut-off shirtsleeves constitute the chorus. My guess is they're wanna-be Broadway show dancers trying to pay the rent. Up a level are some pretty boys, shirts off. They don't do solo strips, but they do pull their pants down every once in a while during group numbers to reveal muscled butts in brightly colored G-strings. The top level are the solo strippers; they have sexpot monikers like Steve Cougar and Chad

Devereaux. Cougar is clearly the number-one naked guy; he specializes in romantic lip-synching to ballads and is featured several times, once in uniform and twice in suits with no tie. No socks either, since these would introduce a severely pedestrian element to the zipless fuck fantasy that dominates the show no matter what the scenario. And here is where I notice that the fantasy propagated by Chippendales is a very limited one, and begin to wonder why.

The solo strippers are all of a particular type. Aside from a few haircut details (one has a Fabio do, another one of those bob cuts favored by pubescent boys on sitcoms), they are so similar that I didn't realize I was seeing Cougar for the second time until I recognized the miniature tattoo on his butt. In a way, that's part of the fantasy—"Oh, I did you before sometime, didn't I, handsome? I seem to remember that cute little bit of ink on your ass. Don't take it personally, baby. I may forget a face, but I'd never forget a tush like yours." Still, the strippers' bodies and faces are remarkably homogenous, even within the limits of what one might expect at Chippendales. They are all tall and of large build, though some of the background dancers are slimmer. They are all white. One guy's name was Lopez, but he sported the same Dick Tracy jaw and pale skin as the rest of them. They have no body hair, armpits excepted.

The themed scenarios in which they dance are tingly clean. One is a faux Calvin Klein ad, in which four or five men strut slowly in their briefs and tank tops, gradually undressing in the light of simulated venetian blinds. When they've all got their shirts off, one strips to a G-string while the others leave. He then simulates masturbation with a giant fake banana on a bedlike structure covered with mosquito netting. Seconds before the lights go out, the banana spews white liquid high into the air. This is as explicit as it gets here: a Florida fantasy, figured in terms of a nationwide ad campaign to provide it with class and legitimacy. Two nearly identical numbers feature men in outfits that imply they work managing the local Hard Rock Cafe or some L.A.

racquet club: purple suit with floral shirt or black suit with color block shirt, both without socks. In another scene, Cougar slowly strips to a Top Forty ballad, stopping periodically to march about in military formation with two other guys in tight white navy uniforms.

None of these men are ever lower-class, nor are they upper-class. The power imbalances that fuel so many fantasies are strangely absent. No dream of fucking the CEO during a job interview is permitted here, no hunky plumber looking under my sink. Just a good, middle-class man with questionable taste expressing his love via a poorly executed lip-synch to a well-known song. Even the longhaired dude in the leather jacket is perfectly manicured and free of any other signs of naughtiness: he doesn't wear ripped jeans, or leather pants, or smoke a cigarette. No five o'clock shadow or cheap white T-shirt or pierced ear or anything whatsoever allows me to imagine he's anything but a guy with a perm wearing a costume. The illusion seems deliberately incomplete.

Where is the UPS man in uniform? Where is the scruffy eighteen-year-old student seducing teacher? The vampire, pale and thin and consumed by desire? The drag queen, slowly removing his clothes to reveal his true identity? Where is the buff construction worker for *me* to whistle at? I'd even settle for the stuff of romance novels: a shirtless sheik stripping for his harem, a pirate king in a black mask, an Indian warrior covered in paint. However, these are probably too politically incorrect, too primal. But hey, what is striptease for?

When a dancer finishes his final act, he descends into the audience in his G-string. Women wave bills over their heads to buy kisses. At best, the man buries his head in her neck while jerking his pelvis about spasmodically; perhaps the recipients of this display have tipped him a fiver, since some women merit only a peck on the cheek. Johnny St. Claire, the longhaired muscle boy who danced in the leather jacket, is particularly tame. He brushes his lips briefly across each woman's skin and darts away with his cash in hand. Still, he is in demand as much as any of the rest;

the women don't seem to want to grab ass or fondle chests. More often than not, they lift their hands high during the embrace, as if wet nails prevented them from touching the dancers. I, however, find myself irritated with St. Claire. "Why isn't he putting out?" I whisper to Jessica. "He should give them what they're paying for."

My moment of irritation was, if I look at it carefully, the first time I have ever really looked at a man as an object, a body without feelings. For a second, I saw St. Claire as nothing but a whore who wasn't doing his job very well, rather than as a human being forced into unwanted physical contact by economic necessity. Sure, I've ogled Brad Pitt at the movies or some lifeguard on the beach, but I'd never before known that an object of desire would touch me for money. For only a dollar, in fact.

Rick, a lanky blond salesman with the body of a surfer boy, worked for a year and a half as a topless waiter in a club outside Chicago. On a good night, there were four hundred women, seven dancers, and four waiters. It was a themed show much like Chippendales, though perhaps a bit more satisfying: no tame group numbers, a beach boy with lots of suntan oil, a Latin lover, my longed-for construction worker. Rick wore tight black pants and a bow tie. Nothing else except shoes. He tells me there was action in the parking lot after the show; he occasionally got some himself, but turned down offers of money: "Come home with me and my girlfriend," women would offer. "You'll be paid." Usually, he says, the waiters didn't have the status for paid sex the way the dancers did. Overheard in the dressing room: "I can't believe it. She gave me fifty bucks just to blow me in the parking lot."

The club had a fair number of regulars, among whom were a mother-and-daughter pair Rick describes as married to the mob. "They had some liquid money," he says. "When everyone else was waving singles, they'd wave fives, twenties." Eventually it turned out the mother was paying one of the dancers for sex, hundreds of dollars. Her husband showed up one day and threatened the owner, making him promise not to let his wife back in.

Still, Rick and his fellow employees didn't see their profession as sex work, but as more of a lark. "It wasn't like they were doing it for the money," he says. "They were already taking home more than two hundred bucks a night. They didn't need another fifty. They were just turned on from dancing naked in front of four hundred women. I never thought of it as prostitution, though looking back on it now, that's what it was." Rick himself would flash a G-stringed hip to a table he served for three or four bucks, and show them a full rear view for seven to ten. "Having your personal space invaded was part of the job," he says of customers who copped a feel, "but it was fun to get paid to flirt with hundreds of screaming, horny women. As a lifeguard, I got paid all day to get a tan, and then got paid all night to show it off. . . . It's not like I was selling myself."

I have no problem with sex work if no one gets hurt, but a guy *is* selling himself—or at least his body—when he gets fifty bucks for a parking lot tumble, or a dollar for a peck on the cheek. That step toward prostitution the Chippendales men take when they cruise the audience in a G-string rather than remaining safely on-stage allowed the only moment of full role reversal that occurred that night, my objectification of Johnny St. Claire. Otherwise, the pseudo-egalitarian striptease acts offered only a faint taste of what it must be like to be a man at a strip club.

In the movies, female strippers very often perform for the benefit of a specific other. When they do these private dances, it is for men with whom they have some deeper connection: the schoolgirl in *Exotica* performs for a man she used to know, allowing him to fantasize about his dead daughter, while the bimbo in *Showgirls* dances for the man she desires and with whom she later goes to bed. In *The Crossing Guard*, Jack Nicholson's character is a club regular; one night he is invited onstage to dance with a stripper in a baby's dress. Later, he goes home with her, as it's clear he's done before. These movies allow individuals in the audience to participate in what I imagine must be a typical fantasy for a man who frequents strip joints: that the dancer is disrobing for his benefit, and his alone. Even if they've never met, they've got something special going on.

At the Blue Angel, a self-proclaimed erotic cabaret, I got to see this fantasy in action. It had been described to me as a hip, omni-sexual place where Drew Barrymore once got so excited she jumped onstage and took off her clothes. I go there with Jessica in search of male striptease, but I don't get it. What I do get is a chance for a close-up view of shaved, pierced labia and a sudden realization that I have never properly understood the meaning of the term *lap dance*.

At the door, a skinny woman with beardlike blue tattoos on her chin takes our money. There are no drinks, no food, no glasses of water. People have brought cartons of juice and soda, but strangely enough, no one has beer. A table of fashion models, male and female, sits up front watching a rather fat, six-foot tall blonde woman with a face like a kewpie doll relieve herself of a shiny black dress. Full nudity, aside from platform shoes; jiggling cellulite. "I bet she's fertile as a cow," the architect type at the table next to me says to his buddy. The only men to perform are a fire-eater and an emcee ("Two Jews walk into a bar . . . and buy it! What's the difference between pussy and sushi? The price!"), but the women show surprising variety. One, who dances an old-fashioned burlesque wearing pasties and a bikini bottom over strange red fishnets, looks about forty. The others are young, but there is a range of skin colors and a total absence of breast implants. I'm sure none of the dancers wore more than a B cup, and many had heavy legs, flat chests, saggy behinds, plain faces. One had a scar on her abdomen. Unlike Chippendales, where the fantasy is orchestrated to be seamless, the girls here crawl around on the stage in the silence following their numbers, collecting their G-strings and other discarded items and sometimes putting them back on before walking through the audience to the changing room in the back.

The most dramatic and somehow shocking act (surpassing even the lesbian dominatrixes—yes, somehow both dominant—

complete with hot wax, slave collars, and gag balls) is performed by a stripper named Chelsea. Petite, with a huge mane of hair, Chelsea, like many of the other dancers, has been strutting through the audience and chatting up the male customers. A pair of fifty-year-old men in plaid shirts, looking like Muppets in this downtown crowd, get an ever-changing pair of strippers filling their extra two chairs. Chelsea, wearing an animal-print dress so short it would not be legal at the supermarket, has concentrated her attention on a boisterous young Asian-American man in glasses and a baseball cap who has been heckling the greasy emcee. Chelsea's been at this man's side much of the night, cracking jokes and criss-crossing her legs. Since the Blue Angel sells no drinks, at first I can't figure out what motivates her cultivation of him; later, in the back room, I see her grinding herself into his crotch as he leans back on a couch. She is completely naked. His hands are on her ass. This must be where the real money is.

Her performance, before the lap dance, begins in a nurse's outfit, complete with cap and a white first-aid box with a red cross on it. After prancing about a bit and relieving herself of some clothes, Chelsea sits on a chair facing the audience. She opens the box and takes out a razor and a container of shaving cream. Spreading her legs, she shaves off all her pubic hair, an activity that appears to excite her no small amount. She uses lots of cream and rinses with red-tinted water from a white bucket. Finished, she oozes over to another part of the stage and, lying on the floor, spreads her legs for the men (Baseball Hat included) at the closest table. They lean forward, peering at her pierced crotch like gynecologists in training. I'm sure the man in the hat thinks she's dancing just for him. And in a way he's right.

The prostitution at Rick's Chicago club was outside the institution, in the parking lot rather than in a back room. At Chippendales the men are secure from solicitation. Very rarely are they alone; when they work the room between acts they wear tuxedos, and never sit down. After the show they are busy busy busy, selling calendars and shooting Polaroids. The romantic scenes the strippers perform do play into the fantasy of the private dance, but since the men don't do lap dances and a quick peck on the cheek is the most a girl can get, no women ever orgasm on the tweedy armchairs of Chippendales the way the men do in the back room of the Blue Angel. If a woman does think Johnny St. Claire is dancing just for her, she can't reasonably expect he'll finger-fuck her under the table after the show for a few extra bucks. When Chippendales guys perform for a particular woman, she isn't cozied away in a back room. She is up on stage being stared at. In the final moment of one number, the G-stringed beefcake at the feet of a party girl in a black miniskirt grabbed her knees, spread her legs apart and pushed his face toward her crotch. She did not look pleased. Earlier the same dancer had grabbed the breasts of another audience member as she sat onstage. Some scenarios are even more extreme. Rick says of his club, "The emcee, he was a fag. He didn't care, he would get on top of [the women] and grind, even in a sixty-nine position on the runway, some old lady or whatever." At the end of Cougar's candlelight dinner dance, he stands in front of his seated companion, puts his hand on the back of her head, and rapidly pushes her face into his dick several times. Afterward we asked Cougar, who was cruising the audience fully clothed, whether anyone ever complains. He says they do occasionally, but not often, and that the woman's consent is never explicitly asked, though he tries to get a feel for how she'll react beforehand. Sometimes, he adds, he just doesn't want to do that number.

Forced fellatio is, I feel pretty safe saying, damn low on the list of average women's sexual fantasies. Even those of us who fantasize about rape probably wouldn't find it entertaining to imagine the gag reflex being triggered. Besides, fantasies of coercion are one thing if they liven up a little solo wanking or add spice to an evening with a familiar partner, and another thing when the unwanted contact is genuine and unexpected. Much the same goes for having an audience of over a hundred screaming people look up your miniskirt or having a man you don't know grab your breasts. Chippendales' notion that such experiences would be sexy rather than bothersome or embarrassing indicates to me a profound misunderstanding of how women get aroused. Or else such moments are meant to deliberately undermine the supposed agenda of sexual excitement.

Any arousal generated by the tame fantasies of Chippendales is dissipated by a switch, somewhere near the man's simulated climax or the momentary removal of his G-string, to a notion of good sex that I can only guess is male. When these guys make love to an imaginary woman, their orgasms are achieved by rapid pumping and the whole of the simulated intercourse lasts about fifty-eight seconds. When they jack off, their exploding bananas or spurting beer bottles spew liquid high in the air, sure winners in any circle-jerk Olympics. But a guy who takes fifty-eight seconds to orgasm is probably a lousy lover; seeing him hump away and then collapse with a smirk of pride just reminds me of bad sex I had in college. And the cum-spurting "money shot" of men's pornography that is being replicated here is a staple of that genre for a reason: it turns men on.

The range of services and style of presentation in strip clubs for women may be limited because there is little demand. Several people I've talked to have suggested that women just don't get off on visual stimulation the same way men do. This could be true, but it also seems like we don't get off on it because we don't get any that's very good, and even that costs more than tickets to the opera. One thing I did realize in going to Chippendales was that I could conceivably be aroused by striptease—just not these bodies, not this music, not these scenarios, not these hairdos. It is really beginning to seem to me that whoever runs the club does not actually want to turn the customers on. Explicit as the show is, it remains good clean fun because it is so weirdly unsexy. And there is nowhere else to go. Here in New York, the city that I'm sure houses many of the most decadent women in the world, the only heterosexual male sex show (S&M clubs excepted) consists of beefy suburbanite men simulating loving, romantic striptease over candlelight. According to the publisher of *The Exotic Dancers Directory,* there are less than ten hetero strip clubs for women—nationwide. Where are the strippers for bad straight girls like me, not bad enough to want a whip across my back, but bad enough to want to see some naked men?

Our culture has a long history of imagining female sexuality as so voracious it has to be controlled and also as so virtuous it must not be offended. In Victorian England, for example, the image of women as loving, but inhibited and delicate, concealed a fear of women's ferocious sexual appetites. Once unleashed they would be impossible to tame, so corsets and strict codes of behavior kept them in place. The notion of extreme virtue went hand in hand with the underlying fear of the female sex fiend, demanding and all-consuming. Our assumptions today are not entirely different: women don't respond to visual stimulation (but we don't have much, so how do we know?); women like large, heavily muscled men with no body hair (but the people I know who like that type are gay men); women won't buy sexual services like lap dances (but what about the women at Rick's club?); women fantasize about loving sex between equals (oh please, just go read Nancy Friday). Could these assumptions—shared by many people of both sexes, and propagated by institutions like Chippendales—mask a fear of what would happen if women could really get off on striptease?

sex lessons
••••••••••••••••••

the point is that our sexual experiences are structured and carried out according to certain rules, even though we pretend they're not. That is why so many people don't notice what is missing from the Chippendales show. It follows rules they don't even know they ever learned. Not only is there the antique social institution of the men's hetero sex show, which lays down definitions of appropriate exposure, sexual contact, and physical attractiveness.

There's also the invisible institution of our society providing almost no similar live entertainment for women. The latter is probably just as important a factor in the dynamics of my ordinary, everyday sex life as the former.

Late Friday night, junior year of high school, basement rec room, a case of cheap beer: Hector Burke, having knocked back a few, explains a secret to the girls who sit around him on the sofa. He is the only boy present, some fluke in the ever-shifting social matrix having left all of us without boyfriends and him admitted to the inner circle. Hector gets girls, but somehow never any who go to our small high school. His girlfriends are named Bitsy and attend single-sex institutions. We don't know how he meets them. The secret he tells us knocks me, at least, into a new realm of sexual confusion. All the rules I thought I knew seem wrong.

"Lubrication," Hector says, speaking of hand jobs (which is really all any of us are up to at that point), "is the most important thing. The Most Important. If you don't have any lotion or anything, just lick your hand."

Lotion? Hand licking? How could these things be introduced into the very neat and clean fondlings that had made up my sexual experience thus far? I couldn't possibly imagine drooling on my hand in front of a boy I liked. I was sure he would find it repulsively unfeminine. And lotion? That was not available in the Camaros and Dodge Darts in which most of my penile contact had thus far occurred, but even if it was, how could such an abrupt move be appropriate? I couldn't imagine fumbling in the dark for a jar of Vaseline. Even if it was conveniently located, using it would mean interrupting the tentative and orderly progression of my teenage gropings—on top of the shirt, up the shirt, on top of the pants in the back, on top of the pants in the front, down the pants a little, then farther, then maybe back up the shirt for a bit, then back down. All that gentle fiddling about, teasingly feminine I imagined, would go to waste. I would have to collect the lotion and then make a direct dive at the penis. With such a startling move things were bound to go wrong.

Lubrication had never been mentioned except as a natural outcome of female excitement that conveniently facilitated various activities—not by my mother, not by the tenth grade biology teacher, not by *Our Bodies, Ourselves,* at least not the parts I had read. How could I know to lubricate what was not naturally lubricated? Now that I think of it, I'm sure many a teenage pregnancy could be prevented if people merely educated their youngsters in the necessary techniques for giving a decent hand job.

My adolescent confusion was a symptom of the reality that sexual behavior—at least for heterosexuals of fairly mainstream practice—is regulated by the instructions people receive from the cultural institutions that surround them. People absorb the instructions, taboos, and standards so thoroughly that they become self-regulated; they don't even admit they have been taught, don't even see where instinct ends and their learned behavior begins. In the broadest sense, this regulation means that they are taught to like the opposite sex, taught what appearances and body parts to find attractive, and taught to be active or passive sexually according to their gender. As a teen, I had obviously absorbed this last idea with inordinate credence.

People learn about sex, as opposed to reproduction, in a coded language that keeps most of the rules invisible. Reproduction we talk about vigorously and loudly. Sex ed classes proudly teach us all to say *vagina* and *testicles* and to approximate the pronunciation of *clitoris.* Most teenagers know how babies are made and the names of STDs. But there is much more to be learned in order to know about sex and how it is performed in our culture: What the common fantasies are. When it's over. What to wear. What noise to make. What parts of it are still unmentionable. And that a blow job has no blowing. Learning these things is very often a rather oblique process. For example, I was completely flummoxed when the man who was my fifth lover commented that I was quiet in bed. I had no idea anybody made more noise than I did. How could I have known? Should I be making more noise? Had I been keeping quiet deliberately, in obedience to some rule of how to have sex that now turned out was not a rule after all? Was it just a leftover habit from early gropings in my high school boyfriend's family recliner? Or was quiet just the natural me? I really couldn't tell which it was. Jessica, on the other hand, has on several occasions entertained tipsy women with imitations of an ex-boyfriend she calls the Hyena. His yelping, canine sex cries did break that unwritten rule about vocalization I had long ago absorbed, particularly because they began long before his pants came off. Fail to learn the rules and find yourself subject to sexual scorn.

We learn the minutiae of etiquette, technique, and response in such indirect ways because the institutions that regulate the expression of sexuality are not about to explain them to us. It is very rare for parents to tell a child that it's better to breathe through your nose when kissing, much less that finding a clitoris is no good at all if you poke it like a typewriter key. School sex education is limited to students making diagrams of the pelvic region and memorizing the effectiveness rates of various kinds of contraception. No teacher ever tells a girl she might fellate her boyfriend (as safely as possible, of course) before putting his condom on, to sweeten him out of any reluctance to using it and ease the awkwardness of fumbling in the dark by bringing her eyes close to what she is doing. The biology class syllabus never includes techniques for cunnilingus, even though it does include the suggestion that people refrain from intercourse and practice safer sex. The health textbook does not recommend the felicitous use of pillows in certain positions or hint at the curious pleasures of delayed orgasm.

Where we do learn about sex is in the backseats of cars, under bleachers, in the hallway at a school dance, or in the bushes. To all of those places that are not quite the bed, we bring our inhibitions, our need to discipline or be disciplined, our desire for comfort, and our judgments. Hardly saying a word, we teach them to each other. And then we hold on to these techniques, limitations, and beliefs with incredible tenacity, perhaps because we learned them in such secret and intangible ways and because their subjects are so unspeakable.

What feels natural has changed. Oral sex used to be taboo. Now it's so commonplace that people forget they ever thought it a crime against nature. Most couples favor the missionary position without thinking about why it seems so natural when many cultures seldom use it and no animals I know of ever do. The tragic heroines of *Show Boat* sing, "Fish gotta swim, birds gotta fly, I'm gonna love one man till I die." In the era of that musical, women's sexual loyalty and limited experience seemed as natural as a fish in water. These days, however, it seems just as natural for girls to experiment in college with a variety of partners. The bodies and body parts that attract lovers to each other also change with the times. Women feel they are "just doin' what comes naturally" as they lust for Prince or Johnny Depp, but both men are runty by the standards of forty years ago. In the eighteenth century, men's legs were displayed in form-fitting pants and stockings that showed off shapely calves. Today, a curvy lower leg has little appeal; men's abdomens and arms are the objects of focus. A woman's ankle, highly sexualized when her long skirts nearly always reached her feet, no longer wields much erotic power in the mainstream. Softer, fleshier ideals preceded the skinny sex objects of the late twentieth century. Genitals will probably always be considered erotic, but preferences in these are subject to cultural pressures as well, as anyone inclined to enjoy those belonging to his own sex can attest.

People never say to themselves, "I will not do it in any position that reminds me of animals or male homosexuals." It somehow just never comes up. They never say, "I will always remember to kiss my partner on the lips because it's more romantic and makes everything seem less carnal." They just do it because that's what's done. They never plan to remain silent, they just do because it seems easy, not admitting that it's because they were never taught to vocalize their desires. No one ever thinks about why lips progress from neck to nipples to genitals and not the other way around. It's just the order of things. In fact, according to *The Hite Report* (granted, published in 1976, but still . . . !) more than 95 percent of heterosexual sex follows the same progression: foreplay, penetration, intercourse, and orgasm (especially male), after which sex is officially over. Perhaps this progression is natural or instinctive in some way, but it certainly shouldn't be the only option.

Well, what are the other options? I have no one to ask, so I try to get some professional advice. At first, skulking around the sex department at my local bookstore, I felt embarrassed that I'd be holding a stack full of near-pornography when some lonely pervert using the bookstore as a pickup joint asked me what I was reading. But I realized rather quickly that it was not my lusts that I was ashamed of: it was the idea that I don't yet know how to have sex properly when everybody else was just born a master lover. Even the lonely pervert will dismiss me as a moron who needs sex manuals. Reading them is really quite threatening to my sense of self, because the idea that sexual behavior is instinctive is so solidly ingrained in me.

That old chestnut, Alex Comfort's *The Joy of Sex,* is structured like a recipe book. The subtitle is "A Gourmet Guide for Lovemaking" and its chapters are titled "Ingredients," "Appetizers," "Main Courses," "Sauces," and so on. The reason for this structure is that cooking is one of the few skills most people learn from a book rather than in school. There is no shame in checking *The Joy of Cooking* for instructions on deveining shrimp or how long to bake a potato. The battered reference book provides not only basic technique but innovative suggestions for serving or varying meals. And who on earth has just one cookbook? People stock their kitchens with lessons from faraway lands and alternative approaches: the foods of northern Italy, the spices of India, vegetarian delights, spa cuisine. They display their gravy-stained spines with pride, evidence of their versatile interest in new tastes and techniques.

The Joy of Sex circumvents the discomfort many readers must feel in learning sexual behavior from a book by couching the experience in terms that make the educational experience familiar, even though it is not. Dr. Comfort reminds me in the introduction that this is a menu, not a rule book; and it does read more like a list of restaurant specials than a how-to guide for cooks. Activities are described, but instructions are rarely given explicitly. Comfort tells me that some people are excited by rubber, masks, voyeurism, stockings, and women dressed up as horses; some people do it on horseback, while bathing, or on motorcycles. He does not tell me what activities might be worthwhile performing in a rubber dress, how to avoid falling down in the shower, how the whole horseback thing gets going, or what on earth the horse outfit entails (a saddle? a tail? does he carry a whip?). He is merely informing me that some people like these things, and if I want to figure out how they're done, I shall have to do it myself.

In other places Comfort gives highly specific instructions about objects without explaining what to do with them once you have them. "Don't use super-cooled ice, let alone dry ice." Okay. Now what? To have intercourse standing up, he says, "Many women need to stand on two Manhattan phone directories with the Yellow Pages . . ." But he gives no specific suggestions for how to screw effectively with one foot still on the Yellow Pages, a mystery that I would be grateful to have cleared up. With occasional exceptions (each variation on penetration from behind is given a separate entry of its own) *The Joy of Sex* presents activities in an extremely oblique style—which is, I think, a major reason for its enduring popularity. The book remains a classic because, although it seems explicit, it does not challenge our notion that the details of sex come naturally. Because it is so objective in its presentation, rarely advocating any practice as especially fun or stimulating, it allows people to leave in place the rules that so far have governed their sex lives.

The sex department of my local bookstore has a small rash of titles by Dr. Ruth Westheimer, who has hit on an approach to the sex manual that Americans are even more comfortable with than the illustrated smorgasbord *Joy*. She borrows the food metaphor from Alex Comfort, but filters all explicit material through her persona, which she describes as Grandma Chickensoup. "We are happy to share the discoveries we have made in the kitchen," she writes. "So why shouldn't we feel just as comfortable exchanging recipes for better sexual functioning?" She says she ends her radio program by saying, "Have good sex!" just like a grandmother saying, "Eat! Eat!"

The persona is a major component of her books. It is not only comforting and unthreatening (as opposed to sex advice books by famed madams or M.D.s), it also makes sex seem as wholesome as a home-cooked meal. "Let's talk about cucumbers..." she writes. "Nothing nasty or sleazy about a cucumber. A nice, natural green penis. Any seventy-year-old lady can keep it openly."

Dr. Ruth's cheerful recommendation of a vegetable dildo betrays all the anxieties she expects her audience to have: What if someone knows I masturbate? What if I'm doing something perverted? Dr. Ruth likes her sex paraphernalia clean, natural, and preferably undetectable. No one has to know—it's so organic it's invisible. While she does recommend openly keeping a shelf of erotic reading material, she strongly emphasizes that "sexually explicit literature" is the term she prefers, rather than "dirty books." She doesn't even like to use the word *porno* because of its shameful connotations, although she acknowledges that for some people her clean and technical phrases take the fun out of things. Dr. Ruth is not one to talk dirty. In fact, she is so reluctant to shock her conservative audience that she speaks frankly about homosexuality, disease, and oral sex only in chapters specifically designated for such topics. Elsewhere, they are never mentioned. Still in print, *Dr. Ruth's Guide to Good Sex* (written in 1983) includes no information on HIV transmission.

I don't doubt that the wholesome image of sex she is working to create is much needed, though it propagates many of the same limited notions about pleasure that the Chippendales show does. The public library copy of *Dr. Ruth's Guide for Married Lovers* I found had the chapters titled "Masturbation" and "Clitoral and Vaginal" ripped out. Also, "You Say You Love Me But You Don't Even Come." The person who can't even bring himself to photocopy such pages at one of the nearby copy machines is a person who needs Dr. Ruth's comforting, natural view of sex rather desperately. Presumably it was the same repressed vandal who wrote "a pretty smart bitch" underneath Westheimer's name on the title page.

Dr. Ruth's famous face smiles out in bold color from the front cover of many of her books, but most sex manuals I'm looking at feature either a small black-and-white photo of the author trying to look physically appealing, or no photo at all. I'm sure marketing considerations make this the most advisable approach. I had my doubts about a book entitled *Erotic Games* when I saw the author looked like Newt Gingrich with a dye job and a cheap suit. He's probably an incredibly sexual being, but he really doesn't look it. I'd generally like to imagine that advice on how to give a good hand job is being given me by a fantastically preserved woman in her sixties, who still gets it at least five times a week from an Adonis whom she doesn't have to pay. Vanessa Redgrave, say, or Eartha Kitt. However, Dr. Ruth's lack of status as a desirable sex object actually aids her cause. With her educated, Freudian accent and miniature stature, she manages to teach sex techniques without ever being remotely arousing. "I don't come across as a voyeur," Dr. Ruth claims. "I am a concerned and authoritative adviser." In other words, she is not needy or excitable herself. She never tells anecdotes about her own sex life and her explanation of how she became a sex therapist mentions neither her own initiation into sex nor her marriage. It is sex education without the sex.

In general, the basics according to Westheimer are: Try to have foreplay. Try to do it in more than just the missionary position. You women, masturbate if you've never had an orgasm and stimulate your man's penis if it isn't erect. You men (mainly), try not to always fall asleep right after. Some information is better than none, but Grandma Chickensoup revels in the one-liner and makes suggestions so pat and obvious that it seems amazing to me any-one in this country ever manages to have sex at all if they don't know this stuff. The first explicit instruction (how to masturbate, for novice females: a bubble bath, a mirror, the handle of a hair-brush) does not occur until page 107. Dr. Ruth later explains how to perform fellatio: imagine the penis is an ice-cream cone. This is the closest she ever comes to explaining how one might go about the "stimulation" she so often advocates for that organ.

Like these other books, Margo Anand's *The Art of Sexual Magic* uses the metaphor of a menu to ease the awkwardness of adher-ing to her prescribed ways of sucking and fucking. She is, how-ever, much more detailed and orderly than any other sex-manual author I have encountered. She suggests I plan my sexual rela-tions and write out a schedule-menu that involves "setting the table," "hors d'oeuvres," "soup du jour," "starters," a "main course," and "dessert." The sample menu she includes involves a heterosexual couple spending some time together from 7:00 to 8:30 P.M., then engaging in a "caressing and teasing session, with feathers." At 9:15, a "self-pleasuring session," and at 9:35, "magi-cal congress," which is Anand's name for intercourse incorporating the visualization techniques and delayed orgasm she has described in the body of her book. Magical congress takes fifty minutes, and at 10:25 the couple celebrates with chocolates and cognac. Anand then reminds me to keep my own personal menu flexible, in case anything spontaneous arises.

Spontaneity is overwhelmingly absent from the exercises Anand gives in her book. My beloved younger man and I, intrigued by her detailed explanations on how to achieve full-body orgasms, good instructions on finding the G-spot, and carefully illustrated fondling techniques, broke into nervous fits of laughter when confronted with instructions to wear magical robes that conve-niently open in front, to prepare a space with our own special power objects, and to remember to hug after it's all over. Given how complex her rituals are, a person might actually be compelled to interrupt cunnilingus to refer to her book. What happened to the thrill of doing it on the bathroom floor, the intrigue of not knowing what underwear lies under that button fly, the rush of fucking each other only minutes before running out the door to a meeting, or even the basic curiosity of not knowing what your lover will do next?

Anand stresses the importance of going through the book sequentially (no soup before you set the table!). "Ritual," she writes, "takes raw sexual energy and organizes it into a discipline of delight." In her first book, *The Art of Sexual Ecstasy,* Anand explains that during her initiation into tantric sex, orgasming fully clothed with a cripple named Rampal, she at first rebelled against the controlled approach to excitement; but she figured she already knew how to have wild, spontaneous sex. Maybe there was another way.

At the end of an hour-long sex frenzy involving stimulation of the man's perineum, delaying orgasm, and lots of oil-based lubricant, she instructs: "Repeat this process as many times as you wish. Bring the session to a close with a Melting Hug. Shiva, thank Shakti for her willingness to give you new dimensions of pleasure. Take a short break and then give feedback. End with a Heart Salutation." Although she writes a lot about transcending our collective attitudes about sexuality by celebrating our genitalia, renouncing shame, and sticking a gloved finger up the man's anus, the process of consciously adhering to an ordered progression of activities is one of the largest inhibitions she is asking us to overcome.

Half business etiquette, half new-age prayer, the erotic practices Anand recommends are suffocatingly intimate, so much so as to be unthinkable to me and my beloved. Though I consider myself relatively adventurous, I could not under any circumstances perform the exercise in which my lover was supposed to stare closely at my genitals while I gave a speech in the voice of my crotch, followed by a question-and-answer period. I could not call my vagina an enchanted garden and require him to ask permission to enter it. I could not form a support group of four to ten friends in which each of us would tell everyone else, using "concrete and practical" examples, what aspects of our sex lives we are dissatisfied with, and agree to keep a journal of our daily bonking to share with the group.

I know I'm being sarcastic and shallow while Anand is sincerely trying to create a new context for sexuality, a new level of receptivity and comfort through the ordered exercises she's presenting. I just can't help it. Anand's exercises really do challenge my most firmly held notions about sex. I may not believe what I'm doing is natural, exactly. I accept that my sexual practices, like most other peoples, are structured by the culture that taught me about them. Still, I think of intercourse as a private, spontaneous act, not something to be scheduled and planned, not something to be discussed with my friends or family except in general terms. These notions—so far, at least—I haven't overcome.

public displays of lust

actually, the idea of sex as private is a fairly complicated one. Perhaps because Mommy and Daddy and the sex ed instructor tell us so many times that our private parts are private and no one can touch them without our permission, a lot of people want to expose them pretty badly. That self-affirming lesson about personal space also carries a hidden injunction: Keep your private parts private. Keep your sex acts private. So while Anand's group exercises seem ridiculous because we hold so firmly to the idea that sexual privacy is natural, we are also often tempted to go public with our sex lives and body parts in certain limited ways. The thrill of disobeying the rule of privacy is part of why so many people like striptease and go to watch it in groups. It is why the girls I knew at college used to flash their breasts in the campus bar and on the quad. Maybe it's why women choose to pose for *Playboy*. And it's why people fuck in public.

In *Kink: The Hidden Sex Lives of Americans,* Susan Crain Bakos writes that there are more than two hundred swingers' clubs in America. In the course of her research, she went to parties where people had sex with multiple partners while others watched. She visited a sex club where, for a ninety-dollar admission fee, a couple can have sex with strangers in a public space. She also reports that the distribution of homemade pornographic videos is a thriving business. Ordinary people with pimply backs and tan lines point a camera at themselves and screw on a bed for a few hours. Then they mail the video to a distribution house, which sells copies to any willing buyer.

People who aren't willing to swap partners or record their orgasms for posterity still disobey the injunction to privacy by fooling around in public or near-public places. Two kids I knew at summer drama school shocked everyone by humping in the bathroom of a bus during a field trip and returning red-faced to their seats. Couples on the lawn in Central Park entwine only yards from picnicking families. They are fully clothed, but their hands are suspiciously hidden and they're not exactly lying still. People make out in crowded movie theaters and parking lots. These behaviors are more ordinary, perhaps, than mailing out home-sex videos or screwing for an audience in a sex club; but the same disobedience lies at the root of both.

So strong is the injunction that even when a PDA (public display of affection) involves nothing more than holding hands or brushing lips in greeting, many people find much to dislike. I do notice that critics of public affection never complain about parents showing love for children, or about couples in their seventies walking arm in arm. It is not the physical contact people seem to find unpalatable, but contact with an implied sexual component, even if the gesture is as tame as holding hands. The most articulate objection to PDA has come from some members of the homosexual community. A number of gay advocates have argued that kissing or holding hands in public is a flaunting of heterosexual privilege in an age when queer bashing still prevents many same-sex couples from doing likewise. To engage in such displays is to reassert the social and political status of hetero- over homosexuals.

I myself don't object to PDA. I like to hold hands with my boyfriend as we walk down the street. I kiss him hello and I kiss him good-bye. It's possible I might even grope a little in the darkness of a movie theater, but only if there is no one sitting next to me, and only during the previews. The instinct to do these things stems, I think, from an affectionate relationship between lovers, although not everyone indulges in them. And while I'd rather not be witness to any active massaging of body parts usually covered by a bathing suit, I'm always glad to see people expressing love for each other openly when hate and disdain are so much more common on the street. Still, it is interesting to observe how many people comport themselves so they may be identified as sexually involved to even the most casual of observers, and I think the instinct to be affectionate is very often being filtered through a series of social anxieties that go deeper than just violating the rule of privacy, though that is part of it.

A number of the people having heavy public sex must be turned on by the possibility of being caught. These people, I bet, do it hiding in bushes, lying on rooftops, crammed in a closet at a party or in a doorway down an alley. But the people who fool around in an environment like a crowded movie theater or on the lawn in Central Park are not playing with the scary possibility of being discovered. Everyone can already see them and they know it. They must be excited by the display, of which one element is the assertion of one's own sexual value: I'm having sex and you are not. I've got a boy/girlfriend and we get it on and I want you all to know that this makes me an important person. The kids on my drama school retreat, or a couple who join the mile high club and then whisper what they've done to their seat mates, these people aren't actually screwing where anyone can see them, but they are advertising their sexual adventurousness and their success at finding a mate the same way the movie theater couple is.

Like public sex, displays of affection are motivated by an assertion of couplehood, hetero or homo, in a culture that considers
singles second-class citizens. People without partners, or worse,
without even a date, are portrayed by the media as sitting home on
Friday night with a bottle of wine or a pint of ice cream, sighing
sadly over reruns of *The Love Boat*. If you're not in a relationship
and you haven't gone into therapy about it, you must have some
kind of serious block. Your friends will discuss your sex life behind
your back, wondering why you're so incapacitated in your personal relationships. Why doesn't anybody want you? Is your
orientation under question? Are you frigid? Did Uncle Bonzo
abuse you at family reunions? Or is it just fear of intimacy? Why
can't you commit? As they analyze you, your coupled friends walk
hand in hand through the park, doing so partly because they love
each other and like to have their fingers entwined, and partly
because it signifies to them that they are emotionally balanced
and sexually active, successful competitors in the romance marketplace. This unspoken ascendance of the coupled over the single
is the reason people act more openly affectionate with each other
on a street full of strangers than they will in a group of friends. It
is not that physical contact alone is unpleasant to witness. It's that
PDA closes off the couple in its sexually successful world, full of
pride in its achievement, and most folks hesitate before asserting
that partnered dominance over people with whom they usually
interact as individuals and equals.

keeping score
....

at my junior high school, every March brought Fifties Day.
This was an unsurpassedly ridiculous event, and probably influ-
enced our collective sexual experiences in countless insidious ways
for the next several years. More likely inspired by the nostalgia of
the aging principal than by our preteen love of the bunny hop
(though love it we did), it was the most hyped of our few school

dances. It allowed us to dramatize our masculinity or femininity in leather coats or poodle skirts and enter an environment in which some kind of stunted sex act might actually happen. In other words, everyone would dress in fifties clothing, and at the end of the day we would all take off our shoes and go into the cafeteria for a sock hop. Lots of people started going steady in that dark lunchroom, but the first half hour of the dance was painfully awkward. All the lights were turned off and a DJ would spin jitterbug tunes. No one really knew how to dance in couples, and the boys weren't asking anyway, so we girls would bunny hop around, wiggling our butts. When we got tired of that, we'd do chest exercises ("We must! We must! We must increase our bust! The bigger the better, the tighter the sweater, the boys depend on us!"). Then we'd put on lipstick and kiss the boys' cheeks. In the light that seeped in from the hallways, the boys would check one another out, counting kisses. They all wore rolled-up jeans and white T-shirts and lots of hair grease in imitation of the Fonz, and many of their faces were covered with red smudges. It was better, I suspect, to have a collection from different girls than a lot from just one, but certain girls were also particularly prized. The redder the better.

People effect the advertisement of themselves as sexually active, albeit usually to a smallish audience of friends, by keeping score. Perhaps they don't want to risk the vulnerability that a public display of affection implies, or they don't have a regular partner and want to avoid some of the stigma attached to the single person: The scorekeeper may be labeled as infantile or afraid of commitment, but he or she will never be labeled frigid. Documenting sex allows people to assert control over the most fragile, intimate parts of their lives.

In 1993, a group of more than twenty-five boys from California who called themselves the Spur Posse splashed across the news media for raping and otherwise molesting a number of young girls. One of the main things the Posse did was have a point system to keep track of their sexual conquests. They competed for high scores, and were so eager to get points that they staged gang bangs and forced intercourse with middle-schoolers. The high scorer was Billy Shehan, nineteen, with sixty-six points. The Spur Posse's failure to comprehend that people with vaginas are human beings just like people with penises makes them one of the lowest life-forms on the planet, but they are not so unlike the baby Fonzies on Fifties Day. They were caught up in the sexual documentation compulsion, putting metaphoric notches in their belts. In a way, I can identify with them.

Last year, after drinking a bottle of red wine, my friend Marnie and I made lists. Marnie is a computer genius and owns three pug dogs named Small, Medium, and Large. She made her list, but actually I just showed her mine, which I started at age sixteen and have kept, somewhat erratically, ever since. Kissing and sex are such intimate activities, even when done with a stranger, that I don't want to forget my partners. I also want to know how many of them there are. The names of all the boys (and men) I've ever kissed are written down in order, with a star next to those I've screwed. The first few are written in pink pen with little hearts over the i's. There were seventeen, starting with Ace from the toga party, and eleven stars. Not too bad, I thought, and I'm happy to say the numbers have gone up since then; but Marnie, the little tramp, had kissed forty-four boys and one girl. It took nearly an hour to make her list. Some were just vague memories with no actual names attached, like "boy with the necklace at the Weezer concert" or "cute actor who was waiting on line for the bathroom with me." I felt like a prude until she admitted she had only six stars. "My mouth's been busy," she said, "but not the rest of me."

Another night a few years ago, at a bar in an Italian restaurant, my old college friend Laurel and I made up lists on wine-stained paper napkins. Of course I hadn't brought mine with me, so we both did it from memory, reminding each other of indiscretions we'd been hoping to forget, adding in names with little arrows to keep the chronologies correct. Foolish drunken yuppies tried to pick us up, and we squealed and hid our napkins in our laps.

My friend Roxy has several lists: one of everyone she's slept with, one of everyone she gave blow jobs to but didn't fuck, and one of everyone she's kissed. But, she says, the kissing one didn't really work out. Was she supposed to count that kid who threw himself at her in the second grade, or the big lug two years ago she smooched just to be polite? It was too hard to work out what to include, so she gave up that one. Jessica, too, understands about my list. She not only has a list of all the people she's slept with, she has a list of all the people her ex-boyfriend has slept with. I think writing names down is both a check for normality (Are my numbers okay? Is my friend the same as me?) and a conduit for nostalgic reminiscences—not to mention a few bitter sneers.

I know it's not nice to say so, but women do occasionally measure, though usually only when we're young and curious. A friend of mine dumped one of her college boyfriends because his penis was only as long as her pinkie and she just couldn't get that excited about it. And my friend Abigail felt one that was as long as an octave on the piano. She also kissed nearly every boy on the second floor of the dorm at our summer drama school—not really on purpose, but since it happened she reported back and gave them marks. Colin Westphalia was supposed to be the best. I had the chance to kiss him once, but I turned him down. That was before I knew he was number one on Abby's scale. I never got the chance after that, though he did write me a dirty note once. Instead, I was the frequent victim of the tongue-first approach. This technique, though certainly employed by other young men of my acquaintance, was the specialty of Lew Mason, my makeout partner for a heady four weeks and my escort for the end-of-summer formal. Lew was gorgeous in a weasely sort of way and was a primo date because he had a car. Problem was, he kissed as if the tongues were supposed to meet before the lips, diving into my mouth like a water snake and wriggling around with great vigor and enthusiasm. I didn't give him a rating because he was so cute and I was so inexperienced that I had trouble evaluating the situation clearly. In retrospect though, he was a C minus with extra credit for effort.

The point is, Abby's handy evaluation of the second-floor boys' abilities was similar in purpose to the Spur Posse's point system: a way of recording personal experience for the information of a small community—in this case, a clique of randy first-floor girls. Like the Spur Posse, my girlfriends from drama school through graduate school have felt the need to measure and document our sexual encounters.

Nor are we alone. In a local gift shop I found two slim volumes entitled, respectively, *The "Him" Book* and *The "Her" Book*. They each open with the same poem: "From this day on I'll keep complete / A record of all the boys [girls] I meet / Because among them there may be / The one who'll mean the world to me." Inside, each one is an address book with a twist: they have room for photos, plus space designated for nicknames and a description of each entry's personality. Ostensibly aids in a quest for true love, the books assume there will be so many contenders that the owner will need notes and photos to keep track of them all, the way a casting director would. The rhyme gives lip service to the importance of monogamous relationships, while the books themselves celebrate and encourage promiscuity. I think this contradiction is an important indicator of our double desires for permanence and for variety in these post–sexual revolution days. One thing keeping score does is allow us to remember and hold on to each experience—to prevent it from slipping away by recording it, the same way photographs memorialize a party or a vacation. This way we can lend permanence even to fleeting encounters. Keeping score gives us a sense of solidity that allows us to take pleasure in variety, which might otherwise seem like a hazy series of barely memorable contacts.

In *Four Weddings and a Funeral,* Carrie (Andie MacDowell) and Charles (Hugh Grant) compare how many people they've slept with. She has thirty-two. He has nine, and feels like a bit of a schlump in comparison. On an early episode of the sitcom *Friends,* Ross (David Schwimmer) admits that he's had sex with only one woman, now his ex-wife. His buddies tell him how sweet that is, then make fun of him behind his back. In a later episode, Richard (Tom Selleck) tells Monica (Courtney Cox) she's only his second lover; she confesses to a higher number, mentioned offscreen. In the next bedroom over, Ross—now somewhat more experienced—is nevertheless feeling threatened by Rachel's (Jennifer Aniston) count of five. In *Clerks*, Dante (Brian O'Halloran) feels like a stud for having slept with twelve women when his girlfriend Veronica has had intercourse with only three men. He basks nonchalantly in his status as the more experienced lover until she lets it drop that she's performed fellatio on thirty-seven guys. "Oh my God, I feel so nauseous . . ." he moans. "Why did you have to suck their dicks? Why couldn't you sleep with them like any decent person?" In *Reality Bites*, Vicki (Janeane Garofalo) watches her one-night stand stumble out the door. She immediately picks up a notebook to write him on her list, but she can't remember his name, although she knows he is number sixty-six.

In *Four Weddings*, *Friends*, and *Clerks* the women are all more experienced than the men, who feel various levels of discomfort at the situation. Though it shouldn't have to be this way, men's scorekeeping gets a much worse rap than women's, largely due to crimes like those of the Spur Posse. That is why the men portrayed by Grant, Selleck, Schwimmer, and O'Halloran are all so inexperienced. The numbers on TV are markedly lower than the numbers on film, but in each case experience adds to the woman's appeal. Their lists make these women desirable, make them seem independent and sure of themselves. Still, those we see make the lists in front of their men do it flirtatiously and a little apologetically. Vicki of *Reality Bites*, alone and most likely hungover, makes hers with a cold practicality that is much closer to the truth as I've experienced it. Lists may evoke nostalgic memories or feelings of competition among women when we scribble them down together, a feminine bashfulness that distracts attention from the reality of a lengthy catalogue when presented to our lovers, but when we are alone we just want to know how many penises we've engulfed.

Keeping score allows people to check the normalcy of their own activities by playing at deviance. Revealing our intimate secrets (and those of our partners) seems racy and decadent, but we're really just reassuring ourselves that we are "doing it right" by setting up some concrete system by which to evaluate behavior. By covertly measuring a penis in the middle of a blow job so she can tell her friends about it, a young woman removes herself from the immediacy of sexual contact and the vulnerability her position implies; likewise the man who gives himself points after a night of lovemaking. The shiny, slick surface of competence and conquest people often present to the world is a false revelation, a superficial confession. It professes openness as a means of better securing the privacy that, I think, is one of our most unshakable beliefs about sexual experience.

This is an age when AIDS and other sexually transmitted diseases have so infiltrated the public consciousness that every new encounter is evaluated according to the measure of risk taken. Each new romance becomes another set of stats to be listed in the catalogue of one's sexual history. Did he use a condom? Did she swallow? Did she ever inject? Did he ever experiment? In this strained, suspicious environment, public displays of affection affirm the emotional safety of couplehood. Ways of keeping score, in contrast, celebrate promiscuity, a celebration that allows us to remove ourselves from the emotional aftermath of sex. Perhaps these two nearly opposite modes of documenting sexual relations are surfacing now in our culture as ways of calming and controlling people's relatively newfound anxieties about disease. They imbue sex with either the social stability of coupledom or with the casual flippancy accorded the acquisition of a new nail polish or a pair of running shoes. They allow people to view sex as a validation, an entertainment, an accomplishment. Anything but a threat.

the fetishist within
••••••••••••••••••••••••••

When one of us has a new lover, my girlfriends and I go shopping. Two winters ago we went and I bought a little black bra with stripes of mesh. There was underwear to match. It won the unqualified approval of Marnie (computer whiz and dog lover) and Jessica (adwoman and tennis goddess), plus two college-age salesgirls. Daring, but not trashy. "You're getting the last set," the salesgirl told me. "Your boyfriend is a lucky guy."

I put it on my charge card and Jessica, Marnie, and I went out for pizza to discuss the relative merits of performing oral sex and what to do about Marnie's boyfriend's polyester shirt collection.

"Oh!" said Roo, luscious bongo player and the (temporary, as it turned out) object of my affections, later that night. "You're wearing stripes!" He was pulling off my dress and he did not look happy.

"This," I told him, "is the result of the lingerie shopping trip. Foxy, right?"

"I like that thing you wore last weekend," he murmured, trying to kiss me.

"How can you not like this?" I cried. "This was approved by all my girlfriends. It's been certified as sexy."

"I don't like stripes," he confessed. "I like solids."

Unbelievable. I was fucking a fashion critic.

I told him I didn't like tighty-whities. Then we threw all our clothes on the floor and forgot about it.

On the shopping trip, Marnie and Jessica and I were indulging in the exact kind of sexual self-display I've been talking about. I was advertising my pretty decent sex life, the salesgirls were congratulating me on getting laid, and my girlfriends were hearing a distinctly varnished version of what Roo was like in bed. Our banter allowed me to be daringly intimate and to protect my privacy and vulnerability at the same time.

Roo and I were having a conflict over our mutual objectification. Our preferences were not in sync. And while we were able to transcend the momentary disenchantment people sometimes feel with a partner, what happened shows how much clothing creates sexual identity and how much potential it has to affect sexual experience. Like the costumes in a strip show, underwear creates a sexual scenario. It affects not only the mood and arousal of the viewer, but the experience of the wearer as well. The outfit a person wears for sex—even the most ordinary, everyday underwear—is slightly performative, because sex involves being looked at by one's lover in an aggressive, appreciative way that's very different from how one is looked at ordinarily. People flaunt their bodies in ways that would be unacceptable in public, and the exposure makes them feel vulnerable, especially in a society like ours in which self-display is such a complicated issue. The clothing people wear in moments of sexual exposure is critical in how they experience it—as lewd, romantic, rapacious, teasing, or embarrassing.

Back in college I had a boyfriend who liked me to dress up. Nothing too out of the ordinary: knee socks and short skirts (the Catholic schoolgirl look), or a red teddy and thigh-high stockings (the New Orleans whore look). Actually, almost all my boyfriends have enjoyed a garter belt at one time or another. What was different about this guy was that he needed it. We'd start to fool around, but he couldn't get excited until I put on the clothes. Then I'd leave them on for the whole encounter, whereas your average horny dude rips the lingerie off as soon as he can get the bra strap unfastened. The thrill is in the exposure.

To me, the drama of sexy lingerie lies in the idea that my black lace bra may be arousing, but what is underneath it is better still. The man who throws that bra across the room in shreds is a man who lusts after the woman who was wearing it, a man who can't wait to see her body undressed. The guy who wants me to leave it on during sex is being excited by the idea of black lace, not by the person he is touching. If his excitement always dissipates as soon as I'm naked, I think the two of us are better off apart.

For some folks, everything has to be perfect or there will be no sex happening whatsoever. The definition of perfect varies, of course, for each individual. But whether the preferred scenario involves solid-color lingerie, high heels, or even scuba gear, sexualized objects have the potential to overshadow the body trembling inside.

In her book *Public Sex,* leather fetishist Pat Califia says that a common misapprehension about fetishists is that they don't see the person beneath the leather harness: "Sadomasochists are often accused of substituting things for people, of loving the leather or rubber or spike heels more than the person who is wearing them." Califia argues that it is a mistake to confuse a turn-on such as lingerie or leather with the objectification of one's partner. She says that if a costume gives pleasure to the wearer as well as to his or her partner, the wearer is not objectified at all. Besides, most people respond erotically to certain objects, substances, and body parts. The fetishist loves his wife even if he loves her shoes a lot, too; and it is a rare woman who doesn't feel the least bit sexy in high heels. For Califia, there is a no clean break between fetishism and "normal" sexuality. Instead, there is a continuum of interest and response, a spectrum that ranges from mild turn-on to monomania.

Though Califia doesn't say so explicitly, I assume she includes body parts such as breasts and buttocks and substances like sweat and spit in her continuum of erotic to fetishistic response. She's not just talking about whips and chains and water sports; more mainstream activities and sexual stimuli can also be fetishized. In her book *Fetish,* fashion historian Valerie Steele points out that most scholars and doctors discussing fetishism ignore the meanings implied by the objects chosen and write as if all fetishes were the same. But as Steele shows, a fetish for rubber is a very different thing from a fetish for fur. One recalls babyhood, the body sliding in a bath of its own fluids; the other animizes the wearer, expanding the hair to mythic proportions and cloaking the body in a symbol of the wild.

Even everyday underwear exaggerates gender and creates images designed to generate arousal. That's not so far from what fetishists do. Victoria's Secret, probably the most popular lingerie retailer in the country, sets up a deliberate double fantasy. The consumer is complicit in the illusion that the store's atmosphere and the products it sells are remnants of the bygone Victorian age: timeless lace, old-fashioned perfume bottles, delicate underclothes with a naughty, yet innocent appeal. There is an illusion of educated tastes in the classical music tapes produced under the store's label and the calligraphy used on the sale signs. But these are illusions we are meant to see through. The image is a bit off-kilter. The plush peach carpet feels like a hotel lobby. The synthetic fabrics and bright colors contradict the Victorian concept. In the catalogue, models in lacy negligees reclining in four-poster beds give way to Hawaiian-print bikini girls by an aqua pool. Even a high school girl from Arkansas knows that a model in black lingerie does not usually adorn the cover of a Tchaikovsky cassette. She knows that soaps and perfumes come in prettier packages at Crabtree & Evelyn on the other side of the mall. And she certainly knows that the red garter belt and stockings she is buying for her prom are not the stuff of Victorian romance. They are for a hot night with her steady, for the thrill of being trashy, for the fantasy of being a whore. Her synthetic, electric blue undies are not simply fun and inexpensive, whatever she may tell her mother. They are tawdry, plasticky, high-tech hooker panties. Beneath the sanctioned fantasy of old-fashioned delicacy at Victoria's Secret lies a futuristic bordello; bright colors, bright lights, breast implants, wall-to-wall carpet, polyester and nylon.

In the clean, open expanse of the department store's first floor and on the practical, slightly dusty shelves of the local army/navy shop, men can buy white underwear with an elastic waistband. The classic Y-front, or tighty-whities, is a juvenile look. The man who wears them is saying, "The underwear I wore at eight is just as good now that I'm thirty. In fact, I only just retired my Spiderman Underoos. I still watch cartoons on TV in the morning. I eat sugar cereal for dinner and jack off at least once a day. Twice on Sundays."

A few years ago, Calvin Klein did his best to change the tighty-whities juvenile image by plastering buff torsos, sometimes with semi-hard-ons, on billboards across the fifty states. More recently, however, his notorious "kiddy porn" ads have featured scruffy, underage models, acknowledging that the effect of little boys' underwear on grown men is to create a slightly emasculated, adolescent sort of appeal, as opposed to the hypermasculine sexiness his earlier ads strove for. This is why, in my opinion, men who are hairy or heavily muscled look better in boxer shorts. They can't possibly achieve that young, just-weaned appeal. They look like mama's boys. The mature-looking man in tighty-whities still lets his mother buy his socks and underwear. He's looking for a girl just like the girl who married dear old Dad.

Boxer shorts convey a wide range of meanings. The man in the cotton-poly underwear, stretched out around the waist and worn to handkerchief weight, plays the role of the intellectual or family man. He may even have seventies-style piping along the sides of his white shorts, indicating a disregard for the loose fit and bright patterns popular today. His erotic appeal is that of the dependable man, the man who doesn't lose his underwear in an hourly rate motel. His clothes are not eaten by the ravenous drier at the local launderette, but washed at home in comfortable, slightly disheveled domesticity. He keeps his underwear until it wears out. This is the man who cooks his wife dinner, who wears a beard, who diapers babies. His stretched and faded undies show his vulnerability and reliability simultaneously.

The man in silk underwear is reveling in an overt sensuality that's relatively rare, because it's a little bit feminine and a little bit lewd at the same time. Silk implies a lush, slightly threatening sexuality: the man who leaves his shirt unbuttoned, who wears a number of rings, who has an uncle in the Mafia. This is a man who's willing to try pretty hard, who isn't buying into our culture's expectation that men be nonchalant about their sexual attractiveness. He's willing to hand wash his skivvies each week so he can enjoy the slick slide of that fabric across his ass, and so he can demonstrate his sensual nature to his lovers before they even reach the bed. Silk underwear suggests a man who knows the name of last month's centerfold, whose bed has satin sheets, whose Jacuzzi is always hot.

Brightly colored boxers with cute designs send the most self-conscious message of all. Men who spend their weeks in serious pinstriped suits and their weekends in Levi's have no hesitation about covering their genitalia with pictures of reindeer, happy fish, or big red hearts—even Mickey Mouse. Actually, often Mickey Mouse. This fashion choice is an extension of the Underoo mentality common to boys beneath the age of nine, for whom the superhero that hides a person's pecker indicates the wearer's own magical powers. Still, the bulging thighs of the Incredible Hulk and the fantastically pointy breasts of Wonder Woman are far more sexual than any of the cheerful polka dots or cute cartoon animals that adorn adult boxers. Shorts of this kind—although obviously aiming for a certain kind of childish playfulness—deliberately avoid the sort of vulnerable sexual self-consciousness implied by the adolescent appeal of the tighty-whities. The boxers with Garfield the cat on them can't possibly hide a nervously arousable, soft set of genitalia and a pimply bottom housing an occasional hemorrhoid. They can't possibly, because they are invulnerable in their covering of publicly recognizable symbols of cheerfulness. This explains why the Wall Street lawyer in the pinstriped suit is sporting happy-face undies: the suit and the boxers both provide a protective layer of apparent invulnerability, one for the members of the firm, and one for the wife at home.

Tan, synthetic women's underwear in shapes so large the navel is covered, heavy, stretchable corsets, and thickly buckled bras are sold mainly in small, dark undergarment shops in neighborhoods that have yet to be gentrified. The very enormity of the items, their faux-flesh color and their constricting nature seem designed to inspire a fetish of some kind. Those heavy bras are often padded. The waist is cinched in by a corset or control top. Look at this underwear when a woman is wearing clothes. Her body is highly sexualized: boobs forward, belly in. Her figure is a hard surface. The tan color suggests that the nylon is masquerading as skin. Although the garments rearrange the body so it cannot be ignored, they also deny their own presence. Their poor attempt at invisibility has the sorry charm of flowers held behind someone's back. The flower bearer pays service to the gesture of surprise rather than genuinely attempting concealment, just as the woman in the flesh-toned padded brassiere gestures toward an idea of a woman's body that is pleasing in its curvaceous modesty, even if its artifice is transparent. The wearer's lover probably allows her to undress in private, remaining complicit in the lingerie lie.

The trendy Wonderbra is likewise a gesture toward the curves we have learned to think of as womanly. Unlike the beige pads, however, it screams to be noticed, discussed, and analyzed whenever possible. The squashed-together cleavage spilling out over the foam-filled microcups is unreproducible in breasts without a bra. That constructed, bursting look recalls Restoration-era flirtations, in which artifice reined supreme; men padded their crotches and flexed their stockinged calves as they pranced about in enormous powdered wigs; women drew beauty marks on their faces and boarded up their chests until their boobs popped out the top of their corsets. No woman just happens to be wearing a Wonderbra; they're not comfortable. She puts it on to be bawdy—publicly, playfully erotic. "I bought a Wonderbra," Ruth announced to me, "and I hate it! I wore it to dinner with Steve. I asked him if he noticed anything different, and he asked me if I got a haircut." Roxy wore hers (with nothing else on top) around the house when her roommate's mother was visiting, so excited was she to have cleavage for the first time. His mother didn't seem upset, just interested in how the cleavage was created. So, whether it works or not, the bra makes tits a subject for discussion and display. You can call them tits when they're in a Wonderbra, you see; but not if they're wearing white cotton.

"You know what I've been wondering about?" asks my college friend Phyllis. Phyllis can sew her own clothes, edit videos, and cut people's hair, but she defers to me on questions of undergarments. "I've been wondering about thongs," she says. "I saw black thong underwear hanging up in two of my friends' bathrooms. It changed my entire opinion of them as people."

The bisection of the butt that thongs create has only recently become a mainstream aesthetic for women's underwear. I think it's popular because women get a sexed-up feeling with a thick piece of fabric between their butt cheeks. Ruth swears she had an orgasm from running several miles wearing thong underwear, although most women won't admit to anything of the sort. They say thongs are cute, and much more comfortable than regular bikinis, so that's why they wear them. But they are lying. First, thongs are very rarely flattering. I know, I've tried wearing one. If I place it absolutely perfectly, it looks tolerable, but most of the time it's wiggling around more to one side or another, hanging too loose or wedging too tight, a far cry from the perfect crease you see in the Buns of Steel videos. Looks, aside from a convenient absence of panty lines, are not the reason for the thong's popularity.

Second, many women who wear the underwear will instantly condemn the woman who wears her thong in public. There was a hyperactive little sexpot in my college aerobics class who wore a thong. She had a ponytail up on the top of her head and she waved it about and shook her booty like the whole class was just invented for the joy of moving her most wiggly parts. Phyllis and I, grunting in sweatshirts, hated her guts. What was with that thong? we asked each other. Who did she think she was? The same irrational bitterness applies today. Secure in our black one-pieces, toasting ourselves on Jones Beach with a pile of magazines and a jug of lemonade, my friends and I ridicule some poor woman with her tush intentionally hanging out. "That is not nice at all," I say. "Why did she have to show us that?"

Why are we so catty? Because those thong girls are publicly revealing a sort of anal eroticism most women—many of them thong wearers themselves under their jeans—are not comfortable displaying. My girlfriends and I, in our predominantly straight, predominantly white, middle-class, urban social world, place only certain body parts in the foreground when we want to appear sexy: legs, cleavage, maybe a bare back in the summer. All the others are off limits. Showing off your butt, in tight jeans, short shorts, or a thong, is branded tacky. The thong is the worst, being, as it is, practically a Wonderbra for the nether regions. Our discomfort stems from our reluctance to admit publicly that butts are erotic, whatever we might do in private. Phyllis later buys a thong, but does not become a convert to its glories. "I feel like my farts can't get out," she tells me when she's wearing it. "Something's blocking them!"

One of the markers between a sexual fetish and an attraction is the level of necessity. Which partner desires the role the underwear or object implies? People with only an attraction or preference for a potentially fetishized item are more likely to simply wear it themselves without requesting that their partners do anything: the girl buying thigh-high stockings for her prom, a guy in a leather jacket, me in my mesh stripes (which, by the way, I continued to wear), or a young man I once dated who would persist in wearing tight black Speedo-style undies. I didn't like it, but I never asked him to change because clearly he felt attractive in them, which made for better sex. When my girlfriends and I shop for lingerie, we are likewise looking for what makes us feel particularly sexy. I don't think any of us has closely analyzed our partners' preferences beyond noticing a positive response to a push-up bra. So while we are shopping for classic symbols of female desirability, we are really buying facilitators for our own desire.

If it is the partner who requests the stimuli of leather or lace, I tend to think of the situation differently. Although Califia contends that the fetish object does not replace the lover, she is talking primarily about sexual relationships that begin with a mutual interest in a fetish. A couple who met in a leather bar don't need to discuss whether wearing leather during sex makes either of them uncomfortable. For a more ordinary sexual relationship, probably begun with a few drinks and the missionary position, one partner's request that another stimulate him by means of a near-fetishized object can be problematic. Your average person gets uncomfortable and feels eclipsed when a pair of thigh-high stockings begins to dominate all sexual encounters, or when one body part seems more important than the whole it's attached to. Witness me and my would-be Catholic schoolboy.

Perhaps, though, what we really fear is our own response. As I've shown, there is fetishistic possibility inherent in even the most everyday of underwear. Are we just hiding our own fetishes under the sheets, not even admitting them to ourselves? Why is it that one woman I know wears only white underwear, or another always paints her toenails? Would they like their partners to do the same?

Steele separates fetishism into four levels. Level 1 is only a slight preference for certain kinds of sex partners, stimuli, or activities, and would not be called a fetish at all. Level 2 is a strong preference, Level 3 a need for specific stimuli in order to become aroused, and Level 4 a situation in which the stimuli take the place of a partner. Steele later complicates her definition, claiming that fetishism is really only an exaggeration of normal sexual response for most men (so studies show). One way to define fetishism, she says, is not by the action but by the mental activity that surrounds it. That is, does the guy jacking off into a pair of high heels behave pathologically and destructively about it, or is it just an enjoyable hobby? Steele also argues that many clinical definitions of fetishism contain unspoken biases against homosexuality.

By Steele's basic breakdown of the fetish continuum, you might say I have a mild fetish, though it is such a common one that it basically goes unnoticed, and it doesn't require anything of my partner. I feel unsexy if I haven't bathed, and I don't want to encounter my boyfriend in the faded cotton panties with the stretched-out elastic I wore when I was single. I am reliant on certain conditions, even certain objects to achieve arousal—a clean body and relatively new underwear. I might manage to have sex without these things, but I probably wouldn't initiate it, and I might even put off my lover's advances. Perhaps I am not so different from the man who needs his rubber jacket.

On the other hand, the tools of cleanliness (the soap, the bathtub) do not excite me. My underwear doesn't excite me either; I can wear the black mesh stripes all day and never feel aroused. The condition necessary to my arousal is not the presence of a stimulus; it is the absence of something I find unsexy—my own body being dirty or frumpy. I haven't invested cleanliness and lingerie with any sexual attraction of their own.

There's a difference between feeling desirous and feeling desirable. But feeling desirable can also provoke desire; it certainly does for me. Certain conditions or objects might turn a person on, or they might be *necessary* for him to get turned on. And an innocuous turn-on can suddenly, surprisingly, become necessary. Or it might be necessary only sometimes, with some people. It might become arousing to his partner, because it signifies his or her desirability. Conditions: privacy, rubber sheets, handcuffs, or the lights out. Objects: large breasts, a hairy chest, a riding crop, or a corset.

My point here is that the relationship between fetishism and more mainstream erotic behavior is not a straight-line continuum, as imagined by Steele and Califia. It is a maze, circling back on itself continually, a dark, underground labyrinth in which a traveler must feel his way. Near the entrance the light of the everyday shines bright. The person deep within the darkness, clothed in leather or bound in handcuffs, may feel herself miles away from that sunshiny starting point, but it is not really a long journey at all. The maze has looped back toward the beginning. The corridors run alongside one another. Only a thin wall separates the hard-core fetishist in the depths of the tunnels from the young man in Mickey Mouse boxer shorts just coming in the front door.

🌀 🌀 🌀

A common denominator in the stories I've told about sexuality is the need to gauge one's normalcy. I'd bet that some people don't feel this need. I'm certain some people claim not to feel it, because when I raise this question in conversation I get many ardent assertions that my friends just do what comes naturally—without worrying about rules, or technique, or what anyone else is doing.

What comes naturally. Hah. Sexually, I think, most people are walking a twisted middle road between extremes that both frighten and fascinate them; our social rules and institutions keep them from those extremes, limiting them to very specific behaviors that are sanctioned as normal, and labeling those behaviors "natural." My friends' very insistence that everything comes naturally is evidence of how important that label is to them.

A lot of guys I knew as a teenager lost their virginity to a girl I heard about only as "Easy Fuck Ashley." One in a tent. One in a car. The others, I don't know where. I never met Ashley in person, though I saw her across a room at a party once. I remember honey blond hair and no makeup. She was tall, and a little thick around the middle. Not what I had imagined, which was a kind of cartoon version of a slut, defined entirely by her accessories: candy red nail polish, high heels, short skirt, teased hair. And even though Easy Fuck Ashley looked like an ordinary, outdoorsy girl with German heritage, she was nevertheless a mythical figure, a shrine to which an inexperienced boy could go to shed his innocence.

The idea was that Ashley was undiscriminating; she would do it with pretty much anybody, anywhere, so the guy didn't have to know much about how to have sex, or how to behave before and after. Nor did he have to be attractive, or popular, or rich, or even kind. If Ashley had been a prostitute, the financial transaction would have entirely changed the myth she embodied. Then, it would have been clear what she got out of the fuck, which would not have been so "easy" after all, costing the boys their dignity and their month's allowance. As it was, I think the fuck was easy not only in the sense that convincing Ashley wasn't difficult; it was easy in the sense that the "easy fuck" doesn't have to be a "hard fuck." I imagine there was little pressure to be hard, as opposed to flaccid. Sex with Ashley was nonjudgmental. Also, it may have been the opposite of a hard fuck in the sense people mean when they say, "I fucked him really hard" or "Fuck me harder, baby, please." She might have been gentle.

What was really going on, I'll never know. Maybe Ashley was a miserable, stupid girl who got used by those boys and had to have four abortions before she turned twenty. Maybe she was a sex goddess with an open mind. What I do know is that all those boys felt themselves in need of an easy fuck, which suggests that in general they found fucking difficult—which is my point.

Really, I don't think any fuck is easy, just as I don't think any fuck is natural. And that's not necessarily a bad thing—it just means every encounter is a complicated negotiation between safe norms and extremes, extremes that might be repugnant or thrilling. The norms might be enforced by one partner, disrupted by another. Every encounter is an adaptation to the other body in the bed. Each involves the construction of identity on an intimate level through the (possibly unspoken) declaration of likes and dislikes, and through the process of self-display. Each is a negotiation between the body's natural state and artifices like underwear, hair spray, hair removal, and perfumes. It is a dialogue with old lovers. The difficult fuck, the hard-not-flaccid fuck, the hard-not-gentle fuck, the hard-to-get fuck—this is the sex we covet and dream about, probably because of its complicated hold on our identities. The Easy Fuck is only a phantom we see when we're alone in the dark.

revealing

spa treatments
....

"Welcome to Us," lilts a pink woman squeezed tight by purple fabric. "For facial you take the elevator," she continues. "Press the button that says C for clinic."

I examine her pores. They are round and clearly visible, even on her forehead, as if they were steamed open on a regular basis, primed to absorb the nutrient cream she applies throughout the day. The elevator arrives.

Something about spa treatments makes me paranoid. Very likely the Madison Avenue spa is a front for some kind of secret plastic surgery industry. Radical refiguring operations on human subjects are conducted under cover of Scandinavian nurses armed with seaweed wraps. After hours, the soft seats of the waiting room and the heated whirlpools of the spa level are filled with bandaged bodies. This is where mob wives go when they need a whole new face, and the former Mrs. Bellini lounges carefully in the hot tub, making sure the gauze around her chin does not get wet. She has not got the aquiline nose she had hoped for, but otherwise the transformation is completely satisfactory. She takes a plane for Australia next month. She and her fellow patients—most voluntary, some involuntary—sleep much of the day, tucked away in the back rooms, allowing the Madison Avenue spa to turn a neat profit in its legit incarnation.

Stepping off several floors down at the clinic, I stand stupidly in the hallway, waiting for somebody to notice me. The lights are dimmed low: the people in white who cluster at a desk several yards off look like nurses working the night shift. Finally a short woman in her fifties comes toward me and grasps my hand. Her fingers are strangely cold and greasy. She examines the slip of paper I hand her and makes a pouty face. "Oh. You're not with me." She pretends to sulk. She leads me down the hall to a tiny room with a swinging door. The room is all white, furnished with mirrors, a La-Z-Boy recliner, several lamps on pivoting arms. I change into a robe and await Helga.

Helga will be doing my facial. She is in her forties, and her skin has the moist, white appearance of a fish underbelly. I think it must come from the rigorous use of sun protection at all times, and from spending her days moleing through the dark spa corridors. She gets me in the La-Z-Boy and covers me with a sheet.

I have a damp paper towel over my eyes. Helga looks at my face under a giant magnifying glass. "Dry, dry, oily, a few pimples. Combination skin!" she announces. "I give you for combination skin, two masks." I am a little humiliated at her open commentary on my pimples—something no one I know ever discusses. It is impolite, like pointing out someone's bald spot or beer belly. Of course, it is Helga's job to analyze my skin, so perhaps I'm offended by her lack of euphemistic or medical language. She might have said I had clogged pores, or acne, or problem areas. The word *pimple* is so loaded with greasy, swollen, teenage pain that I really think she meant me to feel chastened by it.

Helga leaves, returning with a glass bowl filled with boiling water and herbs. She places it under my chin and makes a tent with towels over my head. The steam will open my pores. "If you get too hot," she says, "make a window!" She opens a gap between the towels and smiles in at me. Then she smears cream on my hands and surrounds each one with a plastic bag, the kind you put vegetables in. Each greased, wrapped hand then gets inserted into a large, heated oven mitt, plugged in by the wall. This is the "hand treatment," a gentle cooking of the flesh that will leave my hands feeling exactly as they did before. When my pores have been steamed open, the facial follows. Its purposes are rather mysterious. There's a face massage, cleansing (lotion is put on, then wiped off with a cotton ball), the squeezing of pimples, and two masks of indeterminate function (nourishment, treatment, something like that). I submit to it all blindly; the damp paper towel still covers my eyes.

When it's over, Helga sends me back upstairs to the salon level, where the woman squeezed by her purple dress conducts me to Bertram. Bertram, like three other people at colorful desks in the front lobby, is there to take my payment and push products at me. He is a herring of a man, moist like all the others and white, white, white. He wears a gray suit and glasses with heavy black frames. His nose is a trifle snouty. Helga, he tells me, has made certain recommendations. They at the Madison Avenue spa have sixty different kinds of products, and I need one or four of them.

"No thanks, I'm a soap and water girl myself," I smile, hoping this indicates I'll be broke enough paying for the facial and refuse to spend $18.99 for Sea Creatures Cleansing Lotion.

Bertram looks at me in horror. "Well, you'll see Helga recommended cleansers for you. That's because soap leaves alkaline residue on your skin which can clog pores." He shows me the sheet on which she has checked a few boxes. I am relieved to see I escaped being recommended for eye and throat creams, oxygen treatments, line solutions, camphor masks, and collagen products. Bertram treats me to a lengthy lecture on the dangers of soap.

"I'm just too lazy to do all that," I say, as firmly as I can.

"We at the Madison Avenue spa don't believe you should have to go through a whole long process!" he pushes. "You just say to me, 'Bertram. This is what I'm willing to do,' and I'll give you a product that will suit that."

"I don't want a product, Bertram," I say, and pay the bill.

A visit to the Madison Avenue spa's second location (also on Madison Avenue) is more Ian Fleming. I am here for something described in the brochure as a "body treatment." The square, white room is lit by yellow heat lamps, spotlighting a bed that faces an enormous round mirror. Brigitta, dressed in nursey white, gives me towels to drape across myself, an ironic gesture toward modesty in this miniature theater designed for the lighting and reflection of naked bodies. She puts a smelly green cream on my limbs, my abdomen, and my back, then rubs it off. It has a texture like dry rubber cement. This she calls a "body peeler." Then I'm asked to stand while she covers the table in plastic and steaming purple towels. She gives me nothing to wear except the miniature towel that was draped over my behind, and I stand there, awkwardly, trying to figure out how to make it cover everything I'd like it to cover. Suddenly, the level of bodily revelation has drastically increased without my consent. I can see myself hunched over in the giant mirror, cringing at the unexpected exposure. The illusion of respect for my modesty has been shattered.

I get back on the bed and am wrapped in hot towels, then in plastic, then covered in blankets, and finally submerged beneath a floral comforter. Brigitta puts something damp over my eyes and leaves me, swaddled and toasting, to rest.

The round mirror has cameras behind it, I am sure. The Peeping Tom Society, Manhattan branch, makes black market videos for sale to future serial killers. The buyers sit home in their basement rec rooms, reading books by J.D. Salinger until the delivery arrives. Then they settle onto couches littered with cigarette butts and the remains of convenience store burritos and jack off while watching naked blond matrons get massaged. It costs more for videos of Marla Trump and Carolina Herrera. The pedicure videos sell only to a specialized market, but the Peeping Toms place discreet ads in a certain kind of publication and find themselves well rewarded for the effort. Body treatment videos, like the one I'm in, include a mummification ritual. The society prides itself upon a wide range of offerings.

Eventually Brigitta releases me, wipes me free of the last of the green cream, moisturizes, and spritzes me with rose water. Ninety dollars.

Next stop is the subterranean spa, deliberately hushed. A foggy smell of incense hangs in the air and a dish of fortune-telling cards sits by the receptionist. The walls are painted brown, the lights are dim. I am suspicious of it. I wouldn't be surprised at all if it turned out that the subterranean spa was the indoctrination site of a secret cult. Regular customers, seduced by dizzying aromas and the oily touch of the masseur, are gradually weaned onto an addictive drug mixed into the refreshing herbal tea they drink after treatment. Once hooked, when they crawl every morning to the door for a fix, they are discreetly invited to experience the pinnacle of relaxation and introduced to the worship of the ape goddess, in reality an apoplectic gorilla housed illegally in a compound upstate. In order to approach the ape goddess's serene enjoyment of sensual plea- sures and stunning flexibility in the joints, new inductees must place their SoHo loft apartments in care of the subterranean spa staff and go to live in a communal adobe hut on the compound. There, they exist on a diet of refreshing herbal tea, while their assets are quietly disposed of by the wily masseurs.

I am here for the ultimate in luxury: foot massage. My "coor- dinator" arrives, a buff young man with an earring who whispers greetings. He brings me a pair of sandals in my size and leads me through an underground hallway to a bathroom. I am to change into a robe. There is a shower there, filled with soaps and sham- poos, but I am not invited to use it. Am I supposed to shower? Or am I not supposed to? The music of chirping birds and strumming harps is meant to soothe my jangled nerves, but a discomforting sense of not knowing the etiquette overwhelms me. Perhaps tak- ing a shower is the expected courtesy to someone working on my body, or perhaps to do so would be a presumptive appropriation of the facilities, a transgression into a space not specified for my use. I am also uncertain about how much clothing I should leave on under my robe, though it can't much matter for a foot massage. Is keeping my underwear on a sign that I'm holding on to my inhibitions, or would taking it off be some sort of weird sexualization of the massage, eroticizing a contact that is actually only legal so long as it is not eroticized? As Sallie Tisdale points out in *Talk Dirty To Me,* it is legal to pay someone to rub your back but not to rub your genitals.

The coordinator leads me back to a dark, second lobby. There are no windows and only a soft glow of light, but the table here is covered with self-help books. They are mainly of a spiritual nature—tapping the creativity within, connecting with the true self, et cetera—but a bright yellow tome called *Getting Organized* is also present. It so happens that I read this when I was about thirteen and desperate for entertainment at Granny's summer house. It consists of advice on setting up a personal filing system, the best way to alphabetize your bookshelves, and how to arrange a medicine cabinet. I spend a few minutes in dim self-improvement until another customer enters. We smile at each other shyly. I wonder if he took a shower and whether he is naked under that robe.

The massage, when I get it, is somehow utterly ordinary. The pinched little person in black who rubs me suggests in a mildly superior tone that I should get psychotherapy for my back pain. I feel sorry for her working all day underground, breathing incense and never seeing the sky. At a certain point she stops the massage and asks what I want to have done next, as if she's run out of ideas. I ask her what my options are.

"Shiatsu, Swedish, hand reflexology."

I find it strange to be asked to take responsibility for my own pleasure, am surprised that the course of events was not locked in place once I made an appointment for a foot massage. It is disturbing to think that the pinched lady is ad-libbing. Aren't I paying her $75 an hour precisely because she knows how to do a foot massage longer and better than my boyfriend? Her asking me what I want next highlights our relationship (I am paying her) in a way that is very different from how it would appear to me if she hadn't. Lying nearly naked on a table, unsure of the protocol, unsure about what to wear and whether to use the shower, I felt like she was in charge. And while in a way that vulnerability was unpleasant, it is also partly why I'm here—to abdicate responsibility, to relax in passivity, to accept what is given me. And to profit from her expertise. Now, her question has made it clear she is not in charge at all. Maybe she wants me to know that, and know she resents it.

I return to the sunlight by the same route as I left it: self-help lobby, coordinator, changing room, coordinator, incense lobby. The receptionist reminds me to tip.

Why do the spas make me so paranoid? Why do they seem so much like a front for something else: secret plastic surgeries, the Peeping Tom Society, or the cult of the ape goddess? It's partly because they don't produce anything visible. What are the results? A mud bath does what, exactly? Detoxifies? Smoothes? Nourishes? To be honest, I cannot see or feel a difference thirty minutes after it's over. A massage may relax me, but I tense up again before dinner. A facial seems like an extended elaboration of what should be, at most, a three-minute face-cleaning. The only real reason to get these things done is because you enjoy the process: the physical contact, the smells, the care.

My discomfort at both the Madison Avenue spa and the subterranean spa was based on the fact that they both offer essentially one service: bodily pleasure. The facilities are remarkably secluded, and the behavior there markedly ritualized, so much so that the elaborate decor and careful, whispered contact make getting a massage or a facial seem dirty, even unnatural. Otherwise, why have such elaborate contrivances to render the environment wholesomely natural, hypersterile, and intensely private?

Revealing one's body to a stranger who is being paid violates our culture's injunction to privacy in certain ways (don't let people you don't know touch you, don't receive pleasure in a public building). The violation necessitates the exaggerated seclusion provided by the darkened corridors and windowless rooms of the spas. The excess personnel, Bertram and the coordinator, serve as buffers between a client's regular life and the strange transaction of currency for physical contact. Bertram and his fellow salespeople work right near the door. They seem like a team of receptionists, and the first-time client needs direction from them to find the woman in the purple dress. When it's time to pay, Bertram takes my credit card to the purple woman's desk to ring it up. He isn't really needed as a cashier. He's just meant to sell me some tangible products, earning money for his company and reassuring me that I haven't paid just for bodily pleasure. I have got something to show for it, a tube of oxygen cleanser. Likewise, the coordinator is hardly necessary. Perhaps sometimes it's so busy that he's desperately needed, but the day I went the process seemed wholly ceremonial, especially when I had to wait for him afterward to take me back to my clothes. In both cases, the minor obstacle courses involved in entering and exiting the spas functioned to dissipate the almost claustrophobic intimacy of the actual services.

Spa workers can exact subtle punishments by confronting me with the unsavory aspects of our contact. The pinched lady's interruption of my massage to ask me what she should do next made me feel unsure that the service was worth the money. More important, it made me uncomfortable about my position as a paying customer receiving what might be a degrading service to provide. It is much the same way during a pedicure, where the pedicurist kneels below me and buffs my wet feet with a pumice stone. Her subservient position creates a much more delicate climate for the service than does the relatively equal status implied by the face-to-face manicure. One gesture overtly deferential or one small indication of discontent on her part will disrupt my equilibrium, reminding me that maybe there is something not quite right in paying this tiny Korean woman to kneel before me and fondle my feet. I behave submissively—ask her where to sit, apologize for my awkwardness, thank her repeatedly, never ask questions about the procedure—to avoid the punishment of seeing her submission made clear.

The obvious question to ask is why people are so uncomfortable with paying for physical pleasure. They must be, or why would the spas provide such carefully designed climates and such structured interactions? Since I myself find nothing immoral in sex work except the horrendous conditions and persecutions suffered by so many of the workers, I am surprised at my own discomfort with receiving a related service when the provider is healthy, well paid, and under no coercion.

Underlying my queasiness about receiving body work and beneath the spas' precarious buffer rituals and hygienic-natural atmospheres is an assumption that the body is unpleasant. Receiving such a service suggests a physical neediness based in undesirability. Of the man who goes to prostitutes, there is always the possibility that he cannot get sex any other way; he is not attractive enough for a good-looking woman to sleep with him for free. Of course this may not be the case at all; he may enjoy the thrill, like the freedom from commitment, or have certain predilections that are not easily satisfied. But casting a shadow over any consumer of commodified physical pleasure is the image of the anonymous john: the smell of an unwashed body, the shame of a small penis, bad breath, weak arms. If his wife won't suck him, he must be kind of gross. The sex workers tolerate him only for a fee.

It is the same with the pedicurist. I cannot assume she enjoys touching all those people's feet. It's probably worse than giving fellatio for money; in my experience, it's much harder to get someone you love to rub your feet and cut your toenails than it is to get him to perform oral sex. And almost no one will squeeze your pimples no matter how much they love you. Even massages, which are relatively pleasant to give, require physical generosity that many people don't often extend to other adults outside a sexual context, if then. Going to a spa for intimate physical contact, clinical and shrouded in hot towels as it might be, is something very close to acknowledging that no one you know wants to touch you that way. And that you wish someone did.

My friend Roxy used to live in an apartment that had small plastic tubes attached to the toilets. When I asked her about them, she told me the landlady was a devoted practitioner of colonic irrigation, so much so that she had customized her bathrooms to accommodate her habit. I passed some judgments of my own on that landlady, and on the colonic customer at the spa where I underwent sensory deprivation, too. I thought of them both as neurotically fastidious and yet weirdly open to invasive practices—not to mention pervertedly interested in their own bowel movements.

Lots of spas offer colonics. They're getting very popular. The idea is that you've got a lot of impacted crap in your colon that is impeding the absorption of nutrients, causing intestinal problems, and flooding your bloodstream with toxins. According to some people, you probably have ten pounds of unwanted "material" lining your lower intestine. A lot of clients are willing to pay a good deal of money to have that material flushed out of them through pressurized tubes.

I should say up front that I am not going to get a tube stuck up my ass for the sake of literature. I am more afraid of the colonic irrigation machine than I was of doing heroin, so much that I'm perfectly willing to talk about it from a standpoint of total colonic virginity, no matter how revealing that is about my neuroses, my sexual practices, and my general cowardice. I am willing to bet it's good for you, if practiced in moderation, but I have three major problems with colon hydrotherapy. The first is that it repulses me. I really, really, really do not want to have something pushed up my bottom so I can watch superconcentrated toxic shit flow out of me through a plastic tube. And even more really I do not want to do that in the company of a stranger.

Second, people who advocate colon therapy preach a doctrine of asceticism and fear. They use semiregular fasting as a cleansing technique and they point out food toxins everywhere: in your pasta, in your bottled juice, in mixing complex carbohydrates with proteins. If they knew about my Oreos, and my beer, and my coffee, I'm sure they'd be thoroughly disgusted, shocked as they are by a mere bagel. This dietary hypervigilance is couched in terms that advocate the acceptance of the lower intestine as a beautifully functioning thing. One colon therapy newsletter I read specifically related our social anxieties about our butts and our processes of elimination to the rise in eating disorders. Accept your ass and its interior, it implied, and a healthier body and mind will be the result. But at the same time, the person working to accept her ass is given a cleansing diet that denies her much of her pleasure in eating, and I don't think depriving oneself and rigidly monitoring food intake promotes self-acceptance. The frequent fasting seems to me like it would attract eating-disordered patients and foster their disorders with a rhetoric of health. Also, while celebrating the colon and restoring it to optimal function, people are at the same time reinforcing the idea that their internal organs are dirty and need regular flushing to remain clean. It seems to me that we are already preoccupied enough with how dirty our bodies are. Underarm deodorants and vaginal douches and Odor Eaters are quite enough, thank you. I don't need to be told that my insides are filthy as well.

Third, the language of the alternative health industry conceals the simple truth that enemas are something people pay sex workers to give them or get in front of them. I've read about it in Dan Savage's sex column, and I've read about it a lot on the internet. "Hot enema equipment" is available from a sex supply company in Fort Lauderdale. Frank E. Ball of the Fraternity of Enema Buddies has written a manifesto of anal eroticism entitled *The Eneman's Companion*. There is a "colenema" community united by chat rooms, mail-order catalogs, e-mail newsletters, and a group called the Ladies' Enema Auxiliary. Therapy for some people, for others colonic irrigation is definitely sex—so much so that the Index of Colonic Therapy Centers protests the innocence of the practitioners it lists with a disclaimer that would be ludicrous for any other medical service providers: "These are legitimate health care professionals . . . Do not embarrass yourself by phoning or visiting them for pay-for-play sexual favors."

Like people getting other spa treatments—facials and pedicures and massages—those getting colon therapy are paying for a physical service that is only inches away from paying a prostitute. The difference is that when I get a massage, I am overtly paying for pleasure. When I get a facial or a pedicure, I am paying for beauty, or for "pampering," and the service is acknowledged as a luxury. Colon therapy, on the other hand, is administered in spas, but always under the guise of health care. It involves more intimate physical contact than any of the other services, and it more rigorously denies that intimacy and the pleasure it conceivably supplies.

The extremity of bodily exposure involved in a colonic is perhaps the primary reason I cannot bring myself to have one. Even in a rectal exam, you get to lie on your back. Offering your anus up for inspection by a stranger is, I think, fantastically intimate. Despite its antiseptic, alternative medicine image, a colonic is closer to sexual service than other body treatments. The exposure and the proximity of the process to prostitution are probably sources of pleasure for people who are not so uptight about such things, but for me they pose a problem. One part of my reluctance, of course, is that colonics involve penetration, which is scary if the orifice is unfamiliar. And another is that they involve shit. If I can't bear the judgments passed on my pores by the employees of the Madison Avenue and subterranean spas, I certainly can't bear the critical analysis of my poop.

So much shame is attached to our bodies. It is a component of how we think of ourselves every day. When we choose a bathing suit, cut our nose hairs, take a shower, or use a tampon, we are confronting our discomfort with the organic state of our physical selves. Shitting is the most shameful of bodily events, and the colonic creates a lot of anxiety—in me, but in other people too, I think—because it embodies that shame in a physical process that is sexual (though we've been taught it shouldn't be) and cleansing (which reminds us we are dirty).

The treatment rooms in spas are superprivate and services one-on-one because inside those rooms a taboo against public exposure for pleasure is being broken. The bodily revelation—whether it's pores, calluses, or genitalia—is sufficiently unlike our normal social and sexual interactions to make us uncomfortable. The paranoia is heightened by the judgments passed upon the client by the worker—Bertram's critique of my cleansing ritual, Helga's loud commentary on my pimples, the pinched lady's advice that I go into therapy. This is a safe place, the environment screams; but that's because the services are silently, subtly, anything but safe.

nude beach

I am soaking up the sun with number 24 on my boobs, and my dominant sensation is that of being an impostor. These are all the real nude people. I am just a fake one. Of course that's ridiculous. I'm just as bare as anybody else, and many people's white behinds testify that they're not regular inhabitants of this sandy Eden. Still, the sensation persists. It's not that I'm ashamed to be naked, exactly. Actually, I feel better-looking without clothes than I do in my bathing suit. It's more that public nudity is so novel. I feel like someone else doing it, like an actor in a play.

Lying down and peeping from under the brim of a baseball hat is my preferred mode of operation here. I am an observer. But as I stand up to go swimming and walk down to the water, that changes. I cease being an impostor-observer and abruptly become a full participant in nudity, offering myself for inspection by who-ever might choose to look. Does anyone? Not particularly. They are reading trashy books and eating taco chips. But I have never felt so naked, so much on display. The water is too cold for swimming, and I find myself prancing along the edge of it, strange breezes under my breasts and between my legs. Two twelve-year-old boys, both in bathing suits, one with a burst of red hair and a farmer's tan, walk by. They are carefully scoping, gathering information.

This beach was colonized by nude sunbathers in the early seventies, and some of the nudie, hippie flavor of the early days still remains. Young men with long hair and beards rush splashing into the waves, or sit, posing slightly, on ancient rocks that lift them out of reach of the ocean's spray. Women lie encumbered by sun hats, novels, and beach umbrellas, if not by bathing suits, in positions that allow them to keep an eye on their little naked children. People unaware of how seriously erosion is cutting away at the colored clay cliffs indulge in natural facials, coating their skins with cool sludge.

There is a couple I know who spend their summers here. He is called the Beach President—very short and bearded, radiating youthful energy. During the year he's a professor at a small, bucolic college. There is even a painting of him hanging in his department, or so he told me at a cocktail party, his booming chuckle sounding distinctly of Italy. She is tiny, always tan, with a crisply forceful character. They have a gaggle of children and grandchildren who form an unending parade through their summer house, but still the DeCellos manage to go every afternoon and remove their clothes on the local avenue of sand.

I only come to the nude part of the beach alone. When my family suns itself as a group, we don't discuss going naked, nor even lying with our suits on in the nude zone. Instead we bring beach chairs and stay with the textiles, staring out at the curve of the horizon in sun-induced stupor. We wave at the DeCellos when they tramp through our field of vision.

It wasn't always like this, everyone's bodies wrapped up in stretchy fabrics. In the seventies, my family stripped and cavorted with the nudest of the nude. There is a great photograph that Granny always threatens to destroy. It is slightly yellowed with age so that its color scheme is dominated by those orangey browns so popular for clothing and home decor in that unfortunate era. It shows the summer ritual: we'd have a big cooler full of drinks and icy fruit, and everybody of my mother's generation (maybe four adults) would go naked except for big round sunglasses. In the picture, Mom and my aunts have all-over tans and foxy shag haircuts. Granny herself wears a bikini bottom, but the picture is still an image of a brief moment in the history of our nation when people were naked around their families—and even brought their Instamatics.

In 1977, anthropologist Jack Douglas and two fellow scholars published a study of one particular nude society, a beach on the California coast. The anthropologists "went native," as the saying goes, spending most of their time tanning in the buff and calling it work. Douglas found there was intense peer pressure to get completely naked. The white marks left by bathing suits were called "POW (prisoner of war) bracelets," since they indicated the suit wearer's imprisonment in social constraints. Someone covertly hiding his penis with a towel might be publicly teased. The antagonist would say, "in a lilting, squeaky voice, 'Oh, I just don't dare show my thing to the world because I'm scared it isn't as big as the others.'" A person hesitant to shed his or her clothing was "gently shamed" with injunctions to "get honest." Douglas even witnessed a ritual he termed the "nude beach rape," someone having his or her clothes forcibly ripped off. The rape was "raucously enjoyed by all" and performed only if the victim didn't seem uptight. It was, Douglas tells us, a helping hand for those who didn't "have enough moral fiber to get honest." In this community, there was shame in being ashamed, and judgments were passed not on the body but on people's insecurities.

The pressure to be naked, figured in moral terms, was combined with condemnation of explicit voyeurism. One of the slogans of the seventies beach culture, "nude is not lewd," was designed to separate public nudity from punishable sex crimes. *Bare With Us,* a seventies guide to nudist parks, claims that nudists believe no part of the body is vulgar or obscene. Though Douglas observed huge amounts of sexual activity, from public masturbation and sexual intercourse (nonvigorous, he is careful to point out) to clothed voyeurs peeping through binoculars, it is the latter who were considered to be violating the tenets of nude morality by imposing a taint of perversity on wholesome behavior. Ogling and even erections were deemed perfectly acceptable so long as they caused no one to feel threatened. Actually, the offended person was more likely to be condemned than the exhibitionist. The general attitude toward displays such as public masturbation was that the display itself was natural; if it bothered the viewer, then he or she had a hang-up of some sort.

Those days have faded. People no longer streak through Harvard Square or proclaim loudly their right to a clothes-free environment. The idea that it's healthy to expose your nether regions to as much sun and fresh air as possible (a tenet of some early naturist publications) has been replaced by fear of melanoma. The singles scene that perpetuated much of the nude beach activity in the seventies has gone underground to private swingers' clubs, or taken the more conservative form of the happy hour meat market. But nudist culture does still exist—on the beach, in the home, and in certain resorts and communities designed for that purpose. It seems to have gotten quieter and maybe less sexed up, but it is definitely here to stay. According to Phil Vallack's insane self-published treatise *Nude as a Newt,* there are ninety parks sited for nudity and fifty unsited clubs in the United States. The naturist newsgroup on the internet gets far more action than the Woody Allen fan group or Discussion of Vampires and Related Topics. *Time Out New York* ran a cover story recently, subtitled "All the Nude That's Fit to Print," that reported an art gallery opening in SoHo where the guests were all entirely naked.

I am spread out by myself in the nude zone, peering from under my hat. The guy next to me sports a belly like a beach ball. He is a snorting bull of a person, tamed by his wife. He lies at her feet. She, demurely attired in a floral bathing suit with a little skirt attached, devotes herself to knitting. He is reading poetry, lying on his stomach as if it's a pillow that's supporting him. A woman passes by me, on her way up from a swim. She is in her forties, very trim and tan all over. She reaches her blanket, just a little farther inland than mine, and joins a man who is reading the paper in a beach chair. She kneels on all fours, legs spread wide, and proceeds to arrange her blanket and dust the sand off it and get something from the cooler and get her book out of her tote bag and in general to perform such an extended series of activities, all with her anus and vagina pointing to the sky (and right at me) in the most exposing of postures, that I begin to wonder if she is doing this to turn her husband on. He keeps reading the paper. An enormous pasty man with a halo of brown curls melts beneath a beach umbrella, far from the crowd. He's got a horror novel and a bag of peanuts, and he sits so that he looks precariously balanced, as if he'd tip over at a large gust of wind. A man in his late thirties wearing an old-fashioned fisherman's cap lies some distance to my left, face up among a group of friends who are lying on their stomachs. "I feel like a role model," he says proudly.

During the first few minutes of each nude jaunt I take, I feel a temptation to judge people, to compare them and evaluate their beauty, but that urge is somehow diffused by the environment of the beach. People are, despite their idiosyncrasies, remarkably homogeneous. I think I'd have trouble recognizing anyone I know, especially if I wasn't expecting to see him. No one looks especially gorgeous. No one looks especially gross.

I watch a series of paddle-ball competitions: father and son, a couple, a pair of jocular college boys. The men exhibit a very different silhouette when naked than they do wearing the baggy bathing suits that are popular these days. It's rather startling to see how small their hips are, and I am preoccupied by the penises flipping about in their tan, shriveled-up states. More than anything else, I find the nude beach humorous. People's butts and scrotums and boobs, flopping in the ocean, squeezed against beach towels, proudly yet limply taking the air. Everyone looks slightly, sweetly foolish.

At first, I think that nudity isn't sexy, maybe because there's no mystery, maybe because of the foolishness, maybe because tan lines exaggerate sexual parts and without them people's genitals and breasts just blur into their legs and shoulders. But after a bit I notice the nude beach has changed the way I look at men. I have seen so many people naked, now. Big, small, white, black, ugly, beautiful. Then one day I spot an attractive man who is wearing shorts—not even a swimsuit, but shorts with a belt. He's skinny, white, with dark shaggy hair. I think he must be a potter, a painter, or maybe a chef. There he is, standing among a group of naked men, and it is only a logical progression of thought to undress him in my mind. This is how I begin to wonder—drinking soda on the stoop of the general store near the beach, buying lobsters at the local fish market—what *all* the men around me look like without clothes. I've heard guys say they do this—imagine women naked—but it's certainly never been part of my daily ponderings about shop boys and fishmongers. And now it is. I have a better sense of the possibilities than I did before; I can imagine all the details so much more vividly. Public nudity has sexualized my imagination. What fun.

When I spot the DeCellos on the nude beach, I roll over so they won't be able to identify me. I find something decidedly charming about their love of nudity, but there is an anonymity to the beach that is a condition of my comfort with it. I don't want to see them naked and I don't want them to see me. I have never conversed with a naked man who is not my lover, and have no sense of what subjects and body language might be appropriate. Do I kiss Dr. DeCello hello, as I do when I see him elsewhere? Should I cover up, or pretend it doesn't matter? And perhaps talking to the DeCellos in the nude would make me aware of their sexuality and vice versa. In a perfect world such an awareness would be absolutely fine, but in this one it most certainly is not. They are friends of Granny's, and I will have to see them at a cocktail party next day. It's a little like being naked in front of your boss or your students. The social positions we usually hold would be unsettled without clothes to mark status and identity.

The DeCellos never do seem to see me. Probably, they can tell I don't want them to. They understand that most people are uncomfortable on some level with being nude in public, even if they're brave enough to try it on the beach. In fact, a 1996 *New York Times* article reports that high school students from all areas of the United States no longer shower after gym class. They don't want to be naked in front of one another. A school district in Pennsylvania had to drop its mandatory shower policy after the American Civil Liberties Union threatened a lawsuit. The lawyer, who represented an overweight girl who felt humiliated by the enforced public nudity, received a deluge of support letters from people remembering their own shame in school showers. The *Times* offers two main reasons for people's discomfort with enforced nudity: poor body image, partly in response to a media swamped with perfect physiques, and fear of homosexuals. I think it's also for the same reason I hide from the DeCellos on the beach: people have no idea how to behave. What are the rules?

David Sedaris notes in the title essay of his bestseller *Naked* that some nudists he talked with would not use the proper words for genitalia, preferring euphemisms like "thingee." At the resort he visited, there were rules against intoxication, against sitting on anything not covered by a towel, and against wearing clothes in certain areas of the camp. Sexual reticence and rules for behavior fill the gap left by eliminating the rule against public exposure. Sedaris himself tries to relax by imagining he is naked in a doctor's office, where—as I interpret it—he would feel more comfortable because the rules for behavior by naked parties would be even more clearly defined than they are at the nudist colony.

Douglas's California naturists condemned voyeurs, and *Time Out* reports that it is rude for nudists to look too closely. If someone's gaze becomes particularly sexual, "other nudists surround

the object of prey, thus cutting off the ogler's view." On the internet, vehement discussions rage about what constitutes proper
behavior when nude. Of course, there are lots of naughty sex
postings ("I have a big butt and I like to show it to everybody!"
"I want to see some naked bitches"), but a large proportion of the
messages revolve around etiquette and morality. Are nipple and
genital piercings appropriate, or do they draw attention to sexuality when naturism is not about sex? Should people who shave
or trim their pubic hair be condemned for drawing attention to
their genitalia if they are nude in a family situation? What should
be done in the case of an erection? (Answer: lie on your stomach
and think about baseball.) How should children be introduced to
nudism, and are food fights appropriate?

Outside the boundaries of formalized nudist communities, the
rules for naked behavior are harder to decode. They are never
openly discussed, but when they are broken, even subtly, the environment becomes very tense. The sauna at my gym is a mini nude
culture; not quite a community, since the inhabitants change frequently, but established enough to have some unspoken rules for
behavior that I have managed to learn—if not follow. One day a
few weeks ago I was sitting alone on the top bench of the little
wooden room. I was on a towel, which is a courtesy nearly everyone observes since most people enter the sauna wet from the
shower, but also because there's a slight feeling that your bare
butt might have something disgusting on it that it would be rude
to deposit on a public surface. I was naked. Through the small
glass window in the door I saw the profile of a woman who
looked so remarkably like my friend Sunshine from elementary
school that I stared openly, wondering if it might be she.

The woman caught my eye and I realized I was mistaken, but
she opened the door of the sauna, walked in, and sat down across
from me. She wore a Walkman and was dressed for exercise: running shoes, sweatpants, tank top. She carried a magazine, which
she began to read. The tinny sounds of dance music leaked from
her headphones. The tension was palpable. My nudity and the

action of putting lotion on my legs suddenly seemed grossly inappropriate. I felt like an exhibitionist. I had broken the unwritten code of our locker room: don't stare at naked people and don't stare at people when you're naked yourself. If nudity is happening, everyone is blind.

The woman who was not Sunshine was also breaking the unwritten codes of the sauna: don't rustle papers, don't make noise beyond talking, and don't come in fully clothed. Especially with shoes. These rules keep the naked people safe. People wearing bathing suits or wrapped in towels are wearing only minimal coverings; the contrast with nudity isn't much. But next to fully clothed people, we naked ones feel much more exposed. No loud or sudden noises should startle us either, which is important since we feel so vulnerable, and minimal talk ensures relative anonymity and freedom from unwanted comments. That day, though, the sauna was a social environment containing only two people. The one-on-one scenario reduced the complex etiquette of public nudity to its most essential component: the person with the most clothes on gets to be queen. She was less vulnerable, even if she was breaking more rules than I was. I pulled my towel around me and skulked out the door into the cold.

It strikes me that tacit blindness in nudist settings is first of all a rule that is constantly being broken, and second of all a rule based on the shame of naked people. You might think that naked people wouldn't find it shameful to be nude and don't mind being looked at. But then why condemn those who look too closely? Perhaps they are pretending they're not ashamed, and establish certain codes of etiquette to prevent their embarrassment from surfacing into consciousness. What the codes mean is that naked people end up requiring a certain kind of behavior from other naked people, or from clothed people, and in that sense have a certain censorial power—"Don't look at me closely," "Don't touch," "Don't comment on my nudity," and so on. Blindness is supposedly a supremely accepting way of behaving around exposure, indicating that the potential viewer is so mellow that a giant erection or huge mastectomy scar is really a most ordinary sight and not worthy of her attention. But it is really about compensating for people's discomfort with being looked at.

public baths

the Poseidon Baths have been around since 1892. The entrance is on a slightly ratty block of an old Eastern European neighborhood. A fat man with a Russian accent sits behind a funky counter stacked with eucalyptus oil, Dead Sea mud, and disposable razors. He locks my valuables in a box and gives me towels and a rather makeshift bathrobe. On coed days, the brown felt curtains that separate the locker rooms from the lobby are drawn back, so that on entering from the street I am immediately confronted with penises, whisking briefly out of undies to descend into bathing trunks.* Women are maybe 20 percent of the clientele, but none are changing out in the open, although it's clear we're expected to. The closet marked DRESSING ROOM is filled with extra paper supplies, as if it is unthinkable that anyone would ever need it. I change in the lavatory. There is something more embarrassing in undressing before people than there is in being totally nude in front of them. Proximity makes a difference too; on the nude beach the penises are always at least ten feet away. Here, they are within reach.

Near the back lockers, farther from the door, men take their time undressing. They have their backs to the crowd. Pale behinds in various unsavory shapes moon me as their owners call back and forth in locker-room jabber. A man in his sixties, white hair erupting from his face, jokes loudly with a younger Latino guy, short and mustached. "I was talking to this girl down there," he barks, gesturing at the stairs leading to the baths, "and I finally

*Since my visits to these baths, the locker room has been divided in two: one section for men and one for women.

ask her to give me her phone number. Turns out she's a professional! It was a nine-hundred number." He laughs uproariously at his own gullibility, and the mustached guy tells him they're both just crazy hounds. Their banter consists of reminding each other of their eccentricity and even misery: how much one hates his wife, how much the other hates his shrink. It's an unusual twist on the cliché of men in the locker room, bonding over scores on the playing field and in the bedroom.

Here, watching men of all ages and sizes change their clothes, I feel invisible in a way I do not at all once I go down to the baths. There, it is no longer a nude environment but a bathing-suited one in which I am part of a female minority. There are four heated rooms (two saunas, one steam room, and one "radiant heat" room that looks like a medieval dungeon), plus showers and a chilled swimming pool. A plastic sign on the wall reads "There is no place like this place anywhere near this place. So, this must be the right place."

There are no elderly women on coed days. Only men, old and young, and women under forty. The elders are loud, confident, flirtatious. Some wear only a towel, even though shorts are provided and required. Several of them talk in Russian. Two men in their sixties tease a young Korean-American woman in a black bikini. "She don't look married, does she? . . . Korean, Hawaiian, what's the difference? Why don't you sit next to me?" The woman laughs and looks around for her husband. He is off in the steam room.

An ancient bather wears only a soggy blue robe which falls open with admirable regularity. I get an extended view of his pecker in the sauna, our toes nearly touching as we both sit on the top bench. We discuss the heat. A gentleman with hair on his back shaves his face and head. Another guy yells with abandon as the cold shower sprays off him, moaning and groaning in a manner so vigorous it would be unseemly even in the bedroom. Here, I find it quite shocking. The men of my own generation, white indie-rocker types, stay silent and keep their eyes down. Like me they are nervous, unfamiliar with the tradition of public baths and the behavior expected of them.

Wednesdays are for women only. The curtains that separate the lobby from the locker room hang down for privacy. I go into the baths totally nude beneath my robe, but am somewhat abashed on entering to see a small mouse woman in spectacles, wearing boxer shorts and a jog bra. Her hair is tied up beneath a towel and she is reading a mystery. Perhaps, I worry, I'm not meant to be naked after all. But I am soon reassured. It turns out the mouse woman is a regular, always dressed the same. Nearly everyone gets naked on Wednesdays and stays that way. I go every other week for a number of months, sometimes with my friend Marnie.

Past the entryway, the baths become another planet. In contrast to the boisterous splashing and moaning contributed by the masculine element, the mood on Wednesday is hushed. Conversations are sotto voce, and drowned out by the gush of the pool's fountain. Two women in their early forties wash each other's upper bodies with soapy loofahs. One is white and wrinkly, with the long gray locks of an aging hippie. The other is black and curvy, with brightly colored beads tied around her waist. They wave hello to me, although I've never seen them before. They want to look at my tattoo, but barely stop scrubbing in order to do so. Are they lovers, or not? At first I think they are, but later I am not so sure.

Perhaps their contact treads a line between the sexual and the merely physical, as so many behaviors do in this subterranean marsh. A tall woman with cascading braids sits with legs apart, lower body covered in shaving cream. One hand on her labia, the other slides a razor up her inner thigh. Another, a European blonde, does the same thing, standing and chatting to her friends as she takes the hair off. In the dressing room, an octogenarian, her young companion helping her to stand, squeezes her flesh into a black teddy worthy of Frederick's of Hollywood. Downstairs again, an old Russian woman who works at the baths, her bikini top creeping to her waist as she moves, scrubs a Rubenesque lady with a soapy brush made of wet leaves. The treatment is called a *plotza,* and unlike massages which are also offered, it is done in a public space, and by a worker whose status as such is somehow confused by her nakedness. She seems much less removed from her client than the workers at the spa, partly because of how undressed she is, and partly because she, too, is soaking up the luxurious heat of the dungeon room like all the paying customers. The blurring of the boundaries—between public and private, physical and sexual—is one of the major characteristics of this nude culture. There is more body contact here than on the beach or in the sauna at my gym, and more conversations between strangers.

A very thin and attractive woman standing by the mirror is putting chemicals on her scalp. "Are you dying your hair?" Marnie asks her, intrigued.

"What?" The woman looks irritated.

"Are you dying your hair?"

"Am I coloring my hair?" the woman corrects. "Yes, I am." She turns away.

"Oh, that's cool," says Marnie. We scurry off to the sauna, invading the privacy of the mouse woman, who is holed up in there with her book. We speculate as to why the hair-dye woman was offended. Is it intrinsically rude to comment on any aspect of another person's body when she is naked? Or is it just unkind to notice someone is covering up gray hairs? In the all-female culture of Wednesdays at the baths, women come with plastic boxes full of supplies: shampoo, lotion, pumice stones, conditioner, mud packs, nail files. Some smear their entire bodies with a heavy black mud. Very often they color their roots, shave, take the calluses off their feet. Marnie and I rub the dead skin from our legs with rough towels. Such activities are performed with a silent assumption that the rituals are still private; they would not likely occur in mixed company or in another social context, so the nature of the activities defines the basement haven of the bath as a private space, although it is open to anyone with the right set of reproductive organs and nineteen dollars to spare. The silence surrounding the rituals is also a way of keeping them private. However obvious and even sexualized the display, it is not meant to invite comment. Beauty secrets are not shared here so much as revealed.

At the Poseidon Baths I find a pleasure in nudity—and in witnessing the gradual acclimation of myself and others to it—that is what I imagine the DeCellos feel on the nude beach. It feels, more than the sex I've had, more than decorations I choose for my body, more than holding hands with my boyfriend in public—natural. Although it isn't completely. I think the underground environment of the baths, as opposed to the wide open spaces of the beach, make it easier for me to get comfortable because it provides some of the privacy we usually accord nudity, and also because it is single sex. Its challenge to the taboo against public exposure is rather mild. On the other hand, the relative absence of privacy, in comparison to the almost secretive atmosphere of the spas, creates a context where shame can evaporate—partially, if not entirely.

A Latina girl, probably nineteen, arrives with her friend, both wearing one-piece bathing suits. While her friend is in the dungeon, she sits with me in the steam room. My eyes are closed, and when I open them, I notice she has peeled down her top, experimenting with the feeling of being nude in public. Minutes later her friend bustles in, chatting in Spanish and tying up her hair. The girl quickly covers up again, reluctant to show her body to someone she's actually intimate with. For her, I think, and certainly for me, the anonymity of the baths makes a difference in our comfort with nudity. Granny's friends are not going to pop out from behind a sand dune, and the people I speak with are never in any superior or subservient relationship to me, like the people who perform spa treatments are. The only person to whom I have any defined relationship is Marnie. She and I have known each other since college, shared bathwater and pillows and sodas and clothes. At first, we clutched our towels around our waists, but as the weeks went by and we acclimated, the towels started being used

for other things. Having naked conversations, drifting in and out
of steam rooms and showers, slowly became as comfortable as the
other small physical intimacies we've had over years.

One of the principles behind sweating in a sauna or steam room
is detoxification. Like colonic irrigations, flushing water through
your pores is meant to rinse away the poisons that have seeped
into your flesh, but the process here is gradual and self-regulated,
as opposed to a sudden event perpetrated by a spa worker in
rubber gloves. It is openly public, rather than ostentatiously private. Slowly, over the course of a couple of steam-soaked hours,
the naked bodies of the bathers reveal themselves as surely as the
beads of sweat bubbling to the surface of their skins; when they
emerge, peeling free of robes and suits, the soul is cleansed. An
elderly Russian woman is squired down the steps by an eleven-
year-old girl. Both hide their bodies in floral nylon. The
grandmother wears both a cotton cap and a towel on her head.
But after an hour of breathing in the hot air of the dungeon room,
she is transformed. The towel has been removed, her top has come
down, she has splotchy marks on her skin from the heat.

One woman wears a wool hat, and another wears white cotton socks. As these come off, each person seems suddenly less
exposed. Instead, she just is. On my last day there, the mouse
woman slips off her jog bra and plunges into the pool. Like me,
she has shed her shame in the protective climate of the Poseidon
Baths.

I do think there's a connection between physical exposure and
emotional exposure. That's why Jeff showed me his stomach
when we got high. It's why ThEnigma won't take his shorts off in
front of the camera. It's why Jessica and Marnie and I go lingerie
shopping. I wouldn't want to be naked for very long with most of
my friends, though. The brief exposure that occurs during a quick
change of clothes is probably the limit. And with some of them, I
don't want to be naked at all. I've known plenty of people for ten

years who have never seen my stomach or my thighs, nor have I seen theirs. And we like it that way. I don't think, however, that I'd care if those same people saw nude pictures of me. Hell, they can tape them up on their refrigerators for all I care, because photographs aren't intimate. A body in a photograph is static and invulnerable. All the imperfections are much smaller than they are in real life. There's no movement of flesh over muscle, no emerging goosebumps, and no immediacy. The exposure has already happened. It's over.

It is not, then, the exposure of my body that's frightening, but being there for it, witnessing reactions to it that I have no way of controlling and that have no defined etiquette to structure them. Not knowing where to look, how to sit, what to do with my hands. To be undressed for hours, lounging and chatting as I have with Marnie, requires a huge degree of trust.

Bodily exposure can be liberating, or demeaning. It can invite both intimacy and unwanted assumptions of it. It is judged as immoral in some cases, and as morally superior in others, because it demonstrates freedom from inhibitions. The social contexts in which it occurs—paid physical service, sexual encounters, public spaces that sanction nudity or contexts in which it is deemed aberrant—strongly shape a person's experience of exposure, particularly in the ways the spaces construct (or fail to construct) privacy and rules for behavior. I also think the pleasure we take in bodily exposure (as opposed to public displays of lust and affection) is very much contingent on how much control we have over it.

An example: Back in the seventies, when my family went together to the nude beach, there was a year I decided to wear my bathing suit after all. I was probably nine. Sunshine and I pretended that summer that we were mermaids. We spent a lot of time diving off one particular flat rock and seeing how far we could swim underwater while keeping our legs together like fishtails. We would take our arms out of the sleeves of our one-piece bathing suits and plaster the suits over our nonexistent breasts to look more mermaidesque. The suits would inevitably fall down whenever we dived off the rock, and sometimes they would even end up around our knees. "Ohmygod," we would call to each other, rubbing the salt water out of our eyes. "My suit almost totally came off that time!" Then we'd work them carefully back up to our chests before establishing ourselves once again on Mermaid Rock.

I think this halfway shift into the socially sanctioned shame of puberty, when little girls and boys learn to cover up their private parts and become self-conscious about their changing shapes, was both a rebellion (against my naked mom and aunts) and a conformity (to the larger American beachgoer rule against exposing female chests). It was also a way of repeatedly exerting control over our exposure. We would relinquish control each time the water pulled our suits down, but that was always safely underwater, where nobody could see. Then we'd assert control by yanking the suit up again and arranging it carefully in proper mermaid style. The risk was nil, the context supersafe, because even if my unformed boobies did pop out of the water, the naked people on the shore wouldn't care at all. The fun was in pretending they would, and in knowing they wouldn't, really.

Aside from sex, luxury and medicine are the two main reasons people get naked with each other. Medical contexts, which I'll get to later, involve a practical agenda and a protocol that reflects it. The patient gets naked, and the doctor remains clothed. She touches the patient's body in order to find out information or administer a treatment that has a highly specific function. In luxury environments, the protocol is blurrier because the purpose is blurrier: pleasure, rejuvenation, detoxification, energizing, beautification, moisturization, relaxation. The kind of context set up for bodily exposure in spas and medical environments is one-on-one and highly privatized. But public environments such as saunas, locker rooms, nudist colonies, and nude beaches eliminate the injunction to privacy (about nudity, if not about sex acts) and set up other, compensatory rules.

These days, having absorbed the bodily shame we learn at

puberty and finding the nude beach less than safe because it's less than anonymous, I skinny-dip in secret. It allows me to avoid worrying about rules, or etiquette, or even exposure. Swimming into the deep water secure in my suit, I scramble out of it while treading water and commune with the fishes in my natural state. The thin piece of nylon that keeps me clothed onshore floats in one hand, billowing with seawater. Only the other mermaids can see me nude.

shaved head
....

In the interest of understanding bodily exposure and how it affects social interaction, I have decided to shave my head.

"You can't do this! I'm going to cry if you do. Why would you do this to yourself?" Fred is my aerobics student. He is a former fat person, and speaks in a high, persistent voice. He has taken my class several times a week for two years. We have never had a personal conversation. "I'm going to call Roberta and tell her not to let you do it," he says.

Roberta takes aerobics, too. She and I chat in the locker room, sharing body lotion and updates on our love lives. She is engaged to marry a hairdresser. "Roberta changes her hair every week," I answer. "She won't care if I shave my head."

"You can't do this!" moans Fred, standing by the stereo as I rewind the music for my next class. I should never have mentioned anything about it. I was just making small talk. Why does it matter to him? What makes him think it is appropriate to try to influence my appearance? Why is he so invested in what I look like? I am suddenly aware that this man spends three hours a week or more looking at me jiggling around in black spandex. He's upset because I'll be ruining his floor show. Or, God forbid, his midnight masturbations.

"It'll grow back," I tell him, and walk away.

Olivia is a public high school senior. She and I meet once a

week for a tutoring session. "The Bible," Olivia tells me, "is like
a book on how to live. It tells us how to act, how to dress, what
makeup to wear, everything. Women are not supposed to shave
their heads."

"Is it okay for men?" I ask.

"For men it's okay," she laughs in her warm French accent.

"But what if I'm a really good person, I do everything right,
except I shave my head?" I say. We are talking quietly in the
shabby library of her school. Our hour is almost up.

"Well, the Bible also tells women not to wear pants, but I don't
believe that part of it," she answers. "I believe it's not how you
look but what's inside that counts with God."

"I hope so. Because I'm still going to do it."

"I'll pray for you," she tells me as she stands up to leave.

"I have to warn Grandma B.," says my father. She is coming
for a visit to celebrate her eightieth birthday.

"Oh no!" screams Grandma, on the phone from south Florida.
"Promise me you'll wear a hat when I take you to *Show Boat*.
Promise me you'll keep it on!" Later she calls back to say she
was just teasing and she's sure it will grow back quickly. "But
couldn't you just imagine doing it instead?" she asks. "Wouldn't
it be almost the same?"

"You may be sacrificing your sex life," warns my friend
Holden, who uses a number of expensive products to keep his
hairline from receding.

"You'll have to wear a wig when we go out," jokes Jeff.

"You're going to love it," says Tom Comet, chainsaw juggler
and fire-eater. He hasn't had hair for three years. "It's addictive,"
he tells me. "I wish I could be permanently bald." Somehow I
think Tom's idea of pleasure is different from mine.

"What's the big deal?" asks Laurel, who has gorgeous curls of
her own. "I know lots of women who are bald. It's very sexy."

"Can I cut it?" asks Phyllis. She already has an electric shaver.

"Can I take pictures of you?" asks Marshall, her boyfriend,
who does street photography in gritty black and white.

"Can I watch?" asks Jessica.

"Can I have the hair?" asks Marnie's boyfriend, Harry. He wants it for an art project.

I say yes to everyone. Why not? By shaving my head I am asking to be looked at. I am interested in finding out what happens when I remove the everyday signs that identify me as normal to the rest of the population. What happens when I strip myself of my most natural protective covering, and bare my skull to the sky? Will people treat me differently? I expect the climate will be cold. Raindrops will splatter off my head and strangers will stare. Who will love me? Who will want to fuck me?

"I'll still play with you," says Jessica. "I'll make sure the other kids don't tease you."

Haircut day, Phyllis, Marshall, and I drink beer and watch sentimental dramas on television. Marshall is going to take pictures and Phyll will shoot a video. I have become their art project. Phyll does four different haircuts on me before we get to the skull— groovy shag, twenties bob, Audrey Hepburn bangs, *Rosemary's Baby*. Finally, she buzzes it down. It takes several times over with the shaver to get it short enough, and even then there's hair left. Rubbing my hands over my scalp covers my palms with fuzz, so in the bathroom, I put my head under the sink. The warm water stings, and thousands of tiny hairs pour down the drain. When I stand up, I am bald. A shadow of brown rings my head, but the skin is clearly visible. I feel naked.

In the pale blue, beaded top I'm wearing for Marshall's pictures, I look like someone in one of the photographs Diane Arbus took right before she killed herself: inmates of a home—whether for the emotionally disturbed or mentally disabled I'm not sure— dressed up for church, maybe on Easter. The women's faces look androgynous, even masculine—no makeup, no self-conscious, socially acceptable smiles. Their shorn hair and lost expressions seem dissociated from their formal holiday clothes. In the mirror, I catch myself like that—head separate from body, unadorned and vulnerable atop a hard, sparkly costume.

The next day, I stay in bed all day wearing a wool cap and heavy sweater, with a scarf wrapped around my neck. I have never been so cold. When I try to sleep, the skin of my head touching the cool pillow is distractingly sensitive. My head seems too small for my body. It is this little naked ball atop a huge lumbering frame, weighted down by the heavy clothes of winter. My scalp is dry—scaly with the irritation of the shave and dandruff I had never noticed before. I smear heavy moisturizing cream on it several times a day and it seems to get better. I have a mole on the left side of my head that has no color, maybe because it has never seen the sun until now. It's just a white bump, like a wart. It is repulsive, this uncovered area of skin bubbling up. I feel ashamed to have been hiding something ugly about myself.

Still, I immediately try to cover it, make myself a new disguise. I can wear scarves and hats, but people will ask to see my head anyway. I know they will. I dig an old eyebrow pencil out of the medicine cabinet and try to color in the mole. I have moles on my face and arms—so long as this one is brown, it will look relatively normal. But the pencil will not take, and poking the mole to try to get some color to rub off is uncomfortable. So I try black eyeliner instead. This works okay, but it's artificial—a mole blackened into a beauty mark like an eighteenth-century courtesan would wear.

I am shivering in my bathroom as I experiment frantically with cosmetics. I know the mole isn't really that bad, but I have relinquished control over my appearance and I want to get it back any way I can. I've got to decrease my sense of exposure. I put on eye makeup. Without it, I feel like my features are invisible—tiny gestures on a great expanse of skin. I have a small nose and pale eyelashes. My jawline is soft, and when I put on my wool hat to go outside, the bald head beneath the colorful rim makes my face infantile, the blobby features of a giant baby. So I mark my lids with dark brown shadow to assert my presence in the wide ball of flesh that is my head.

I have always been a good girl. I'm not supposed to scare people, or turn them off, or make them anxious for my welfare.

And I don't. I never look mean, I never look tough. I always wash,
I brush my teeth, I use a napkin when I eat. I look healthy; I project normalcy, competence, physical stability. All this, no longer.
With a scarf on my head and my body covered in layers of clothing to keep out the cold, I look like a cancer victim. My
stepmother, a doctor, says the scarves I've been wearing remind
her of watching people go through radiation therapy. A girl I
know from aerobics, when I tell her I shaved it myself, confesses
she thought I lost my hair to chemo. My boss at the gym fields several phone calls expressing concern about my health. A drug
dealer in Washington Square Park asks me if I'm okay.

But if I bare my head, I look harsh, even mean. My stubbly
scalp says to people that I don't care about the unspoken rules of
our society; I have broken one already—girls have hair, look
pretty—and I may well decide to break another. I am a skinhead
with Nazi sympathies, a sidewalk punk with safety pins through
her nipples, an escaped lobotomy patient. The short man with the
wispy mustache who calls "Beautiful" or "Pretty eyes" to me
each morning as I pass his doughnut cart is effectively silenced. I
no longer have to cringe in expectation of his unwanted compliments. There is an unspoken threat in my naked skull. It looks
repulsive to me, the little hairs growing in, the uneven curve of
my head, the baby hairs remaining just above my temples.

I know I shouldn't feel sorry for myself. I chose this. It was meant
to be a rejection of conventional notions of beauty and an experiment in bodily exposure. Instead it is proving a painful encounter
with the sense of fragility I have when insecure of my appearance.
Some people, beautiful as they may be to their loved ones, feel
ugly all the time because of some perceived imperfection—a big
nose, heavy legs, even a balding head. Others have to face the
world's displeasure with how they look because of obesity, a
handicap, heavy burns, or birthmarks. Still others face it because
of the choices they have made to flout convention—people with
facial piercings, mohawked hair, or cross-dressers. I assume this
last group puts up with any censure they encounter because of the

pleasure they derive from how they look, or because of the political statement it implies. But I have done something that is, I
think, unusual. I have deliberately altered my appearance in a
way that I do not find attractive, cool, or enjoyable in any way.
It's funny, because I never much liked my hair. Certainly, I never
considered it as fundamental to my attractiveness or respectabil-
ity. But now I see I loved my stringy, split-ended mousy mop and
the protection it gave me. It held my entire sense of self in its
ragged strands.

I don't want the people I work with to see me. I don't want my
ex-boyfriend to, either. He leaves a message on my machine but I
don't call him back. He will be sorry for me and think I've lost
my looks. He will forget the good times we've had in a strange
combination of repulsion and pity. I don't want any men to look
at me at all. I'm suddenly aware how many of my friendships
with them are based on some underlying sexual tension, which I
am confident will dissipate now that my head resembles a vul-
ture's. I go out anyway, creeping into social interaction nervously,
but with determination.

"Did you really do it?" asks Fred, who is waiting outside the
aerobics studio as I arrive with my key.

"What does it look like?" I say.

"Your hair, your beautiful hair!" he moans. He doesn't say
anything more, though. He seems silenced by the reality of my
visible skull.

"I thought maybe you joined the Hare Krishnas," says a
woman from my class in the locker room later on. She explains
that in China, where she is from, women shave their heads only
for religious reasons, so she assumed I had undergone a spiritual
conversion. She seems relieved to know I'm just eccentric.

"Can I touch it?" asks my friend Barry from graduate school.
He rubs his hand on my head.

"I have lotion on it," I say, worrying he'll find it greasy and
repulsive. He looks at his hand and then wipes it on a napkin.
"Really, I do," I say. I start to explain about my skin being dry,

but this sounds even more disgusting than an oily head, so I change the subject.

I go to lunch with Jeff. He calls me "baldy" but otherwise seems not to notice. As we pull our hats on before pushing outside into the cold air, I tell him about how I've transformed my ugly mole into a beauty mark. The story seems funny to me—I'm admitting my vanity and laughing at my attempts to salvage it. "Oh," he says with evident relief in his voice. "So that's what that was!"

I brave a friend's birthday party at a bar downtown. There, a literary gentleman with a few beers in his system starts petting my head. People have been touching it all night, but this man doesn't stop. He pets and pets and pets. "Enough of that!" I finally say.

"It's good you stopped me," he says, looking off into space with mild embarrassment, "because I couldn't stop myself."

"I have to ask you," says a drunk young man I knew in college. "How does it feel to spend your whole life being very sexy, and then suddenly one day, you're not? Because it doesn't look good. If people are telling you it does, they are lying."

"I thought they might be," I answer.

"They are." Later, he wraps his arms around me.

"You're just flirting because you're sorry for me that my head looks like an ostrich's," I say, laughing.

"Yes," he says. "It's a mercy flirt." I am grateful to him anyway.

"You look like a militant lesbian feminist!" cries a man who owns a cell phone. Funny, because I'm wearing a skintight dress and shiny lipstick.

Grandma B., who heroically braved all the sidelong glances aimed our way at the *Show Boat* matinee, takes me to a department store. Two girls behind the cosmetics counter ask me about my hair. "I could never do it!" says one. "But let me tell you, my boyfriend always says, 'If you like a girl and think she's pretty, imagine her with no hair. If you still find her attractive, you should date her.'" They chat with me and Grandma B. about lipstick shades and engage in a typical female ritual: affirmation of appearance. They praise my skin and my bone structure, telling

me how well I pull it off. Sinéad O'Connor, Sinéad O'Connor. In
their compliments, I hear the kindhearted understanding of young
women with beauty troubles of their own, but I also hear the slick
patter of cosmetics salesgirls. Grandma B. seems to hear a validation of my social acceptability. She pulls out her credit card and
buys me some makeup.

The series of interpretations people assign my lack of hair is, I
think, typical of what we do when confronted with the exposure
of a body that doesn't seem normal. We need to find an explanation. I answered phones in a talent agency one summer where
actor Evan Handler was a client. Handler has since written a
book about his successful battle with leukemia (which left him
permanently without hair), but his illness was never discussed in
the office. He'd show up, looking healthy and cheerful and bald
as a cue ball, with a bandanna wrapped around his head. I
invented a number of stories to explain his appearance, most of
which were based on a weird combination of stereotypes and mis-
information. Mainly, I figured he had been meditating heavily in
Tibet, but I also wondered if he was into S&M. I have found
myself engaging in this same interpretive process in the locker
room at my gym; there is a bodybuilder there who is totally flat-
chested, a woman who's had a mastectomy, an anorexic, a
woman with facial hair, and a woman with numerous body piercings. Whereas to everyone else there I am respectfully blind, I
have stopped and explained these aberrant bodies to myself,
noticed them, and assigned them meanings. And now I am one
of them.

Finally, with a week's growth on my head feeling like a blessed
coat of fur, I run into Roberta, the woman from aerobics whom
Fred enlisted to prevent this catastrophe. "Girl!" she cries. "I
heard about your hair. Let me see it!" I pull off my scarf and she
screams in delight. "I shaved my head, too!" she cries, and pulls
back the bangs of what I thought was her straightened hair.
Beneath the wig, pushed flat with a black headband, is a tiny,
patchy Afro. Validation! Companionship! Another bald woman!

The very person who was supposed to prevent me from shaving my own head has been a baldy all along!

Turns out Roberta has been having thyroid problems, which are now pretty much under control. When her health was at its worst, her hair was falling out in chunks. "A whole braid came off in one piece," she tells me. "I wanted to cry. Clumps were coming off all over, so I had to shave it. I always wear a wig, though. That way I can change the style every day. Black as I am, I do not want an Afro." She leans forward to show me the top of her head. I can see the wig's plastic scalp.

We go out to lunch. Roberta brings Claire with her, who has only an eighth inch of hair. Bald chick party! Actually, Claire does not look bald. It's more of a pixie look. She doesn't feel bald either, but people bother her about it all the time anyway. Her mother hates it. Her brother hates it. She has to explain herself a lot, especially when she goes home to the islands for holidays. But she has no regrets. "I used to spend three hours a day under the drier," she says, raising her eyebrows in disbelief. "Three hours! And that was with the biggest rollers in my hair. I don't have that kind of time."

Though I am hiding under a kerchief, I tell Roberta she should consider baring her head. African-American hair is so often worn extremely short that she seems less exposed to me than I do. But she says no. She likes the wigs, and she'd rather wear one than pay to have braids done. "But it's really different now than when I used to wear wigs for fun," she comments. "Because now that I'm bald I have to wear them. No one else can tell, but I know I can't go out without one on. My fiancé did not want to see my head. He's really into hair. 'Don't show me!' he said when I first shaved it off. Now that it's grown back a little, he's curious to see it, but I won't show it to him. He didn't want to see it then, I'm not going to show it to him now."

I think the distress is about losing control, more than it is about how we look. It's about not wanting our appearances to dictate our lives, and needing to choose the contexts for physical exposure. Roberta doesn't want her health problems to influence her looks, willing as she is to talk about them. She wants to decide how she appears each day, and is sad because she feels she can't go without a wig. Claire chose near baldness to escape the tyranny of endless hair preparation and the conventions of feminine beauty. She's happy that way because for her it's about controlling her time (no curlers, no drier)—and her image—without regard for social pressures.

And although I, too, chose baldness, I have relinquished the kind of control Claire has gained. I am spending all this extra time fiddling with scarves and lotion and eye pencils. The bleached blond shag I wore last summer seems like a glorious fantasy now. Instead of celebrating my departure from conventional standards of beauty, I have been trying to get back to them. And I can't. No hair gel, rubber bands, or bobby pins can change the shape of my head, and my lack of hair has become the single most noticeable factor in how I look. And instead of celebrating my physical exposure like the happy nudists on the beach or in the baths, I've become less accepting of it every day. It is no longer voluntary, and the judgments made about my body are far more comprehensive than those of the spa workers. No matter what I wear, the meanings people attach to a bald woman in our society—cancerous, angry, lesbian, hyperreligious—stick to me. I wish I didn't care, but I do.

As my hair grows back, the doughnut-stand man begins to bother me again. I am ashamed to say that for the first time I relish this mild harassment as evidence of my attractiveness. It is so different from the nervous inquisitions I suffered as a bald woman.

I have been ridiculously vain during this period. A frustrated vanity, that is. Being relatively pretty in the eyes of the mainstream has its problems—people assume I'm stupid, men call to me like a dog on the street, horny aerobics students pressure me for attention—but I had not realized how easy it was for me to be accepting of myself and my physicality before I shaved my head.

It hasn't taken much to disturb my pleasure in my body, to make me look down in shame when an acquaintance passes me on the street, to hesitate going to a party because I feel so ugly, to choose clothes that render me invisible. Not much to make me feel humiliated on a daily basis at my own involuntary bodily exposure. Not much at all. A haircut.

healing

the new age
....

In the early seventies, as I was entering kindergarten, my mother entered the New Age. She may have dallied there previously on a few youthful acid trips, but by 1971 she was totally immersed. She painted the ceiling of her study a deep purple and burned candles there at early hours of the morning. So while I was coveting Barbie's beach house and a certain miniature oven that would allow me to bake real live cakes, Mom was eating granola and swallowing seaweed tablets. While I learned to put on my own shoes, she took off her bra. When I got a tricycle, she got a mantra.

We soon abandoned the apartment with the purple ceiling for a communal home full of hippies. The house was four stories high, including a renovated attic, and every floor was cuddled up in brightly colored wall-to-wall carpet. No one wore shoes inside; the foyer was lined with wooden shelves, sagging under the weight of work boots, Birkenstocks, and my own dirty blue sneakers. The house's inhabitants sometimes forgot to wear clothes, and a lot of them smoked marijuana on a daily basis. "It makes people feel good," a friendly lady in a dashiki told me once. "It makes people feel good, but the president doesn't want us to have it." In the pantry, huge crates of apples and oranges rested on the floor. A chart detailed who was responsible for cooking each night, and the dinner table sat twenty. One big room downstairs was the music room. It held nothing but stacks of Donovan records and an old upright piano on which I had lessons. The residents of the house would gather there in the evenings and do yoga-based exercise involving round meditation cushions and a lot of chanting. The sound of *om* would resonate through the house, temporarily interrupting my absorption in *The Waltons*.

The residents chanted before meals as well, twenty people holding hands around the supper table, *om*ing as a way of saying grace. The food there was healthful in a now outdated way— brown rice and tofu, honey instead of sugar, oatmeal cooked with apple juice instead of milk. The new-age health regime meant that little attention was given to taste, color, or smell—the senses were abandoned in favor of an inner orientation. Interest in nutrients replaced the greedy joys of the tongue. Some people fasted, and others adhered to rules I didn't understand: They didn't drink liquids with meals; they combined proteins, abstained from dairy products, and so on. My mother didn't make me eat anything I really hated. I was allowed to have fruit or cottage cheese for dinner instead of cashew spaghetti or vegetables cooked in tamari. I spent my allowance on candy.

When I got to be a teenager, my mom's hippie lifestyle posed a problem. She was smoking pot, having boyfriends sleep over, and meditating two hours every morning. How was I supposed to rebel?

I became a carnivore. I devoted myself to the consumption of as many pigs and cows as I could possibly ingest: steak, and sausage, and bacon, and slices of ham. I'd get my dad to buy them for me when I saw him on weekends, and I had a stash in my backpack of beef jerky and spicy pepperoni sticks from the corner drugstore. I also became a preppy, earnest in my pursuit of madras plaid and various other trappings of conservative democrats with lots of money. I read *The Preppy Handbook* and fantasized about shirts with little alligators on them. I even dreamed of wearing a uniform and going to a boarding school where teachers were very strict and we had to be in by curfew. Last, I became a media junkie, as much as was possible with only five channels and a ten-inch screen. I watched late-night shows in my bedroom with the volume turned off, committed copies of *Tiger Beat* to memory, and became an expert at Pac-Man in the local video arcade.

Nothing worked. My mother was very accepting of whatever fool choices I made. I don't think she considered beef jerky much of a rebellion when the news was full of stories about kids who killed themselves on PCP. And while she may have worried that my current taste for alligators and Robby Benson would cause lasting damage to my aesthetic sensibility, she kept it to herself. Yet I think my rejection of spirituality and healing practices has pained her over the years. She has always, in a mild and generous way, offered to introduce me to various therapies and techniques she finds useful. Would I like to see her chiropractor? Go to a personal growth workshop? Have my astrological chart done? Did I want to have some therapy? Get my aura balanced? Would I like to join the meditation group? Take some seaweed pills or vitamin E?

"No thanks," I always said. And what I meant was, "I am not you, Mom."

Today, after ten years living on my own, I still categorically reject new-age practices designed to harmonize body and mind: yoga, shiatsu, meditation, Rolfing, acupuncture, chiropractic, biofeedback, Heller work, Ayurveda, aromatherapy. No no no no no. Not for me, all that harmony and energy. Not for me, alignment and renewal.

There are reasons for my rejection. I have thought them out. I think the cleansing rhetoric surrounding colon hydrotherapy encourages self-denial and even self-loathing. Health food enthusiasts place rigid limits on the pleasures of the palate. Spa environments reinforce the feelings of shame that are already too prevalent in our culture. And the line separating spiritual enlightenment such as Samuel Brandon's from total insanity is much too fine for comfort. Plus, I never can see anyone's aura, and my horoscopes in the paper never do come true. But the main reason is that I'm still rebelling against my mother.

She, I think, sees a deep connection between body and mind. Meditation, diet, acupuncture, and aura balancing are her ways of developing and articulating that connection. And although the connection hugely interests me—indeed, it is the subject of this book—her ways are not mine. My idea of meditation is drinking a few beers and lying on the beach.

the doctor's office

then my back goes out. Years of high impact aerobics and fashionably high heels have turned my upper back into a spasming tangle of muscles. I am in daily pain.

I try stretching every morning. I try lying on my floor with a large wooden ball under my back, pressing my muscles into it until they release. I soak in hot baths filled with Epsom salts. No change. I stop lifting weights. I take to lying in bed with a hot water bottle under my back. I do this even in the summer. My vertebrae are chunks of rock candy, grinding against one another as I try to arch backward. I can make my whole spine crackle in a series of small interior explosions merely by lifting my arms over my head.

I decide to take my back to the hospital. Western medicine for me, please: white coats and years of training, sterile gloves and plaques on the wall. Maybe I can get some painkillers.

My doctor, a balding man with stubby, strong hands, has a terrier who is dying. His wife calls while I'm sitting on his table, and he talks to her for ten minutes about whether to put the dog down or keep it alive when it is suffering so. They don't come to a decision. Hanging up the phone, he is visibly upset, and returns to the examination table unsure of what I've come to see him about. I am a little embarrassed to recall him to my aches and pains when a faithful terrier is so near extinction, but I tell him about my back again. He presses my shoulders here and there. They've had the dog for almost thirteen years. Name of Manilow. Does it hurt when he presses? Yes, it does.

"You have trigger points," he tells me. "Would you like some therapy for that?"

"Yes, please," I answer. What are trigger points? I never get to ask. I am hustled out so the doctor can devote his attention to the terrier.

The physical therapist is a tiny French woman named Jeanne-Marie. To get to her I follow a green line of tape through the hospital corridors until I reach the right elevator. The waiting room is full of wheelchairs, each containing a hospital inpatient who appears to be in staggering pain.

Jeanne-Marie takes me back to a curtained cubicle with a padded table in it, leaves while I put on a hospital gown, and then does what she calls "*Ma*ssage." I like her; she is nervous and kind. But she will not press hard during the *ma*ssage and she will not do anything in particular to the part of my back that hurts. She says it's all related anyway and that she's got to relax all the spinal muscles. I am not certain she thinks it matters at all which part hurts, but I tell her every time anyway. "Yes, yes" she says, "but when I do my *ma*ssage I have to go all over." She also vibrates my shoulders with electrical current. Her primary technique, however, is to put moist hot packs on my back and leave me to breathe in the hospital smell and listen to the screams and moans of the patients in the adjoining cells. An old man with a whiskey voice is there on disability leave. He's been lifting heavy objects and suddenly can't move his right arm. People are being given perceptual tests to measure a kind of dyslexia that makes them unable to distinguish shapes and colors. "Which is the circle?" the nurse keeps asking. "Which is the square?" The therapist on my right has a loud, ringing voice. "I'm Sandy," she says brightly to each patient. "Remember me? We're working together on your joint mobility." I fall into a doze here behind the mint-colored curtains, every Tuesday and Thursday afternoon.

After three months of this, Jeanne-Marie pronounces me cured and won't treat me anymore. "You are much better," she says.

"But I'm still in pain," I answer, feeling a little abandoned. "I don't feel better."

"You are much better," she repeats.

In the doctor's office—in the physical-therapy cell of the hospital, the dentist's chair, or the gynecologist's stirrups—there is a tacit assumption that corporeal and emotional states are unconnected. I don't mean that Western medicine has never considered the body-mind connection, nor that certain practitioners don't communicate with and listen to their patients. What I do mean is that the Manilow doctor is interested in me only for my trigger points, the dentist only for my teeth, the gynecologist only for the cells in my Pap smear. They don't care about my mind.

Lying in the hygienic white recliner chair, mouth stretched open by a plastic device, body swamped by a lead apron, I find myself incapacitated. Dental technicians are X-raying my teeth, a fairly standard procedure, but the plastic device hurts like hell and it is penetrating my favorite orifice in a highly invasive way. I do not understand why the lead apron is placed over my stomach when they've put nothing over my brain. The brain seems to me like something that really really really needs to be protected from radiation, especially radiation directed at the head. Jerry Seinfeld's grin exhorts me to floss every day and a fuzzy kitten poster tells me to "Just Hang in There." The hygienist wears fake nails underneath her rubber gloves, and she is guilty of withholding information on how to fill the little cup of mouthwash until after I have pitifully tried to make a single cup last through an entire bloody cleaning. I am less actively hostile to the graying dentist with his drill and his cherry-flavored toothpaste, because he rescues me from the scary hygienist and pays me lots of compliments mixed in with lessons on the home care of molars. He prods me into confessing I don't floss, then congratulates me on the talents of my orthodontist, a flirtatious man with a self-consciously sexy mustache who made my early teen years a torture by taking plaster casts of my mouth on a semiregular basis and prescribing the continuous wearing of headgear, never acknowledging that the first would make me gag and the second would be so painful I couldn't sleep. The dentist tells me I am fortunate to have very good teeth.

When you have something physically wrong with you, doctors search for a physical cause. They don't want to know how you feel about your ailment, or what you think is its source; nor do they consider that your mental state has any effect on your health aside from a generalized notion that you should be "stress-free." If you have something mentally or emotionally wrong, doctors may consider a physiological cause such as a chemical imbalance or Alzheimer's. If you have a life-threatening illness, they may suggest you try visualization techniques. But the experience of going to the doctor's office for a routine checkup or relatively minor bodily ailment is generally one of mental surrender, of subduing the mind because it isn't important in this context.

An example: When I was seven I cut my head open falling down the bright green stairs of the big communal home. I bled all over my mother's white blouse, and my tearful panic was mixed with pleasure—I wouldn't have to go to school that morning, my accident would give me a few days celebrity with the members of the second grade, and my invalid status would probably garner me some biggish quantities of ginger ale. The doctor who treated me said kindly, "I'm going to be washing out your cut. It will sting just a little." He did something, and it did sting, and then he bandaged me with gauze and said good-bye. I had been told I needed stitches, and I was very concerned that he was sending me home without sewing me up—especially as a cut without stitches would carry little importance with Sunshine and my other friends at school. I mustered the courage to ask him, and he admitted he had lied; he had done the stitching while pretending he was just washing off the blood.

Another example: When I was eighteen I got a stomachache from being taken to a health food restaurant by somebody who didn't know it would give me weird childhood flashbacks. I ended up in the hospital, where nurses and doctors alike insisted to me that I was probably pregnant. "I'm on the pill," I told them. "I have been for more than a year. I get my period and I haven't had sex for two months."

"Still," they said. "It's very likely. We're just going to be doing some tests." I would rather have been told I had stomach cancer than that I was pregnant, and I didn't think I could possibly be pregnant anyway, but I started to think that maybe I was, because none of these people would believe me that I wasn't. Should I have an abortion? Should I tell the father? What would I do? Horrible anxiety. Eventually, I was diagnosed with tummy ache and sent home, feeling slightly foolish that nothing was wrong with me, and having learned that it is silly to think not having sex with anyone would mean I wouldn't get pregnant.

The doctors in both cases were kind. They probably knew what they were doing. Nonetheless I was being tacitly asked to leave the thinking to them, to submit entirely to the situation as they reported it, even if it went against my understanding of my physical history and needs. They took their information from my body (with a pregnancy test) rather than from my mind. Or they tried to keep the mind in ignorance (lying about the stitches) so it wouldn't interfere with what they were doing to the body.

The language of Western health care is often about denying pain or minimizing it, which is different from preventing it. Anesthetics and painkillers prevent pain, which is great. But what about situations in which you are going to feel pain, they don't want you to know about it, and they don't want to hear about it later? They like to call it "a little discomfort." We're told that the shot will be over in two seconds. Or the nurse practitioner is "just" going to scrape some cells off the cervix, which might be a bit "uncomfortable." Or the sharp metal pin poking your gums is "only" doing a little cleaning. You won't feel a thing. Or the doctor burns a wart off with liquid nitrogen, explaining that the patient's skin might peel, but saying nothing about the throbbing pain this will entail. They are persistently reticent.

The pain caused by any of these procedures is pretty minimal. It is nothing bad enough to strike fear into the patient's heart. But it is surely bad enough to make her wonder if the pain she's feeling is normal, since her doctor never mentioned it.

As a patient, I am given a free toothbrush and sometimes free condoms, but I'm left uncertain about my relationship to the doctor and his assistants. To them, it seems, I'm only an obedient little girl, a paying customer, a problem to be solved, a troublesome questioner, or a waste of time. It is somehow very difficult to ask anyone anything—about the mouthwash, for example, or the lead apron. The brisk bustle, which suggests that everyone is working very hard on my behalf to get all this over with (which is what I must want), makes interrupting the health workers a disruption of both their authority and my own supposed desires. When they tell me I'm all fixed up, as Jeanne-Marie did, I am expected to feel relief that the process is over. That, in some sense, is supposed to translate into physical relief. I cannot insist that I don't feel better, because l) that will mean I have to keep coming to the hospital, which is unpleasant; 2) an authority figure has told me I am better, and it is somewhat scary to challenge her, especially when I have spent so much time lying naked and vulnerable in front of her; and 3) the hospital doesn't want me, and it is much bigger than I am. It is all very complicated and difficult to negotiate—and I am lucky enough never to have had anything seriously wrong with me.

The assumption that physical and emotional states are unconnected also translates into an assumption that physical intimacy doesn't have any kind of emotional component. When you are sitting in the examination room, this assumption provides a certain security—you yourself will not be exposed, even if your body is.

Show the lady in the white coat your genitals, your tongue, your ass. She won't pass judgments on your beauty. She won't be affected by the sight of you at all—not aroused by your tits, not repulsed by your pimples, not even curious about your moles and scars and wrinkles. You won't have the emotional intimacy that's usually associated with physical contact forced upon you here, because no one will acknowledge the two are connected. This makes the bodily exposure of the doctor's office safe in a way that the pleasurable services of the spas never are. But it also means there are gaps in the kind of care Western medicine provides, gaps I've been looking to close ever since Jeanne-Marie was unable to relieve or explain my back pain.

yoga

d ragging a sleepy, depressed ex-boyfriend in khaki shorts and a two-day growth of beard, I go to a beginning-level yoga class one Saturday morning. A guy we know named Bart went to India a prep-school pinup, and returned a messianic yoga devotee. He's pretty intriguing, sporting the same toothy smile the girls always loved, moving through parties with a sandy beard and a new, fluid grace. He can do the splits and put his chest on the floor. Besides, five people I know have told me yoga cured their back pain.

In a dimly lit room saturated with incense, pale pink paint, and rosy carpet, a soothing woman dressed in white thanks us for allowing her to be of service. A photo of a famed yogi sits on a small altar. Chubby pillows lean against the wall. The teacher begins by leading us in a chant. *Om. Hari Om. Om shantih shantih shantih.* I feel like I've returned to the womb, and it is suffocating. I start to have flashbacks of early childhood chanting, hands clasped around the supper table, brown rice and carrots. Unity with people whose names I don't know. Mutual sharing. Fragments of T. S. Eliot's "The Waste Land" flash by as well. For Eliot, the closing line,

"Shantih shantih shantih," is a deliberately forced and foreign peaceful closure imposed upon the fragments of the poem, a futile attempt to calm the chaos of the "unreal city."

Oh God. The ex-boyfriend and I have bad karma. We would rather have back pain than smell incense and recite wishes for peace and light throughout the world. I don't want quietude forcing down my bitterness, serenity removing my sense of irony. I don't want to feel the energy and harmony of the world when the unreal city of Manhattan rages in dissipated horror just outside the window. My ex, in need of black coffee and a Xanax, doesn't either. We run away in a state of panic, and I resolve never to go back.

But my inflexibility does not serve me well. The spasm near my shoulder blade persists through two new boyfriends, a new apartment, a couple chapters of my dissertation, and the adoption of my cats. I cease thinking of it as an alien scourge to be eradicated by whatever means possible, and begin to think of it as part of myself.

Then one day in August, my friend Holden, degenerate drug fiend turned corporate lawyer, writer of action movies and hopeless romantic, phones to say he's thinking about doing yoga. Holden's milieu is more 4:00 A.M. boogie than early morning prayer, so I'm pretty surprised. But he has back pain, too. "My body is made of peanut brittle," he announces. "I am the man with muscles of unbending clay. I have to do something or I'll crack in two." He promises me we'll go to brunch after yoga class and rebel against the brown rice vibes with a stack of pancakes. I am tempted to try again, if only to laugh at the sight of Holden trying to touch his toes.

So we go one Saturday morning, with our two stale-candy spines and a couple of hangovers. The class begins with chanting and eye movements. Holden, to my uncharitable surprise, is not afraid to chant. His masculinity is not threatened. He is chanting and stretching and having the whole yoga experience while I am sitting in an ironic little state of self-conscious removal during all the *om*s and *hari om*s. "I don't mind it," he says afterward of the chanting. "Actually, I kinda like it."

Eye movements involve looking right and left several times using only the eyeballs. Then up and down, then round and round clockwise, then back the other way. "This exercise stretches and tones the eye muscles," says the instructor, "and with regular practice can even improve eyesight." I try rolling my eyes at Holden in mock disgust, but he is concentrating on rolling his counterclockwise. I try to settle down to be a good student, but the exercises are boring and I have 20/20 vision.

The definition of a good student is very subtly constructed at the yoga studio, as I notice during the course of the next few months. Holden and I go every weekend. Towels are laid down on the floor to mark each student's space, but an aisle is always left in the center of the room, ostensibly for the instructor to move up and down in, but really it seems to me, to provide a pathway to the altar in each classroom. The altar and the open path are never referred to, but any student who, uninitiated in the etiquette of towel placement, unwittingly seats himself in the aisle will be gently asked to move.

The eye movements are followed by the asanas, or postures, which are presented with a reverent respect for each individual's physical limitations. The teacher's instructions to rest in the "relaxation pose" at any time or to modify the poses for your own body do allow each student to work at his own pace, but they also forestall asking questions during the class itself. There is no obvious "right" way to do anything, so there is no need to ask how to do it. Often, then, the goal of an asana and the technique it requires remain opaque through several lessons. In the bow pose, I wonder, should I keep the knees apart or together? In the rabbit, should my chin tuck under, or not? And what part of me would be stretching if I did it right?

I've been told by my teacher not to compete with myself, or my neighbor, and to accept the limits of my body for what they are each day. Therefore I do not feel comfortable asking him my questions in the hush of the classroom, where there are supposedly no "shoulds." But I know he thinks I should not be worrying about how my knees go and that the tacit rule of the classroom is I should not speak. Teachers are available after class to answer questions. The few times students have asked at any other time, the meditative mood has been visibly disrupted, the teacher almost discernibly annoyed.

Near the close of each class we engage in three different breathing practices: a deep three-part breath, a quick series of short exhalations through the nose, and alternate nostril breathing. The last involves contorting the right hand into an awkward shape and closing off the left nostril while exhaling from the right; breathing in and switching nostrils. We are told that this helps balance the left and right sides of the brain. I am resistant. The other breathing practices seem like fairly clear-cut means of getting more air into or out of the lungs. Alternate nostril breathing makes extravagant claims for itself, and requires not only an uncomfortable hand position that has no comprehensible relation to my lungs, but also requires that I count the length of my exhalations (*om* one, *om* two, *om* three) so that I breathe out for twice as long as I breathe in. I don't want my brain balanced. I want my back healed. The two are separate, aren't they?

Also toward the end of class is the yogic sleep. We lie on our backs, heads facing the center of the room. Uniformity is again enforced under cover of a return to a natural way of being and an acceptance of individuality. "This peaceful, open feeling is your true self," the teacher claims. However, if anyone lies in the wrong position, he is gently corrected. We are guided through a process of tensing and relaxing each part of the body. Then our attention is focused on our breath. Thoughts may pass by in our heads, but we mustn't pursue them, just notice them and let them go. If we itch, do not scratch. Notice the itch and return the thoughts to the breath.

I find the yogic sleep pleasant, yet I am wary of it. Am I being told what to think, how to think, under guise of freeing myself from my thoughts? Am I really being true to myself if I silence my neurotic cognitive spasms and don't relieve my itchy eyebrow? Maybe my anxious thoughts need expression and development, not suppression or even release. Is my true self here, lying quiet and still in a neat little row on my neat little towel with my head facing in the right direction? It's a bit like nap time in a Nazi nursery school. Maybe my true self is not so peaceful and relaxed; maybe I'm a little silly, a little loud, a little crooked, a little angry. Isn't that okay?

The spoken and unspoken rules of my yoga studio are designed to create a soothing environment. But they are also suppressing certain urges (to see the teacher easily, to query, to interact with other students, to itch or get up to pee) under a guise of self-acceptance. That suppression is similar to the dietary restrictions I disliked in my communal household and in the colonic irrigation newsletters; it is also pretty close to the artificially constructed hush of the subterranean spa. I have a lot of objections to what's going on here. Why, then, do I feel so good afterward?

I unhesitatingly love the postures themselves, which I barely noticed on my first visit, although they constitute the focus of the class. Most have names that evoke an animal or object: corpse, cobra, mountain, bow, boat, fish, rabbit, pigeon. Envisioning myself as each of these and replicating their qualities—the taught string of the bow, the exposed belly of the fish, the reared head of the cobra—is simultaneously a vacation from my body and a reinvestment in it. Often a pose is followed by a counterstretch that goes in the opposite direction. Forward bends follow backward bends. I become aware that my back stretches almost no matter what other part of my body is being worked. It is startling to be made aware of how many directions I could bend or twist, and to feel where my stiffness limits movement. Holden has an easy time with poses I find difficult, and vice versa. It is true he cannot touch his toes.

Funny: the regulation evident in the instructions for the asanas doesn't bother me the way the chanting and guided thoughts do. I like hearing each instructor use the same phrases as the last. I like the repetitive order of the poses. The muscles along my spine learn to anticipate the next posture and twitch in preparation.

Holden and I have been going now for three months. We have bought sweatpants, and each carry an old towel that we sit on during class. We begin to recognize the other students: an old lady, her face lumpy with age and plastic surgery, is a regular on Saturday mornings. She has removed her eyebrows, and her heavy base makeup slides down her face as she sweats. She has a deep and audible respiratory problem. A shiny black leotard stretches over her bumpy round torso. She is part society diva, part walrus. A tall man with a Brooklyn accent and a thick brown mustache is also a regular. He shaves his armpits, which are visible since he wears a tank top. He knows the Sanskrit chants better than the rest of us do. I think he's an instructor in training. A soft, Eastern European–looking woman with overgrown eyebrows and a rosebud mouth sits opposite me in a tie-dyed shirt. She mixes up left and right. Holden, hunched over his legs and looking perplexed at his inability to sit up straight, seems exposed without his glasses on. I can never get my towel to lie smooth and often get up for drinks of water, dehydrated from the heat of the room and also rebelling against the implied rule that we sit quietly, never disrupting the meditative environment.

Our usual teacher is a young man with long, curly hair, a pretty face, and white clothes. He's a teen idol after three years in India. He chants with ringing enthusiasm. We echo him: "Lead us from unreal to real. Lead us from darkness to the light. Lead us from the fear of death to the knowledge of immortality. *Om shantih shantih shantih.*" I'm not sure what all the words mean, but it's nice to sing a familiar song aloud together.

The eye movements, though still boring, have started to serve a purpose for me. It is not, however, the one I was led to expect. Spending a few minutes on the periphery of my vision, looking but not seeing anything in particular, moving something deliberately that I usually move only instinctively, readjusts my perspective. I remember that I choose what to look at, choose where to direct my gaze. I usually keep my eyes focused a foot in front of my face (on my computer, my book, my breakfast). Like a horse with blinders, I don't look to the side, don't observe the lives and options that are off my beaten path. The eye movements literally remind me to look around, both clockwise and counter.

After five months of classes, I feel flexible. I can touch my head to my outstretched knee and rotate my shoulders in ways that never used to be possible. Along with my tension, I have let go of the ironic distance that kept me giggling in class and have left behind the childhood memories brought up by the chanting.

The codes of behavior enforced here do not all suit me. Not all the exercises feel beneficial. The chanting and nostril breathing still don't have meaning for me. But trying them did not mean they stifled me in fetal harmony with my mother's beliefs. I was not engulfed when I returned to the maternal embrace of chanting and meditation. In fact, I was able to find comfort and renewed bodily strength. I engage fully with what feels right to me and maintain distance from what does not. An emotional flexibility has accompanied the physical.

Mom calls up, as she does every other week. She's still eating seaweed tablets and granola. She's still got her mantra, to the best of my knowledge. But she's put her bra back on. She is doing yoga now, also, after a long hiatus. She doesn't make too big a deal of it, but I think she's pleased I've got some *om*ing in my life. Our discussion is lighthearted. She likes the hand stand. I like the downward-facing dog. Her teacher doesn't make her do nostril breathing. Goldie Hawn is in her class. She laughs when I want to know what Goldie wears.

And a few days later when Mom says, "I've been thinking, would you like to try being Rolfed?" I consider her suggestion. She's made so many similar offers, in so many other years. I have said no, so many times, for so many reasons. Now, for the first time, I tell my mother yes.

rolfing
•••••••••

"**Y**ou're getting Rolfed?" cries my friend Barry, lounging in the afternoon sun. Barry is a literary critic and ballroom dancer. He has an open-faced charm. He loves women, but he sleeps with men. "I've heard some *things* about Rolfing," Barry says, making the word *things* sound like it designates the most carnal of obscenities. "Are they true?"

"Today," I confess, "was my sixth session. This lady felt my butt for an hour and a half. It was all about the butt."

"Exactly!" yells Barry. "That's what I'm afraid of. I don't want people touching my butt. I'm a very bad gay man."

"Well," I say. "She didn't go inside or anything."

"I know, I know," he answers. "It's not that. It's just that I really don't want anyone touching me there. I have issues about my butt."

Me, no longer. After what I've had done, it feels like public property.

Rolfing is the bad boy of the massage world. Its practitioners are not licensed massage therapists, though they do go through extensive training. It hurts. It is physically invasive, as Barry feared, and is known to call up repressed memories. It has even been called violent.

Dr. Ida P. Rolf was born in the 1890s, and became a cause célèbre at the Esalen Institute in the 1970s. Rolf, a biochemist trained in traditional Western methods, studied spiritual healing, yoga, homeopathy, and osteopathy. In the 1940s, legend has it, she met a woman named Ethel, a music teacher who had so badly injured her hands and arms that she could no longer play piano or even comb her hair. Rolf looked at her and extravagantly claimed she could fix the problem. "Do you trust me to try?" she asked. "You can't be worse off."

Ethel agreed to teach music to Rolf's children if Rolf could get her to a point where she could conduct a lesson. They started with yoga-based exercises. After only four sessions Ethel was well enough, and Rolf's kids got their lessons. This was the starting point for the development of Rolf's technique, later known as "structural integration." From that point on, people swarmed to Rolf with physical ailments that hadn't been cured elsewhere. Grace was a woman who had been crippled by a diving accident in her childhood. She always had to have someone with her because she couldn't do even the most basic movements, such as reaching down to pick something off the floor. Rolf worked with her for a couple years, manipulating the soft tissue of the body and lengthening it. By the end, Grace went off to California by herself. Other dramatic cures followed, and by the fifties Rolf had begun teaching her method to others.

Rolf's theory is that the body's connective tissue (collagen) becomes imbalanced and compressed because of stress, gravity, or emotional trauma, impairing muscle function and joint mobility. A series of ten sessions, each working on a different part of the body, can restore balance by decompressing the tissue and allowing for good posture. "This," Rolf once said, "is the gospel of Rolfing: When the body gets working appropriately, the force of gravity can flow through. Then, spontaneously, the body heals itself." Once a body is aligned properly, gravity no longer strains the structure, it reinforces it.

In 1970, there were about 40 Rolfers in the United States. By 1976, there were 180, and the process had received coverage in *The New York Times* and *Time* magazine. Now there's a Rolf Institute in Boulder, Colorado. Rolfing's connection to psychotherapy has something to do with its popularity: "Physical health and mental health," proclaimed Rolf, "it's the same thing." As Rosemary Feitis, one of Rolf's disciples, explains: "When chronic physical tension or weakness translates into emotional irritability or dependence, releasing the physical component allows release through the system as a whole. This can manifest as the resurfacing of a buried memory. Or, frequently, it will show as insight into habitual behavior patterns. As the physical anchor lets go, outgrown emotional responses can change."

One chapter in Rolf's manifesto is called "Many People Refer to This Drama As Pain." In it she writes that pain is created by resistance to an experience. Just as Pavlov's dogs ceased to appear hurt when they learned that physical punishments were consistently followed by an offering of food, so do Rolfing clients cease to feel pain during the process when they experience positive results. The uncompromising physical aggressiveness, even invasiveness, is what allows for the emotional breakthroughs people experience, and hence has been an element in its popularity. In the seventies, Rolfing seems to have been a sort of hazing process the hippie community underwent as a rite of passage.

My mother was not one to be left out. She was Rolfed in 1971, and found it both agonizing and uplifting. One session, she says, was so invasive it was like being raped: a solid hour of excruciatingly deep manipulation of her inner thigh muscles. Still undaunted in her Age of Aquarius pursuit of physical gratification and spiritual enlightenment, Mom switched Rolfers and continued the process. After one of the sessions, she felt like she had wings. In the seventh she had a breakthrough. "The guy was working on my knees," she says, "and all of a sudden I had this incredible memory flash. I remembered everything and understood it totally, all at once. My sister and I were in the back of a car, and my parents were in the front seat. My mother leaned back and tickled my knee and said this little rhyme: 'Tickly tickly on the knee! If you laugh you don't love me!'"

Both Mom and her little sister burst into tears. Neither of their parents understood why they were crying. The reason, which Mom comprehended in a rush of clarity as the connective tissue of her kneecap was being manipulated by her Rolfer twenty-four years later, was that their father, who was generally a very reserved man, used to roughhouse with the kids. These games were almost the only times he would break his stern facade, and the children savored the attention. "But," says Mom, "he used to pinch us very hard on the area right above the knee, where it feels like your funny bone. These shooting sensations would go right up our legs. But if we cried, he got angry. He had no tolerance for 'sissy' behavior. And so my sister and I had learned to laugh instead of cry when we felt this pain, because we didn't want him to get angry and we didn't want him to stop roughhousing with us." Her mother's rhyme forbade the laughter that was the only response Mom knew to give, even to a painful kind of tickle. The conflicting message was incredibly stressful to such a small child.

Flotation tank enthusiast John Lilly was Rolfed by Ida herself. "She was working on my left shoulder. Suddenly I saw myself at two and a half dragged across the lawn by my favorite collie dog, who had his teeth gripping my left shoulder. I was in panic and rage and I had a sense of being betrayed by my favorite dog. Suddenly, as the adult, I could see more of the scene and I saw the dog had been dragging me away from a wall that I had been about to fall over. . . . As she continued to work on the shoulder there was no more pain."

Briah Anson, a Rolfer in Kansas City and author of a book on Rolfing and personal empowerment, says that the process is a way of releasing the history stored in our bodies. Many of Anson's patients report dramatic emotional breakthroughs and describe their experiences with surprising honesty. Some had prophetic visions that helped them understand themselves better. Some recalled incest traumas and confronted recurring nightmares. Some relived their own births.

The sincerity of these testimonies is a little unnerving, perhaps because the language of the Rolfing converts has the flavor of religious zeal. The extravagance of their claims is in noticeable opposition to the disclaimers attached to many treatments in traditional Western medicine. There, recovery rates (and failure rates) are often part of a patient's understanding of a procedure, and strict instructions about ingesting medicine make it clear that the prescription is not guaranteed; human error—that is, patient error—can render it ineffective, and many other factors might make an illness unresponsive to a particular treatment. Symptoms differ, so that two people with the same disease might be prescribed two different kinds of pain relievers. There are always exceptions to rules. Rolfing, on the other hand, lays bare the connection between body and mind so explicitly that its claims become universal. Bodies store memories, which can be released and dealt with by means of connective tissue. The initial prescription for everyone is the same: ten sessions. Something about this universality, and the intensity of faith placed in Rolfing by its practitioners and patients, gives me pause, though I realize that the tenets of the medical world—though more invisible because they are more complex and more mainstream—are believed in with equal fervor.

My Rolfer, Carmen, reminds me of my mother: same height, same short haircut, same rosy cheeks and new-age rhythm of speech. I am having psychoanalytic transference before we've even had one session. In a one-room office in Greenwich Village, furnished with a low massage table, a coatrack, and a desk stacked with books and plastic vertebrae, Carmen explains the principles behind Rolfing. Then she has me strip down to my underwear and parade around the room. No wonder Rolfing brings on emotional catharsis, I think. This woman is forcing me to act out those nightmares you have about strangers seeing you in your underwear.

She takes Polaroids. They are massively unflattering and my thighs are the size of Nantucket. I resolve to throw out this ugly blue underwear as soon as I get home. Then Carmen sits me down at the desk and uses the photos to analyze my posture. As we look at them together, she shows me I lean backward as I walk and that my feet are turned out like a duck's. These misalignments are what she'll be working to correct.

The inspection and evaluation is different from any other bodily exposure I've experienced. In the doctor's office and other places I've gone, the practitioner leaves the room while the patient disrobes; Carmen simply sits at her desk and waits. In medical and luxury contexts, total nudity was avoided out of respect for the client's privacy, or to desexualize the experience of paying for pleasure. Here, my underwear stays on, but the Polaroids disrupt any notions I have about privacy. Even though Carmen promises no one else will see them, I will always know they are out there, somewhere, waiting to embarrass me when I'm old and respectable. The pictures also shift Carmen's judgments away from my actual body, because her comments are directed at the photographs. Somehow, this eliminates the flush of shame I felt when judgments were passed on me at the various spas, and it gives me a chance to ask questions. Last, we have the conversation while I'm still in my underwear, whereas typical medical conversations about a person's body are nearly always conducted when that body is fully clothed. I start to feel comfortable being undressed in front of her long before she ever touches me.

I lie down on the massage table. Unceremoniously, Carmen begins to push her fingers into the spaces between my ribs and around my hipbones, leaving little red marks. Some areas are incredibly ticklish, but she is gentle, and tells me people often have the sensation of something being unzipped inside them as she drags her thumbnail along their ribs. That is a pretty accurate description. I am surprised to find it doesn't hurt, though it isn't what I would call comfortable. It is something close to pain, only not.

When I come back for the second session, Carmen works on my feet and ankles for more than an hour, "fluffing up" my connective tissue. I've worn new sandals that give me blisters, and I'm ashamed of the condition of my feet—red and oozy. I expect her to tell me I shouldn't wear heels because they'll ruin my posture, and that shoes like this cramp my toes and mess up my alignment, but she doesn't say anything. She spends a lot of time on my ankles and knees as well as on the tops of my feet—hard areas of bone and joint rather than muscle. This is definitely not a relaxing massage: I often have to sit up, press against Carmen's hand, or bend over so she can look at my spine. She has me stand when one leg is finished, and walk around the room. It feels radically different, lopsided.

In session three, I lie on my side and Carmen works on the outer part of my leg. She talks about arranging the shoulder, ribs, and pelvis into an even stack, creating space between them. The extra room is supposed to allow freer breathing and less painful crowding of the structures. I have never thought about the possibility of extra space inside my body. Sure, lungs expand and muscles stretch, but the tissues around my pelvis or my shoulders have always seemed fixed in relation to one another.

The session on the inner thighs blew even my mother's open mind. "Inner thigh," it turns out, means a part of me that's very inner, very upper, and not always what I'd even call "thigh." Now is when I fully realize how different Rolfing is from massage. Every masseur I've ever had has assiduously avoided any area that might be considered sexual. All the little sensitive private areas were left alone. Now, Carmen stays outside my underwear, but aside from this one detail her fingers are probing areas even my most adventurous loves have not explored so thoroughly.

Her explanatory pamphlet says that we have now left the superficial fascial planes of the body to work on it's active core, the part that lies closest to the center. Besides the inner thighs, the active core includes the muscles of the abdomen. The psoas muscle (in the front of the hip and up toward the ribs) needs to be loosened up so it can work when I walk. Walking then becomes a more natural movement involving the torso as well as the legs. The abdominal treatment is also supposed to relieve menstrual cramping and gas. What really happens is that Carmen digs her fingers down beneath my uppermost stomach muscle (the one that goes down the center of my belly) and literally lifts it away from whatever guts and organs it's usually resting against. This is unlike anything I've ever experienced—a muscle becoming separated from those that surround it. I feel a deep kindred with all the chickens whose flesh I've ever gnawed apart. I think about how Jack the Ripper had a surgeon's knowledge of the anatomy of the human torso.

"We're all just big Gumbys," Carmen says proudly as she

releases my muscles back to their usual position and goes to work on my rib cage.

In session six, Carmen loosens the tissues of my pelvis from, ah, behind. I lie on my stomach and she goes right for those fleshy bits. It is remarkably unsexy, like a doctors exam, only it lasts much longer and we gossip throughout. These are, I think, crucial differences. The contact is not presumed to be invasive, something to be gotten over with as quickly as possible. Nor is it presumed to be sexually pleasurable, and therefore avoided. The conversation is not restricted to the process I'm undergoing, as it is during most doctor visits; it's about our common ground, subjects that bridge the gap between me as client and Carmen as service provider. Her cat attacks her husband, mine won't come out from under the bed. She dyes her hair herself, I cut mine in front of the bathroom mirror. Still, I wish for it to be over.

Carmen's descriptive pamphlet makes session seven sound like a dream: "The Practitioner works on the fascia of the neck, opens the connective tissue around the skull and face and helps to improve breathing further by opening constricted nasal passages." Turns out I didn't read that last part carefully enough. I arrive at the office expecting an hour of relaxing work on the tight parts of my neck and upper back. To my horror, Carmen is cheerfully laying out rubber gloves. "Today," she explains, "I'll be working inside your mouth and up your nose." Dr. Rolf's theory here, if I understand it correctly, is that the connective tissue around the uppermost vertebrae is best reached by way of various orifices. I suddenly realize that the inner reaches of my thighs are one thing, my butt is another, but the inside of my nose has never been touched by another human being. I do not want to share this part of me with Carmen, or with anyone. The other areas of my body she has touched have been relatively unembarrassing, even when ticklish or sensitive, and I shower before coming, so she hasn't encountered any particularly gross bodily fluids or odors. But there's nothing I can do now about the food between my teeth, and there's nothing I can do about my nose. I wasn't prepared. It's totally full of snot and God knows what else. I need a tissue.

The fear here is very close to my fear of colonic irrigation, although the environment doesn't exacerbate my paranoia. Here is what I am afraid of: the unpleasantness of body parts I have been taught to find unpleasant will be revealed and judged, and mine will be found to be spectacularly more unpleasant than most people's. Forever, if only in my own mind, I will be what I have often feared myself to be: a purveyor of mucus and saliva, a swollen bag leaking unwholesome fluids.

When Carmen does go up my nose, it's not so bad. She tells me about how uncomfortable she was the first time she had to do it to someone, how humorous it is, really. All with her latexed finger poking at my nasal cavity. She doesn't mind, just like she didn't mind my blistered feet. She thinks it's worth it.

"Carmen?" I ask, another day. I am taking off my clothes as we talk.

"Ooh, I like that bra," she says. By this time she's like my oldest girlfriend.

"I keep waiting for this big emotional breakthrough that's supposed to occur."

"The emotional thing doesn't happen for everyone," she replies. "It wasn't like that for me. Although in one of my first sessions, I did have these visions. It was better than . . . well, I took a few hits of acid back in the sixties, and it was better than that. My practitioner was working on my rib cage, and I started seeing this background of incredibly bright royal purple, covered with little green floating amoebas. It was so real! I had to open my eyes to remind myself—I'm still in this room, Arlo is working on me. But as soon as I shut my eyes again, it came back!"

I don't find this story too convincing. Maybe Carmen had stared at a lightbulb too long. Maybe her eyes were tired. I see all sorts of weird shit when I close my eyes and that doesn't mean I'm having some intense mind-body epiphany. Still, I wonder if I'm blocked or something. I didn't hallucinate anything good in the isolation tank, and now I'm failing to have an emotional break-through when other people relive their births or at least burst into tears. I feel like the only one in a consciousness-raising group never to have had an orgasm.

Carmen also tells me she's making my body more stable, more centered, and this will have a psychological effect even if I never have a breakthrough. I'll feel more grounded.

In session nine we finally reach my upper back. I am ecstatic. My saddest of all body parts, the perpetually moping, whining shoulder blade area, will finally get some attention. Carmen works on it for nearly the whole hour. I feel like a needy dog who keeps lifting its leg in the perpetual hope that someone will rub its stomach. Someone is rubbing, and my metaphoric leg is jiggling up and down. It is amazing how different it feels to have a body part worked on that is used to being touched: back rubs are part of my repertoire of physical contacts, whereas very little else Carmen has done to me has been so familiar.

Throughout our sessions, Carmen has told me about her first husband (bad news) and her present husband (fantastic, but piti-fully unhandy around the house). She has told me about her manic cat, Gypsy, and about the country house she's hoping to buy. She's told me about her Rolfing training, her sister with the bad posture, and the time she dyed her hair red by accident. In this session, as my miserable shoulders relax into her touch, she tells me she's been married three times, not twice as I'd supposed, and that with that bad first husband she has a son who is about my age. For the first time it occurs to me that Rolfing is a mutual experience. Carmen has been going through it with me.

On our last day, Carmen says my body's not done yet. The changes initiated by this series of ten will continue for months, or even years. She does some more work on my shoulders and neck and we take another set of posture photos. I can see results: my feet no longer splay outward and I'm no longer leaning back. Carmen points out some less obvious changes, subtle adjustments of balance and alignment.

The most significant part of this experience has been letting someone touch me intimately in a new context, one that is not sexual, social, or exactly medical. In a way it has been like losing my virginity—a gradual acceptance of bodily invasion. Other invasions people experience in this culture are not based on established personal relationships, and therefore I, at least, never find them comfortable. Although people accept invasive touch in a sexual context, we remain terrified of it both in medical and social settings. In the former, contact is impersonal. For example, I'm not sure I've ever seen the same doctor more than twice. A tongue depressor in a nurse's hand can bring water to my eyes. My blood is taken by a new technician every year; my dental hygienist is an evil, hostile woman with a fake tan. All such contacts do is reinforce my body boundaries, reminding me how unpleasant it is to have them crossed. And as for social settings, even a long-term friendship rarely has an element of physical revelation to it. Friends cheek-kiss and hug briefly, touch hands, whisper in ears, but that is all. They do not touch on the beach or at the gym where flesh is dangling out. They pat each other only on the shoulders, hands, and the occasional knee. For a friend to grasp my toes, to smell my neck, to rub my belly or wipe my nose—such things would feel invasively intimate given the way my relationships are set up today. Even with Marnie, my fellow nudist, such contact is pretty unthinkable.

"Don't touch me"—what does that mean? Something emotional as well as physical. Though it lacked the pyrotechnics of a rebirth experience or even an amoeba hallucination, being Rolfed meant developing a relationship with someone who cared for my body and pushed herself across my boundaries. It has been a gradual breakthrough. My blistery feet and snotty nose were touched without judgment and were somehow reinvented as areas without such anxiety attached; my dismay at ugly Polaroids became chit-chat about my bra and analysis of my posture, and my initial need for privacy was all but eliminated. My butt and inner thighs—never extensively touched outside a sexual relationship—now seem sexualized by the context and manner of the touch they receive, not because they are forbidden or particularly private. I no longer think, "Don't touch me."

It seems obvious now that Barry's lighthearted anal anxiety, my mother's memory of having her knees squeezed, and Anson's patients' recollections of incest all have in common the fear provoked by having one's body touched in unfamiliar ways. I came to terms not so much with the pain Rolf describes in her writing but with what I would call discomfort. It is easy to see why being touched in certain places might be upsetting, and equally easy now to see that this discomfort is socially constructed. It can be overcome.

Carmen talked about Rolfing opening up space inside, as if room were needed not only for freer breathing and wider movements, but also in order to let others in. I had been waiting to have this big emotional breakthrough, some intense release of pain, and instead I made space inside, eased my physical boundaries, never until the end seeing what Rolf said all along—that physical and mental health are the same thing.

acupuncture

It's hard to get an appointment with an acupuncturist in New York. Maybe it's the nouveau delights of body piercing, but the people of this city are remarkably inclined to have themselves punctured. I get put on several waiting lists and search out a couple of referrals before I find someone who will take me on. I guess I've got nothing so interestingly wrong that some guy who puts needles into Woody Allen would make time in his busy schedule for me. All I've got are some bad sleep habits, a predisposition to tummy aches, and some stupid back pain. Irritations, you'd probably call them, symptoms of life in a city where calling a doctor's office feels like trying to join the popular crowd.

Finally I connect with Edna, who practices acupuncture, herbal remedies, and cupping. Acupuncture is the most famous element of traditional Chinese medicine. Tiny needles are inserted one quarter to one inch into the skin, often along the meridians—the energy pathways in the body. The idea is that the needles stimulate or unblock the flow of energy, or *qi,* so that it speeds through the body unimpeded. But the meridian theory is only one of a number of mysteriously poetic concepts layered together like sheets of phyllo dough, each touching the other. Theories of the five elements, yin and yang, the fundamental substances, the pulse—all these and more beyond my understanding come into play as the acupuncturist decides how to treat a patient.

Edna is a red-faced woman in a small, three-room office; she has soft-looking, floppy hair and a cozy, pedestrian manner. I was hoping for an acupuncturist with more dramatic flair: Perhaps an ancient man, his cheeks feathered with lines, in a dark basement office in Chinatown, or a towering woman in flowing robes who spends her evenings poring over ancient manuscripts. Still, Edna's round, solid presence is comforting. She writes down a lot of standard information about my health, and spends an unusually long time staring at my tongue. It's a little too red, she says, which might indicate blockage in the liver. She takes my pulse on both wrists and tells me she disapproves of my birth control pills and my aerobic exercise. One, she says, blocks up everything in the lower torso, a bad thing no matter how much it stops you from making unwanted babies; the other sends all the energy up and out of the body, rather than grounding it in the earth.

Just like the doctor's exhortations not to smoke or have unprotected sex, Edna's condemnation of pills and aerobics applies to any and every body that she sees. I tell her these things feel healthy to me, like I'm taking care of myself. She is sure I'm wrong, as if I'm telling her how great it feels to smoke two packs a day, or how the solace of my usual six martinis far outweighs any harm it might do me. The difference between Edna and a doctor telling a patient to curb bad habits is that Edna doesn't threaten disease, doesn't talk in terms of risk for cancer, cirrhosis, or HIV. She talks only of facilitating the movement of energy.

In the treatment room, an ominous set of wires with clips attached to them is draped over a hook on the door. Soothing music plays. Lying facedown on a massage table, wearing only my underwear, I cannot see what Edna is doing, but she tells me she's going to calm the energy in my heart zone and unblock the *qi* in my liver zone, cooling it down. My upper body is tense and needs to be loosened up and energized, and my digestive organs are cranky and need to be soothed. The result of the acupuncture will be a better flow of energy all over, and I won't be so fatigued.

The needles are tiny, about the length of sewing needles, only thinner. In fact, they aren't needles at all to my mind, because needles conduct another substance. They hold fluid, pull thread, or knit yarn. The acupuncture needles are more like pins; their whole purpose is the perforation of the flesh; they carry nothing with them beyond their own cold metal selves. Edna puts them in using insertion tubes, tiny cylinders held against the flesh that help keep the needle in place. Her technique further emphasizes that metal is the substance of value here; it is not the conveyor, but the conveyed.

A little pinprick and Edna's fingers double tapping are all I can feel. Needles go in my back, my neck, my ankles; those on my wrists are the only ones I can see. After them come the cups. Cupping holds a fascination for me because I have read about it as an antique European practice as well as an Eastern one. Related to bloodletting, which was fairly common practice in the nineteenth century and before, cupping uses suction against the skin to draw out impurities. In Chinese medicine, it is meant to stimulate the flow of *qi* through areas that are blocked. In previous centuries suction was created using heat, following some principle of physics I am not interested in understanding. These days, practitioners tend to use suction cups instead, but the general notion is the same: create a perfectly round, giant-size hickey, and something good will come of it. A doctor I know says the old Italians who used to come into her emergency room sometimes bore the marks of cupping. I like the idea that two old women, one Chinese and one Italian, unable to communicate, would bear the same round marks on their backs—a visible, if temporary, sign of a mutual belief.

The cups are four round glasses shaped like flashlights. The handle part twists to create the suction. Edna puts two on the right side of my back, and two on the left, where my ache lives. As my flesh pulls upward, I can feel the layer of skin and fat separate from the muscles and bones.

"Oh," says Edna, her voice surprised. "You do have a lot of energy blocked in your upper back. It's stagnant *qi* in the heart zone. Its turning really red under there." She goes to the cabinet and collects some small objects I can't see. "Oh my!" she says, returning. "They're really quite purple, especially on the left." Her comments seem like expressions of wonder at the greatness of her own procedures, rather than judgments on my stagnant energy. And the cups do feel entirely different on the left side of my back than on the right, so much so that I wonder if the suction has been applied equally.

Edna then lays a piece of cardboard across my back and shows me a small cup filled with a dried herb. "This is artemisia [mugwart] and hemp," she explains. "I'm putting the cup on the piece of cardboard and burning the herbs. The heat will warm the needle that's going into your back. Not all acupuncturists have these cups. I had to send away for them. Some practitioners put the herbs right on your skin and burn you. Anyway, there's hemp in here, so it'll smell a little like pot when it burns." When I look it up in *The Way of Herbs,* I learn that burning artemisia stimulates the immune system and is particularly recommended for all cases associated with coldness and deficiency. My book doesn't say anything about the properties of hemp, but I have no objections to a contact high.

Edna flicks open her lighter and holds it centimeters away from the skin of my lower back. The herbs lit, she leaves the room for twenty minutes. I cannot budge; the suction of the cups provides significant resistance if I try to move my arms, reminding me that free motion of the muscles is contingent upon the freedom of the skin to shift around over them. Even if I could get up, throwing the cups off me with a sickening pop, my back is covered with tiny needles and the burning herbs might scorch my skin. Nothing hurts, but aside from that minor detail I feel like a submissive paying a mistress for domination. Edna has paralyzed me, and I'm picking up the check.

The near-total disempowerment I experience as a patient strikes me as connected to the hyperorganized philosophy of the body that underlies traditional Chinese medicine, at least as it is practiced and written about in America. One of its most basic principles is the idea of yin and yang, opposites that contain and create each other, as cold defines heat, low defines high, inner defines outer, passive defines active. The top of the body is yin, the bottom yang; the front is yin, the back yang; the right is yin, the left yang. This does not mean that the front of my right arm is more yin than anything else. Each opposition functions by itself. A full understanding of the principles of yin and yang is more complex than my description here, but the point is that the opposition of strong to weak, each defining the other, is the most fundamental principle of traditional Chinese medicine. It is not surprising that it infiltrates the doctor-patient relationship.

In the dentist's chair, or trussed in a cast for a broken bone, I may be similarly incapacitated, but there's no philosophy to explain the situation. My discomfort is an unfortunate consequence of treatment, not an integral part of the process. Receiving acupuncture and cupping, my position—yin to Edna's yang—is clear and understood. Somehow this makes it acceptable. She even tells me, during a later visit, that many Chinese patients prefer the needles to hurt significantly, whereas American patients and practitioners aim for minimal pain. Moxibustion, the thermal therapy she performed by burning herbs in a cup on my back, is traditionally done directly on the skin, producing a blister. In acupuncture, as in Rolfing, the patient's interest in—or, at least, acceptance of—pain as a part of treatment relieves the doctor from the Western injunction not to hurt her, or to pretend he is not hurting, even when he is, as my dentist and my gynecologist are wont to do. Instead, pain is accepted and expected as part of the acupuncture process, relieving the doctor-patient relationship of much of its falsehood.

Another major difference I noticed in being treated with traditional Chinese medicine is the medium of approach. Edna's plan for my digestive system is partly to use acupuncture, working through the skin. The herbs she's giving me to take later will help strengthen my system and thereby ease my back pain. She believes the muscles and skeleton are connected to the digestive organs and should be treated accordingly. Western doctors, on the other hand, have prescribed massage for my back, and Pepto-Bismol or something like it for tummy aches. In fact, nearly every Western remedy I know for common complaints other than skin irritation or muscle soreness involves ingesting something: hot tea for sore throats, cough syrup for colds, aspirin for headaches, Prozac for depression, sleeping pills for insomnia.

In Chinese medicine the skin, rather than the stomach, is the main vehicle for healing. It is punctured by needles and suctioned by cups. Skin is the only tangible layer between what we perceive as "inside" and what we perceive as "outside" ourselves. Manipulating the skin is a way of getting the outside in, and vice versa.

On my second visit to Edna's office she treats the front of me. This is somehow better, since I can see what's happening, and worse, since I can see what's happening. She is going to strengthen my spleen weakness, which is connected to my back pain, by means of my ankles. No pins go anywhere near my back; instead they are placed up and down my legs, around my neck, in my wrists, on my chest, and one in the center of my forehead. I make a sorry unicorn, the needle flopping forward between my eyebrows. She again burns herbs, this time in a cup on my stomach.

As she works, Edna tells me of an ex-convict she's been treating at a clinic. The woman's face has been cut away to remove cancer. Her body is covered with skin graft scars and she wears a

swastika tattoo on her hand, right on an acupuncture point. At
the clinic, Edna has been teaching the staff to insert five needles in
the ears of patients, a useful treatment for drug addiction or alcoholism. She tells me of an AIDS patient with chronic, humiliating
diarrhea who found relief from his symptom through acupuncture in the last months of his life. Her descriptions of the work she
does strike me, because I have been thinking of acupuncture as an
alternative medicine patronized only by those who can afford it,
and as a technique used to alleviate minor ailments. An aging
gourmand is relieved of flatulence; a Park Avenue housewife
swears it cured her headaches; a film actor says it relieves his
stress. Ted Kaptchuck's book on acupuncture, *The Web That Has
No Weaver,* concerns itself mainly with symptoms Western
medicine would associate with the flu: headaches, fevers, thirst,
vertigo, vomiting, coughing, and the like. I have been participat-
ing in what Dr. Stephen Thomas Chang claims is a popular
misconception about acupuncture: that it offers only temporary
relief and does not cure. At most in my mind it has been a potent
painkiller, perhaps a tool for anesthesiologists, but certainly not
a medication to use in a crisis like drug addiction, AIDS, or
cancer. Maybe I've been wrong.

The most striking aspect of acupuncture is the theory behind it.
It is an incredibly reassuring vision of the universe. The idea of
restoring balance to the body rather than attacking a pathology is
simultaneously the reason it seems like it could help heal the most
violent of diseases, and the reason I associate acupuncture with
minor ailments. In acupuncture, the world and each individual
human body exist together in beautiful harmony, a harmony that
cradles the severely ill and the fretful hypochondriac alike.

The balances of yin and yang are supplemented by the five elements or phases: Wood, Fire, Earth, Metal, and Water. Their rela-
tions to one another can be charted as a five-pointed star within
a pentagram. The world and the body within it form a neat pack-
age. There are five elements to each component of the universe,
whether intellectual or material. Five emotions: anger, joy, worry,

grief, and fear. Five domestic animals, if you don't like cats: chicken, dog, ox, horse, and pig. Five orifices, even though there are really more, especially on girls: eyes, ears, mouth, nose, and anus/urinary tract. Or alternately, forget the lower half of the body entirely and count the tongue and mouth separately. Five directions (including center) and five seasons (including Indian summer). Five colors, five grains, five kinds of energy, five kinds of physical strain, five sounds, five bodily fluids.

The notion of the five elements is at great disparity with our culture's fundamental belief in the disorder of the human body and the physical universe. I can always find a sixth, or reduce the five to only four. "What about kitties and vaginas?" I want to know. The disorder of the universe has been taught to me since childhood. In picture books and kindergarten lessons we learn what is "basic"—for me, cats and dogs, three primary colors, four food groups, countless kinds of grain. The ox seems no more a basic part of domestic life to me than Fido and Felix in the suburbs might to a preschooler in China.

Westerners see four directions, four seasons as the earth goes around the sun, and leap year every fourth year, but we never connect those with our four limbs or our four-chambered heart. Instead our bodies seem related to the world in ways that can't easily be charted; invisible germs, or viruses, or bacteria are floating around in the air and on the lips of glasses and toilet seats. If they get inside us we have to kill them by drinking foul-tasting liquid. We should also eat vitamins, which are kind of like minerals, only not. And take calcium. Oh, no, don't bother if you're over thirty. And eat oat bran. Well, that's not really necessary. And eat margarine instead of butter. Well, actually it's still fattening, so skip it. And eat honey instead of sugar. No, eat saccharine instead of sugar. No, wait, eat aspartame instead of sugar. And avoid chemicals. Western bodies seem chaotic, ever-changing mysteries that are constantly being understood and then remystified. Their relationship to the world is opaque. We Westerners are continually reenvisioning ourselves and our needs, and we generally consider the environment to be hostile. Ocean air and bathing used to be common prescriptions for those of weak constitution, but now we fear the sun, the salt, the chill, chemicals in the water, sharks, and ticks in the beach grass. It is no wonder we don't see ourselves in harmony with the world.

Stomach problems, back pain, and indulgent sleep habits are all symptoms of turmoil, of a struggle with my environment. I run about to parties full of posers, scramble suicidally through the city streets on my bicycle, push old ladies to get a seat on the subway, and then wonder why I can't get up in the morning. I am locked in my house most of the day, glued to my chair before the computer, trussed to my work in service of my ambition. No wonder parts of my body are stagnating. There is definitely something immobilized yet hyperactive about my life. Although these are ailments that might be called trivial, the cure Chinese medicine offers is not.

Though its theories and practice are dizzyingly complex, they have a stability to offer that Western medicine doesn't. There is order to the traditional Chinese vision of bodies in the universe that remains unchanged despite the latest research or experimental techniques. Kaptchuk explains that the theories originate in ancient texts that are assumed to contain the seeds of everything that can be known. Chinese medicine is complete and self-contained, developing only within its established conceptual framework, which remains forever the same. I think this stability may be part of the appeal of acupuncture for Westerners—at least, it is for me. A real sense of belonging in the world as part of some ancient, balanced structure would go a long way toward healing what truly ails me.

I am no convert, only a dabbler. I am not at all sure my true self is peaceful, harmonious, or flexible. It certainly isn't quiet. I am holding on to the birth control pills, and to my silly, fidgety tendencies, and to my buried childhood memories. And while I don't have much reverence for my doctor, I don't have much for famous yogis, Ida Rolf, or Chinese herbalists either.

Perhaps I am irreverent because no one has cured my back pain. I am really not much different physically from the person I was on my first visit to the terrier owner. Going to yoga regularly for almost two years now has lessened the pain, perhaps, but the imbalance is still there. The real difference is that I think of it as an imbalance, and as an emotional trauma stored in my body, and as a blocked energy pathway, and as the tightness that makes the rabbit pose a challenge. Before, I just thought of it as pain. It's not that I've given up that idea—I'm quite attached to the idea of pain—it's just that I've found some other ways of imagining the same thing.

I have also found, if not a cure, some contexts in which a cure is not the only thing to look for—and, therefore, is not insisted upon ("You are much better"), or executed without my knowledge ("I'm just going to wash the cut now"). Some of the gaps I see in the kind of care Western medicine provides have been filled. The pain involved in treatment can be acknowledged, even sought out and embraced. Areas of the body that are usually untouchable without the metal accessories of the speculum or dentist's drill can become accustomed to a different kind of contact. The mind is not asked to surrender, but to participate. The body I learned to diagram in high school biology, the body of Western medicine, can be reinvented as a series of animals, as a mass of connective tissue, as a place in which space might open up, as a conduit for energy, as a balance of yin and yang.

rebelling

physical fitness

Last weekend I rode my bike along the river, dodging skaters and cyclists, joggers and speed walkers. A few people threw Frisbees for grateful dogs or lounged on the piers, but most of us were intent on getting our heart rates into that target zone, blithely assuming that what we were doing—movement not for enjoyment, not to get anywhere, not to build anything or even to win a game—was entirely natural. People spend their leisure hours working out, "being good" to themselves, without noticing that the popularity of exertion without sport, play, or productivity is actually a highly idiosyncratic social phenomenon.

It amazes me how we embrace physical fitness—hell, we take it to bed with us and buy it flowers the next day—without ever looking at the object of our affections. I have spent eight years working as an aerobics instructor but have only recently realized what a bizarre little world the fitness industry is. It reflects our society's fear of rebellious bodies—bodies that are aberrant, ill, or aging. And that fear is very much tied up with our collective notions about sexuality and public exposure.

I made friends with Phyllis in our college aerobics class. She had braids that hit her hipbones and wore these flowered pants for exercise, a fabric you might dress a baby in. She would do back walkovers after class and was easy to talk to. I wore my high school boyfriend's crew shirt and some hiking shorts. This was before spandex. Lots of us wore two bras at once because we didn't know about jogging bras. We just blasted disco music and bounced around in a wallpapered parlor originally intended for young ladies in hoop skirts, and we kept doing it every afternoon for three years until Phyll and I had acquired jogging bras, and high-tech shoes, and spandex galore. Then Phyll graduated and got sick of it, and I graduated and went right on doing it for money at gyms in Chicago and New York. Only somewhere pretty far along the line I realized I was not being paid for the thing I had always liked, which was dancing around to loud music with Phyllis and laughing at the hyperactive woman in the thong leotard. I was being paid for something else indeed, something much more complicated, and I don't think the people running the health clubs, or the people in my classrooms, have ever given much thought to what was going on.

People go four times a week to the gym without saying to themselves that they are deliberately entering a culture with certain tenets and beliefs. If they joined a chess club, or a street gang, or Alcoholics Anonymous, they would think about their membership. They would ask themselves, "What does it imply that I am part of this group? What behavior will be expected of me and do I want to perform it? With what sort of people will I be in contact? What do they believe or enjoy?" But people think much less about joining a gym. Sure, a guy might consider which is more important to him, a pool or a big free-weight area, or he might reject one gym as too yuppie and another as full of bodybuilders, but he almost never asks himself what values gym culture promotes or how he will be expected to behave there, the way he would if he was joining almost any other institution.

One of the rhetorical standbys of the fitness industry is the phrase "prevents aging." Lifting weights and doing aerobics and stretching out your muscles will "help prevent aging." Of course, what the phrase really means is that the physical effects of aging—wrinkling, sagging, bulging, and hunching—can be staved off. But the language replaces the process of chronological aging, which is totally inevitable, with the cosmetic effects of it, and I think that's significant. Aging is conceived as an unwanted physical process, rather than as movement through time. The aim of fitness—enforced by the environment of the weight room, the bike path, or the aerobics studio—is to exert control over that bodily rebellion. Fitness tries to push the body as far as possible from its pimply, hairy, lumpy, wrinkling self—to perfect it, and thereby honor it and disavow it at the same time.

The historical roots of the current fitness craze lie partly in the health movements of the nineteenth century. In the early 1800s *athletics* meant only outdoor games, but by midcentury people had started doing calisthenics, and a movement called Muscular Christianity took shape—basically, the idea that only the buff go to heaven. Muscular Christians thought the body's form could be perfected, and that preventing bodily decline meant preserving spiritual purity for the afterlife. People also believed that strict exercise regimens would contain unruly sexual energy, breed self-control, and strengthen a man's moral fiber. According to fitness historian Harvey Green, urban gymnasiums functioned like churches—their mission was to help members combat the health and moral hazards of life in the big city.

The fitness trend coincided with the industrial revolution, and with it emerged the metaphor of the human body as a machine, or an "apparatus," as some exercise advocates called it. The idea was that the body's performance could be improved, like that of an engine, by reconditioning its parts. Various bizarre contraptions were developed to help achieve this reconditioning. Newspapers carried ads for large rubber devices such as "the parlor gymnasium" (a giant elastic band with handles), or a set of pulleys that attached to the floor. Men did home gymnastics using "Indian clubs," bottle-shaped wooden objects that they waved around their heads.

Bodybuilding, pioneered in the 1860s under the name "physical culture," was promoted through the 1890s by Bernarr McFadden, who was quite a specimen himself. In contrast to Muscular Christianity, physical culture emphasized sexual vigor. McFadden published a magazine, sold pictures of sexy female exercisers in flesh tights, and added a voyeuristic thrill to his lectures by exhibiting his own scantily clad body as a prime example of manliness.

The ideals of Muscular Christianity were supplemented by the movement for dietary righteousness, precursor to the health food movement and ardent colonic irrigations of the New Age. John Harvey Kellogg and C. W. Post promoted cornflakes, Grape-Nuts, and many more foul-tasting products designed for the convenience of the housewife and the renewal of the small intestine. Kellogg's near-obsessive preoccupation with bowel movements and other digestive processes linked inner cleanliness with godliness. In 1899, dietitian Horace Fletcher instituted a campaign for slow chewing with a similar agenda. He devoted his life to persuading everyone to masticate methodically, a discipline designed to keep the digestive system pure. As historian Hillel Schwartz points out, the late nineteenth century was a time, like ours, in which "the protocols of slimming" were taken "as the protocols for social and spiritual renewal."

After a relative lull during the bathtub gin excesses and war-time deprivations of the first half of the twentieth century, fitness regained its popularity. In the late 1960s, Jack Lalanne started leading calisthenics and had the biggest national show on daytime TV. Forty thousand desperate housewives every month ordered Lalanne's Glamour Stretcher, "a whole gym in a rubber cord." Family-oriented recreational institutions such as the YMCA and the JCC had sprung up in response to the baby boom, the health club was becoming a place to go on weekends, and exercise for its own sake was fully reborn in American culture when, in 1969, Dr. Kenneth Cooper published *Aerobics*. Cooper gave people the basic idea of wiggling around for twenty minutes or more at a time to improve the cardiovascular system, and that same year Jacki Sorensen invented aerobic dance as an exercise program for air force wives. By the time her mantle was taken up by Jane Fonda in the early eighties, there was no turning back. Unknown American runner Frank Shorter's 1972 Olympic marathon victory is said to have sparked the trend for running: Huge numbers of people took to jogging about in knee-highs and short shorts. And although our outfits have changed, we are still doing it, twenty-five years later.

What is this a history of? Sex, technology, advertising, the fight against physical decline. A history of morality, too: the fitness enthusiasms of both the late Victorian age and the post–sexual revolution years could be called responses to upheavals of religious belief. For the Victorians, physical culture emerged as many people were turning away from the church and the moral code it provided. The quest for physical perfection and a clean intestinal tract replaced the quest for spiritual insight. The *Charlie's Angels* generation was bereft of both the stuffy Christian-based morality of the fifties and the sixties faith in peace, love, and John Lennon. The new gurus were Jim Fixx and Arnold Schwarzenegger, later Jane Fonda and Richard Simmons. The regimen of a five-mile run every Sunday morning has now—for many of us at least—replaced attendance at the pastor's exhortations. More important, exercise is something we consider virtuous.

People don't speak of how much fun they have pumping iron or swimming laps, the way they would of sailing or playing asphalt basketball. They speak in terms of discipline and morality: "I was good today," a friend will tell me. "I ran six miles and ate really healthy." Or, "I feel so guilty! I haven't worked out all week!" Why is she guilty about something that harms no one, not even herself? A week of inactivity won't add pounds to her frame or weaken her heart. And how is my friend defining *good*? Her regime is not about kindness or generosity. Instead, the "good" of fitness is about resisting temptation, working against inertia. Just like the preservation of virginity, exercising and eating right are "good" because an outside institution (the church or the fitness industry) tells people they are, and because they involve abstaining from something pleasurable, whether it is intercourse or ice cream. I don't mean to say that exercise and low-fat diets aren't healthy. I just think people don't acknowledge to themselves that they speak about them in moral terms, or what that means about how fitness functions in their lives.

Muscular Christianity and promoters of physical culture sent out mixed messages about sex and exercise in the nineteenth century: Did fitness suppress a person's sex drive, or did it make him more sexually desirable and energetic? Was it an activity that promoted discipline and self-restraint, or was it uncontrollably sexual? The same conflict survives today, and crystallizes in the sweaty atmosphere of the gyms where so many people work out. There, the moral self-discipline of the exercise routine and the desperation of the fight against aging merge with the erotic appeal of barely clad bodies and a climate of sexual availability.

"Pumping iron," said Arnold Schwarzenegger in his bodybuilding days, "is like coming, but coming continuously." His equation of fitness with sex was typical of the late seventies and early eighties. Gyms were the "new singles bars" (said *Mademoiselle*), and they began providing services that promoted mingling and romance—hot tub parties, juice bars, mixed doubles tennis. The Jamie Lee Curtis–John Travolta vehicle *Perfect*, made in 1981, was a dramatization of some essays published in *Rolling Stone* about the California health club scene. In the movie, a fitness fanatic played by Marilu Henner works out with her lover, who is counting her every chest press as the sweat runs down her face: she is working to make her breasts bigger. Curtis, an aerobics "pied piper" with nearly as many male followers as female, is won over by a pelvic-thrusting Travolta. The man-hunting swinger girls who frequent the gym are hurt by a magazine article that paints them as trashy babes who use the gym only to meet guys—but the piece is basically true.

Another early aerobics movie, *Heavenly Bodies,* tells the story of a single mom who finds romance and TV stardom when she starts an aerobics studio. Her toned body and sexy moves gain her a handsome hunk and make her fitness club a social phenomenon. Olivia Newton-John's "Let's Get Physical" video showed Newton-John cavorting with a bevy of muscle boys who were pumping up their bodies.

This media image of health clubs as singles bars has had lasting effects on the fitness industry. The overt pickup scene of fifteen years ago has submerged itself, but its essence remains, fused so fully with the architecture of the health clubs and the technology of the exercise machines that gym members take its presence for granted. The metaphor of the body as machine that emerged with the industrial revolution now facilitates voyeurism as it staves off bodily rebellion.

The gym physique is instantly recognizable: developed pecs, washboard abdominals, toned triceps. You don't look like that from running, swimming, or working with your hands. You get a gym body by stepping into a machine made to work a single muscle at a time, far more specific than Lalanne's Glamour Stretcher or the parlor gymnasium. It's an assembly line physique: twelve reps per circuit, three times through. To work your heart, you log on to a big machine for twenty minutes or more: treadmill, bike, stairclimber, rowing machine. The goal is to segment the body into small, unrelated parts and mold each one to a peak of sexual attractiveness. It is all about affirmation of normalcy: make yourself conform to socially sanctioned standards, keep your body from declining or exhibiting any sort of aberration, and thereby license yourself to display your physique and examine those on display.

The machines themselves are closer to the slave-discipline contraptions of an Anne Rice porno novel than anything else I've seen in real life. Certainly more than anything I've seen in public. People open and shut their legs, pushing against metal slabs that exert pressure on their thighs. They insert themselves into the giant Gravitron and strain through military style pull-ups inside it. They imprison themselves in the abdominal machines, looking out through a tangle of iron bars, moaning as they twist their torsos like sex-starved juvenile delinquents in a prison exploitation flick. It's pretty great, and the architecture of health clubs is designed to allow maximum opportunity for scoping these sweaty scenes of techno discipline. It blatantly caters to the voyeur. Many clubs have windows to the street and wall their aerobics studios in glass. At the gym where I work now, a sheet of glass gives a view of my wiggling behind to the athletes in the weight room and the runners on the track. Of course, I am so busy checking my own self out that I barely notice them drooling, or gagging, or whatever they're up to. What would aerobics class be without mirrors? Just exercise.

My point is that people who work out, myself included, spend hours each week in a space constructed to promote visual examination—of others, and of themselves. In no other environment I can think of have I ever spent a full hour looking at myself in the mirror next to other people. I can't help but check out how they look, how they move, how their proximity affects me, how their bodies compare to mine. And nowhere else in the city can I get a twenty-minute show of a nearly naked man sweating heavily and breathing hard without paying thirty dollars or doing anything illegal: college team athletes working out off-season, built young men in tight white T-shirts, skinny earnest types in baggy plaid shorts, aging artists with veins showing in their arms, spandex boys with broad shaved chests. It's better than Chippendales. I love them all. I don't feel dirty as I watch their thigh muscles straining against the machines. Because it is legitimized by the layout of the health club, I can take my voyeurism of sculpted bodies in metal contraptions in stride.

Ads for fitness-related products also present fitness as embodying a democratic philosophy: You are free. Just do it. No judgments. Achievement is available to everyone who can afford it. In *Muscle: Confessions of an Unlikely Bodybuilder,* scholar turned steroid popper Sam Fussell describes the image of the gym portrayed in muscle magazines: "Gyms are actually a haven of safety in a world rife with disease, poverty, and prejudice. They are the stronghold of democracy, they said, where every lifter, regardless of color or creed, is free to pursue personal physique gains. Just bring a 'positive mental attitude,' and you'll be among likeminded friends in the gym."

The democratic philosophy and the idea of gyms as havens of safety differentiate fitness from competitive sports. In a 1978 essay, Christopher Lasch argues that proponents of fitness are "vaguely uneasy about the emotional response evoked by competitive sports." Lasch says that sports obliterate our awareness of everyday reality by mimicking it, dramatizing our experience of conflict. When people view athletics purely as entertainment for the players (pickup basketball games or intramural Frisbee), or when people exercise for their health alone, sport ceases to provide that emotional release. In other words, the lack of games in the gym is highly significant. These are the athletics of the fitness industry: swimming laps, running on a treadmill, pushing against machines. No one is playing games; they are working—working out. My aerobics students isolate their abdominal muscles and dance complex routines before a mirror. Enormous contraptions help people climb endless staircases and ski miles to nowhere while watching the daily news. Beyond Fred's harassment about shaving my head, nothing has happened in my eight years of teaching aerobics. The tinny sounds of eighties pop were replaced by house and then by the return of seventies disco. Spandex got fashionable. Step aerobics was invented. But that is pretty much it. I had no wins. No losses. No last-minute scores, no near-defeats, no sudden injuries, innovative game strategies, nor Most Improved Players. I had no emotional experiences whatsoever. Only a sense of control over my body, which I ultimately believe is illusory.

Americans are uncomfortable with their physicality, focused as they are on it. People keep their bodies in control by fitting them into machines, regulating their caloric output, keeping their limbs busy. The discipline keeps flesh from excess and relieves people of having to consciously seek an outlet for voyeuristic pleasures. It maintains the Protestant work ethic during those few leisure hours. It promises to keep us from becoming fat, or sick, or otherwise aberrant; it "prevents aging" and makes people safe from the danger of contact sports, from the thrill of victory, from the agony of defeat. By diverting sexual and competitive urges into workouts, we achieve a warped relief from the tyrannies of anger, desire, disease, decline, difference, pain, and glory.

The fitness industry embodies many of the cultural phenomena I'm talking about here: covert scenarios for semisexual gratification and bodily display; use of the word *natural* to justify and explain what is actually extreme and culturally specific behavior; and alteration of the body as a negotiation with socially sanctioned norms for appearance. I also think the practices of the fitness industry reveal a mistrust of the body. It might rebel, and betray us in one of three possible ways. First by disfigurement. People fear ownership of unusual bodies, bodies like those of people who suffer from disabilities, and bodies like those I looked at in my gym locker room, and like I became when I shaved my head: fat bodies, hairy bodies, bodies with parts deemed too small or too large. Second by filth, by which I mean disease and the physical changes that come with it, but also the more everyday evidence of our bodily putridity—the snot and shit that make Rolfing and colonics so potentially humiliating, and the vomit, pus, and sweat that lurk inside us, ready to spew forth at slight provocation. Third by age, the enemy of the fitness industry, which carries with it the threat of dysfunction. Losing one's youthful beauty to the years can be a severe betrayal of the mind by the body; but more important, I think, people fear the changes of habit and temperament that seem to come with the decreased mobility of age. From these fears stem not only the perverse pleasures of personal trainers and step aerobics, but also a multitude of other tiny behavior patterns and rituals that expose our need for control over our rebellious bodies.

gross yourself out

Pimples are upsetting in a way peculiar to themselves. I remember locking myself in the bathroom as a young teenager and ripping into my chin with a sterilized safety pin. Desperate to rid myself of those painful red sprouts, I was determined to dig them up like onions from the earth. I would have removed cubes of flesh with a knife if I could have. I never had very bad skin, but I feared it. I got my mother to buy me a rotating gadget, the very existence of which convinces me I was not alone in my paranoia. It had six different attachments for washing and exfoliating the face. It had a soft brush, a hard brush, a sponge, and who knows what else. I operated it in conjunction with large quantities of Noxzema, followed by astringent, benzoil peroxide, and moisturizer. I considered my time and my mother's money well spent. I was fending off bodily revolt.

Acne is malignant grease trying to break its way through the epidermis, the sour oiliness in my soul coming to the surface. Drying medicines and astringents don't help much. If I apply them before the pustule presses through the skin, they merely redden the area and make it flake. If I apply them to an oozing whitehead, their sting reminds me that my wet flesh has opened itself to the air, insisting on unwanted exposure. Acne remedies do not heal; they enact an acid punishment on the rebellious body. Pimple sufferers feel shame even when it is common knowledge that bad skin is rarely caused by poor hygiene. It is the shame of involuntary self-revelation.

The horror of owning a body inclined toward such filthy behavior has been dramatized in a recent series of children's books called Barf-O-Rama, geared to a preteen audience. The first book, *The Great Puke-off*, is the story of two rival cliques of fifth graders. One group puts cockroaches in the school burritos, and the whole cafeteria goes crazy, "heaving and gacking and extruding large quantities of stomach contents." A gross-out war ensues, the competitors using powerful farts and "diaper gravy" as weapons, one victim spewing "a stream of cream of barf." Finally, the two kids with the highest tolerance go one-on-one, stuffing themselves silly on cotton candy, snot, and pimple juice at the local amusement park, then riding the roller coasters. Neither one gets sick until they kiss, at which point they puke so much they cause a flood in the middle of a crowded schoolbus. The second book, *Garbage Time,* is the story of a boy who, in his efforts to chase a pretty girl quarterback off his football team, dumps a "helmet of hurl" on his own head, causing a whole locker room of players to lose their lunch. And the series spews on.

Vomiting is an event, rather than a condition, akin to orgasm or a sneeze. But puberty is a situation that lasts for years. So it is really unsurprising that on the verge of a mysterious physical change eleven-year-old book buyers would want to read about barf. Nor is it surprising that the moments of sexual tension in the books (the gross-out-war kiss and the strange excitement generated by the pretty quarterback) are resolved by chunder. When a kid's own body is threatening to gross him out with pimples, pubic hair, and weird sexual urges, it's probably a great relief to get grossed out by diarrhea and vomit instead. Those horrific bodily revolts are over in a few minutes. Barfing is also a return to childhood physicality and the simpler concerns of babyhood. Infants spit up all the time, and until the age of five it is not unusual to be sick with some degree of regularity.

Sunshine, when we were eight years old, taught me a trick for grossing yourself out that had a huge effect on me. First, bend your fingers as much as they will bend—but don't make a fist. Then hold your hand away from your body and squint at the back of it. Eventually it will look like your fingers are just little stubs that stop at your first knuckle. A mutant hand. Creepy, huh?

Of course, there were far grosser things we could have been

doing. In truth, we did them. Charity, who always had a blue ribbon of mucus hanging out her nose, could gross out a whole
lunch table without even trying. There were boys who continually
had to have time-outs during science workshops because they
kept eating the bacteria. Barf-O-Rama had yet to be invented, but
jars of fake snot and books on how to eat fried worms were available to those who saved their allowances, and we made avid use
of them. Our class play, which I am proud to announce I wrote
single-handedly, climaxed when six of the characters disappeared
down a giant toilet. It was 1976 and they let us perform it in front
of the whole school.

As my dramatic efforts show, I was as preoccupied with excre-
ment and other disagreeable things as the next kid. But the
mutant hand was really more interesting to me. Even today it
makes me feel funny inside. It has something to do with seeing my
own body as a foreign object. It is my hand, but it doesn't look
like mine. It looks congenitally deformed, and not very usable,
the hand of someone with a very different life than I have.

Whereas squeezing pimples is a fantasy of eradicating filth and
disciplining rebellious flesh, mutant hand is a fantasy of owning
a unique, misshapen body. It's about imagining a permanent state
rather than a sudden event like vomiting. And most important,
mutant hand involves thinking about outward deformity, rather
than inner malignancy.

There was a kid named Mink in the classroom next door to
ours who had a sunken chest. He used to lift up his shirt at recess
and we never got bored of it. One of our teachers had webbed
toes which she would show us if we nagged her. And while I
would never have asked the boy who had polio if I could look at
his legs (at eight I found people with disabilities sad and a little
frightening), Mink and my teacher were in perfect health. Their
physical anomalies were fascinating: icky and somehow not altogether safe. The mutant hand experiment allowed me to try the
same thing on myself, giving me a momentary empathy with bodies that strayed from the norm.

freaks
· · · · · · · · ·

Other people's extreme anomalies have always held an appeal for me that is not exactly pleasure. It is a form of horror linked with intense curiosity, and a little guilt. I do not mean to be cruel, but when I am confronted with a person who is mangled or deformed, I cannot help but look. And I cannot look without a visceral reaction, a twinge of disgust mixed with my interest or pity.

It is easy to find coffee-table books with sensational titles that feature photographs of freak show performers and the garish painted banners that used to advertise them. Many of the images date back a hundred years, to a time when collections of photographs were centerpieces in late-Victorian drawing rooms. In those days, self-made freaks (tattooed ladies, geeks, and sword swallowers) and cultural freaks (people from tribal communities in nonwhite countries) were displayed alongside people with physical oddities and handicaps. Many of the anomalies are startling and pitiful: Myrtle Corbin had a double lower body out of which she bore five children, three from one side, two from the other; Sepentina, the serpent girl, claimed to have no bones in her body other than her skull; Mignon, the penguin girl, had squat, abbreviated limbs. For a bit of spare change, customers could gawk at Flip the frog boy, Ella Harper the camel girl, or the Elephant Man. Somehow though, I am drawn by the people whose bodies are a bit more like my own: Toney, the alligator-skinned boy, was normal except for a horrible skin condition. Grady Stiles, also known as Lobster Man, had fingers and toes that were fused into pincerlike claws. He fathered a family of lobster children and beat his wives. The double-thumbed man, face a blur behind hands in the foreground, is billed as the "best cotton-picker around." These people's bodies seem grounded in the ordinary, but yanked out of control by some unseen force. Or perhaps they are rebelling from within.

Freak shows, unlike gyms, are an explicit context for bodily display. Hence they are a guilty pleasure, like the stripteases at Chippendales and the Blue Angel. The pleasure of watching freak shows is so guilty, in fact, that they've been all but eliminated from our culture, ostensibly because the performers are dehumanized by being exhibited. But perhaps it's also because people are even more ashamed of disgust than they are of lust. Or because we assume it feels worse to display an aberrant body partly clothed than a naked one that's been certified beautiful by the manager of a strip club. Still, freak shows and strip shows are not so far apart, really. We assume it is degrading to exhibit oneself in either situation. We take pleasure in watching these degrading displays, and feel slightly ashamed of that pleasure. Is it the transaction of money we find so shameful? Is it the overt nature of the exhibition? Or is it the visceral reaction of lust or repulsion that these displays inspire? Perhaps it is how close the two are to each other.

At Coney Island, just off Surf Avenue, a sideshow barker draws a crowd. A man stands next to him holding an enormous albino boa constrictor. Families and couples gaze up at them with nervous fascination. Sideshows by the Seashore is a traditional "ten in one." For a single price, you can go in and watch a series of rotating performances. For the past seven or eight years, when I have seen it, the show consisted irregularly of a contortionist, an illustrated man, a sword swallower, a snake charmer, an escape artist, and a man who pounds nails into his face. Like ThEnigma, Tom Comet, the chainsaw juggler, and everyone else in Jim Rose's sideshow, the Coney Island performers were self-made freaks. They exhibited unusual control over their bodies. They could withstand pain or they were extraordinarily flexible. No one in the show was born with anything anyone would call a defect. No one suffered any disfiguring accident beyond the dislocated shoulder that allowed a Latino teenager to get out of a straitjacket while hanging upside down.

Recently, however, the sideshow has begun to feature a bearded lady (or "woman with a beard," as she prefers to be called)—real as real can be. Her name is Zenobia—Jennifer Miller by day. She is young and angry, and when I saw her perform she juggled and made wisecracks until the audience heckled her so much she stormed off stage. "The world is full of women with beards," runs her patter. "Or at least they have the potential to have a beard . . . instead of spending the time, and the money, on the waxing, and the shaving, and the electrolysis, and the plucking. We all know someone who plucks. Pluck, pluck, pluck, as if these women were chickens!" She claims that hair is power—that's why the men don't want the women to have too much of it. And her point is that she is not a freak at all, though she displays herself as one. "Ten times a day," she told *The New York Times,* "I address in the strongest, most forthright terms feminist issues of appearance and dress. I use the platform of the sideshow to defreakify."

The people who run the sideshow tell me about the fat lady who performed there a couple years ago. "Helen Melon," also known as performance artist Katie Dierlam, had an act similar to Miller's in that she talked openly about her weight in a feminist monologue that confronted people's morbid curiosity head-on. She also mooned the audience. The sideshow guys point out to me how different this is than the passive exhibition of Howard Huge, a fat man in a Florida sideshow who quietly stuffs lunch into himself while a voice-over details his breakfast for the audience: sixteen eggs, four pounds of bacon, and so on.

A short film about Miller, *Juggling Gender,* treads the same fine line between feminist assertion and exploitation of freakishness that her own performance as Zenobia does. A long slow-motion sequence in a bathtub serves to answer any questions viewers have about Miller's sex, the amount of hair on her body (a goodish amount on legs, nothing out of the ordinary anywhere else), or her bra cup size (I'd guess B). The sequence ends with an extended close-up of Miller's breasts. The film invites prolonged contemplation of this exposed freakish body, even more than do the sideshow performances in which Miller lies topless on a bed of nails. On the other hand, it offers an alternative aesthetic to culturally standard notions of beauty, and Miller's analytical commentary and emotional vulnerability in the film make her decidedly less freakish than her more showmanlike performances do.

I saw Miller again as queen of Concy Island's annual Mermaid Parade, her hair in a fancy French twist, wearing blue false eyelashes and a blue feather boa to match. She did not wear a dress, the usual attire of bearded ladies I've seen in photographs, but the concession she'd made to social norms of beauty on the day of the parade seemed to me even braver than the beard she wore; it is easier to reject such norms entirely than to acknowledge their appeal when forever barred from achieving them. In dressing that way, making her self-display overt and deliberate, she made herself more fully a freak than she had been in other contexts.

A few blocks away, standing near the kiddy rides with an elderly man and a number of teenagers, I pass a woman with a population of curly black hairs on her cheeks and chin. They've been shaved or waxed recently, but they're growing back. She's wearing a white vinyl minidress and black knee socks. Her straightened hair lies in heavy bangs against her forehead, and she's engaged in a complicated negotiation with the kids about Snow-Kones. I wonder if she's seen Miller reigning over the Mermaid Parade. And whether she thinks the bearded lady is a queen, or a freak.

The sideshow has added a little person this year, too. Koko the Killer Clown is "The Midget That Did It!" I see him lounging shirtless on the barker's platform after the parade, offering himself for observation in a sort-of halfway stance between performance and everyday life. He isn't dressed for a show, or doing anything particular; he is drinking a soda and having a rest. But he is on a stage, and exposing more of his midget body than most people have ever seen of such a person. A man in a Coney Island T-shirt snaps at him, "Are you wearing your costume? The show's about to start." Koko hustles backstage. Later, I see the same man patting him on the head.

Across the midway, a sign is up: LITTLE GLORIA, it reads; THE WORLD'S SMALLEST WOMAN. 29 INCHES TALL. WEARS A SIZE 2 SHOE. $10,000 REWARD IF NOT ALIVE AND REAL. A scrawny teenage boy and I are the only customers anywhere near the exhibit, which stands rather desolate on a blacktop lot. A man is washing off the painted front with a garden hose. We pay our entry fees and go inside.

Little Gloria is a Jamaican midget watching TV. She wears a short floral dress and a hairnet over her graying Afro. She sits on a large, rather dirty cushion, drinking a diet soda.

"Hello!" she says, looking up. Her voice is full of energy, as if she's making an effort at diffusing our tension. "I'm Gloria. How are you today?" She shakes hands with the boy, but does not offer her hand to me. Neither of us says our names in return, perhaps because we feel guilty goggling at this tiny old woman and don't want to name ourselves in the process, perhaps because neither of us expected the exhibit to be interactive. There is a plastic bucket by the television set. "Tips," it reads. "For Medicine." I put a dollar in and ask Gloria if she's been in freak shows before.

"Oh yes," she says. "All my life. In Jamaica before this."

"She can't work!" interrupts a woman in pale pink lipstick who is standing near the exit. I cannot tell if she is Gloria's friend, or merely a lingering, overinvested customer. "Look at her! She's not like you. If you had a big, rich husband, would you hire her to clean your house?"

"Sure . . ." I start to say.

"She can't do it! She can't do the work!" the woman barks. "She can't get around! That's why she have to do this sort of thing!"

Outside, a few families have gathered. "Is it real?" a woman with a stroller asks me.

"She's real." I tell them. "I spoke with her." The woman leaves the stroller with her husband and takes her four-year-old inside.

Last year there was a two-headed human baby on the midway. BORN TO LIVE! the sign read. I look for it this year, but it isn't there. It's been replaced by an exhibit front with a picture of a sexy blonde in a swimsuit: THE HEADLESS WOMAN. CENTERFOLD MODEL DECAPITATED. CONDEMNED TO A LIVING DEATH. . . . WATCH HER BREATHE! I pay my dollar to see a mirror illusion featuring a plump African-American girl in a T-shirt and bike shorts. Later, I ask one of the men who works the sideshow about the two-headed baby. He is slim, dressed in black despite the heat, with long hair and thin beard. Will he tell me what was inside? Yes, he will. Yvonne and Yvette. Two heads, one body, three arms. They lived a few weeks, a hundred years ago, then died. They've been preserved in formaldehyde or something ever since.

"Those kids are my inheritance," he tells me, explaining that the guy who ran that exhibit is a relation of his. Now Yvonne and Yvette have moved out to California. There's another pair, too, the man tells me. Boys, with a single, perfect body shared between two heads. I do not catch their names. "At Christmas," the man tells me, "we take them out, and sit them under the tree. The children should get to have Christmas!" He laughs.

Unlike the Sideshows' self-made performers, Jennifer Miller, Helen Melon, Koko the Killer Clown, and Little Gloria are all exhibiting freakishness based on a *lack* of control over their bodies rather than an unusual amount of it. The "born" freaks don't stop being stared at when the day is over. Nor have they chosen their strange bodies, like the illustrated man. Imagining their discomfort in themselves (which may be entirely a projection of my own anxieties) creates a kind of guilt in seeing them perform, or—in the case of Little Gloria and exhibits like her—in simply seeing them. Is it wrong to look at these people? Is it more exploitative to see them onstage than in the subway? Or is it less so, because onstage they invite the spectator, and earn a paycheck for doing so? Why do I, and other people, want to look at all?

Literary critic Rosemarie Garland Thomson has pointed out that freak shows render their viewers "comfortably common and safely standard" by comparison—in other words they reaffirm our normalcy. I think she has a point, but for me, at least, part of the appeal of looking at freaks is a feeling of recognition. Think about this: the two-headed baby in a jar is exhibited behind a banner out front that says BORN TO LIVE. Why? Because people much prefer a live freak to a dead one. No matter how real it is, the baby is disappointing, because a crucial part of the strange pleasure involved in looking at an aberrant body is a mangled, fearful empathy. Yvonne and Yvette haven't felt anything for nearly a century, and we cannot project our feelings onto them, nor respond to them with the selfish, visceral ache that a living, breathing freak inspires.

Jennifer Miller complains that men respond to her much better than women do, and says she is frustrated with the "hate" she feels radiating toward her in lesbian bars. That complaint helps me understand my response to her and to the other freaks who, like her, seem grounded in the ordinary. I—and from what Miller says, other women—feel threatened even as I feel fascinated, because I can identify with her rebellious body. It reminds me of my own. She shows me what could happen if I lose control.

What I'm trying to explain is that my curiosity about freaks is linked to those moments when my own body seems alien to me. I'm not so much talking about feeling ugly, although that's a related feeling, but about times when a short wave of horror washes over me at my own physique, when I gross myself out. Times like those early teenage excavations of my acne-spotted face; when I look at my toes too long and cannot believe those stubby, hairy things are attached to my body; when I squeeze the flesh of my legs and unutterable shapes form beneath my skin; when I look at my face in a magnifying mirror; when I vomit and realize that inside me is a horrific molten landscape. The mutant hand. These are moments when my body is rebelling, flouting my expectations for its behavior and alienating me from it.

Being bald, once I had done it and couldn't take it back, also created a sense of dissociation, of my body behaving without my mind's sanction; something akin to what I imagine freaks might feel. But why exactly is that so horrible, whether the cause is deformity, or illness, or age? Perhaps death is teasing me whenever my body rebels, taunting me with an immanent putridity I can never prevent. Or am I afraid of old age, the nearly imperceptible changes that will one day make my own body a stranger to me, incontinent and bent double with the years? Or maybe the sense of horror is rooted in my culture's preoccupation with keeping control of the body at all times, keeping in burps and farts, toilet training as early as possible, lifting up breasts, covering genitalia, chewing with the mouth closed. The rebellious body is a social sin. When my body reasserts itself, spewing its insides out through mouth or skin, moving involuntarily, I am violating some of the earliest rules I was ever taught.

I notice that the dissociation I felt as a bald woman was distinctly different from how I feel about the little bit of freakishness that remains to me now my hair has grown back. My tattoo simply gives me pleasure in self-decoration. Other people may see it as freakish—a woman in a Florida candy store told me I'll need a long-sleeved wedding dress, and one former flame could talk about nothing else when I ran into him at a party—but I do not. Self-constructed aberrant bodies—ThEnigma, Coney Island's illustrated man (the late Mike Wilson), sidewalk junkies wearing purple mohawks and safety pins in their noses, the man in my neighborhood who dyes his beard in rainbow colors, or even the bodybuilders at my gym—I view them with a fascination that is a kind of yearning for experience. Those people take risks with their bodies and identities that would be unthinkable to most everyone else.

I don't view physical anomalies with a yearning fascination, but with a slightly fearful one that invokes my own sense of dissociation, of bodily rebellion. Freaks do not necessarily reaffirm my normalcy, as Thomson claims. They remind me of our kinship.

On the edge of sleep, people's bodies twitch. Sometimes I am awake enough to feel my own twitches, the spasms in legs and arms that propel me into the unknown. The mutant hand takes over my normal hand, and the stubby fingers jerk as they escape from my conscious influence over them. My body has a life of its own, which asserts itself more and more as I edge toward unconsciousness. It is not under my control. Nor will it ever be.

octogenarians

the lukewarm pool contains five bathers, two of whom wear the wraparound sunglasses prescribed after cataract operations. They

swim gingerly, heads protected from the sun by scarves and baseball caps, chins kept out of the water. Sometimes they stand, arms
waving smoothly through the chlorine drink, sharing this week's
news. This one did that, that one did this. An old man lies on a
deck chair, covered head to knee with a yellow towel, resting after
his swim. His wife, wearing slippers and a brightly colored house-
dress, shuffles into the pool area and gently wakes him. "Can I
put your hat on your head?" she asks, helping him to sit up. He
doesn't answer.

I am conspicuous in my poolside lounger, wearing a bikini and
drinking bottled water. "Is that a tattoo?" I hear a miniature
woman with snowy hair ask her paid companion.

"Yes," the companion answers. "But it's okay, now. They all
have them."

"Oh, all right," replies the woman, apparently content.

Grandma B. lives here at Pondside Retreat. It is a retirement
community. Nineteen white condo buildings, three or four pools,
a library, shuffleboard court and bowling alley, a community center where Clinton once spoke. Hanukkah dinners for charity and
group trips to Vegas. Gambling on computerized slot machines
once a week at a nearby Indian reservation. Thunderstorms most
afternoons. Pondside is a culture of the aged, a Floridian micro-
cosm whose rituals and relationships are deeply rooted in the
bodies of its inhabitants: what they can manage, what they enjoy,
what is important in the years after eighty. Rhythms of social life,
fashions, and friendships all grow out of consideration for an
antique frame. People here are watching their fears about declining come true, and they shape their social institutions accordingly.

Pondside is in possession of the Amazons. Women run the
library, coordinate fund-raising events, do volunteer work, go to
building meetings, decide where to have dinner, dominate the
poolside chat. The men, disillusioned perhaps with the reality of
a long-awaited retirement, die relatively young. Everyone seems
to be a widow, many people twice over. When a man is visible—
jogging lightly in golf pants, holding a brown paper bag, shuffling

with a lopsided gait down the hallway, timidly ringing a doorbell
to help a neighbor with her recalcitrant air conditioner—he behaves
with a quiet passivity. He expects or offers service with an implicit
comfort in the division of labor and leisure by sex.

Walking with Grandma B., I pass a softly shriveled man, bent
precariously forward and supported by a cane. Gram clutches my
arm. "Let me tell you what goes on in this Peyton Place," she says
when he is out of earshot. Here is what I learn: Mr. Greenbaum is
ninety-six. One day, not long ago, a woman arrived at Pondside's
security office saying she was worried about him. He was expecting her to come over, she explained, but he wasn't answering the
doorbell. She had called and shouted and knocked and rung, to
no answer. She was worried he was sick, or dying, or something.
Security opened up Mr. Greenbaum's apartment to find him in
the best of health, lying naked in the bedroom, awaiting the prostitute he was too deaf to hear calling. "Whenever I feel blue,"
confides Grandma B., "I just picture him spread-eagled on the
bed. You saw him, how small he is. I picture him spread-eagled
and I just laugh!"

Hanging out with Gram's friends, most of whom she's known
for over twenty years, I am struck by their attitudes toward relationships and by their ironic sense of history, both of which seem
like the result of the community's collective physical frailty.

Diane is a smoker, and the ground-glass voice of what must be
a sixty-year cigarette habit contrasts with her upswept blond hair
and wide eyes. She ushers me past her husband, Ira, who is
watching television in their living room. They have been married
since Diane was eighteen. Ira used to be a candy maker. He is
dressed all in pink. He isn't joining us today because he has
Alzheimer's. Diane and I go out to the porch where she plumps
herself into a rocking chair. "This is what you have to look forward to," she laughs. "Rocking."

Diane's aunt Maudie, she tells me, died last April at eighty-six,
only a few years older than Diane is now. Maudie was looking for
love until the very end, and finding it, too, apparently. Having run

away from home at age fourteen, she had been married three times when she came to Pondside, twice to men who broke her bones. "All of her marriages were gentile," says Diane with an expression of mild amazement. Herman, Maudie's third husband, was in the service when they first met. "When he came out," Diane tells me, "they went to stay with his folks. They were real hillbillies. They had nothing to eat. Herman's father was abusive. He beat his wife. He broke Maudie's nose. She in return picked up her foot and kicked him right in the groin. He couldn't walk for four weeks."

Herman was a pipe fitter and Maudie worked as a waitress. During their twenty-seven-year marriage, they moved around a lot, eventually settling in Pensacola, Florida. In her seventies, Maudie would get up every morning, get in the car, and drive to the shopping center to have her free coffee at Albertson's. Everybody knew her. . . . "But all through their marriage she'd been beaten up," says Diane, bringing her focus back to Maudie's painful physical history. "There was no part of her body that wasn't broke. When she came down here [after he died] she was so damn sick. . . . Her outing was going to the bank and going to Eckerts [the drugstore]. But she didn't walk out of the house unless her wig was on right and her colors. Purple and pink were her best colors. Even her car was purple. . . . She matched perfectly. Everything had to be long-sleeved. She had skinny arms and she didn't want to show the markings on her arms. . . . It took till eleven, twelve, one o'clock before you could even tell her you want to go out somewhere because she had to put on her eyebrows and her blue eye shadow. And even her glasses were pink. . . . She was a very sick lady, extremely sick, but as old as she was she was looking for a man. But he had to have three things: He had to have hair on his head; he couldn't be fat; and he had to be nice-looking. But no sex. She wasn't interested in sex, she was only interested in someone to be a companion. She wouldn't cook. She told them plain: 'I don't cook; no sex.'"

"What about just kissing?" I ask.

"That I never asked her!" laughs Diane. "Whether she wanted to be felt up or whether . . . She came in here about three weeks before she died and told me she met somebody at Publix [the supermarket]. A young man. I says, 'You're out of your mind.' She says, 'He's absolutely gorgeous.' She got very sick after that. She wouldn't let me call nine-eleven, and by the time they got there she was gone."

Maudie's interest in romance—her prerequisites for it, as well as its importance to her—is not uncommon at Pondside. I never expected that talking with old people about their bodies—people who were facing the physical decline everyone in our culture is so urgently trying to avoid—would mean talking about sexuality. But it does, although that's not quite the same as talking about screwing. In fact, the romances here seem based on something other than sex, the lack of which is several times mentioned to me as a key condition for a relationship. Physical attraction is important, but contact is not, at least not to the women with whom I spoke. Mr. Greenbaum is considered undesirable because he is a dirty old man, and a ninety-year-old guy in Diane's building was turned down for a date because he is too sexual. Diane also tells me about a male Alzheimer's patient (not Ira) who became "oversexed. He wants [his wife] in bed all the time. She says, 'Who needs it?' He wants it five, six times a day. By me, once in seven months would be fine!"

Marty, an effervescent, birdlike woman, has been widowed twice. Her second husband died nearly twenty years ago, and since then she has dated a bit. Her most recent boyfriend was several years back. "I could remain as a friend with him," Marty said, "but he wanted to get married and I just didn't want to."

"But it was a romantic relationship?" I asked her.

"It wasn't what you would call romantic, but we were very comfortable with one another."

"Did you kiss?"

"Oh yes, sure. Of course."

"Were you staying overnight and things?"

"Oh no, no. None of that stuff!" Marty gently changes the subject.

Of course, some Pondside women take an interest in sex. Even so, the relationships I hear about are established in a practical and efficient fashion, remarkably free of romantic idealism. Marty's ex was snapped up immediately by a woman who was being forced out of her apartment and needed a place to live.

It is open season on men just widowed. "If a man's wife dies here, women start knocking on his door. . . . They must read the obituary!" grouses Diane. Grandma B. tells me the story of two people in her building: The woman, Ann, flaunted a string of pearls given to her by Isaac, a recent widower. The necklace had belonged to Isaac's wife, barely cold in her grave. But "ten days later it was all kaput. . . . Now," says Grandma B., "[Ann's] got another one she goes with. She's a homely looking woman, but she got a hold of this Fishkin. He looks like he's only seventy."

Violet is a relative of mine so many times removed I don't know what the term is. She sits me down in an armchair and stands in the center of her parlor, arms spread wide. "Look around you," she smiles, pointing at the needlepoint pictures lining her walls. "Hobby, hobby, hobby, hobby." A voluptuous woman with a shock of bright red hair, Violet has a skin graft on her calf that is inclined to swell. She sleeps every night in a reclining chair to keep it elevated. "It's very comfortable," she tells me. "An additional reward is that everyone looks at me and says, 'When did you have your hair done?' The back gets messed up, but the front of my hair always looks like it just had a set. They think my beautician is wonderful, but she tells them she's only wonderful 'cause I sleep in the recliner!"

Violet tells me the story of a Pondside man who wrote a lightly fictionalized account of goings-on in the community. He self-published it and passed it around to all his friends. It was based on the well-known promiscuous adventures of Sylvia, an acquaintance of Violet's. Sylvia met a man, Joe, at a dance. Joe's wife would never go out: not to the movies, not dancing, not anything.

According to Violet, the adventuress "finagled him into divorcing his wife . . . he musta been married about thirty, forty years. All the neighbors in that building turned against him for what he had done." Joe and Sylvia married and moved to a new apartment in Pondside. Nine months later, they went to Scandinavia on a cruise. There, he died of a heart attack. They had to ship his body back.

Violet paid Sylvia a shiva call. "I think he deserves thirty days of mourning," said Sylvia. "But then I'm going to start going to dances."

"So," says Violet, "she went to the dance and met a real jerk. I said to her, 'How could you just jump from jump to jump to jump?' She said, 'Oh, this one I really love.'" Next thing Sylvia knew, her new boyfriend was trying to get his name put on the deed to Joe's honeymoon apartment. When she refused, he left her. She wasn't alone long, though. She met Arthur, a nice gentile man, and moved into a different condo in Pondside with him. They fixed it up, he bought a new car, and then Sylvia left him, moving in by herself to an apartment in the same building. She found somebody else, Saul, but Arthur still takes care of her car, washing it and keeping it in good repair.

"Saul has no family, no money, but they became very, very close," Violet explains. "She said to me, 'I don't care if he can't afford to take me to nice restaurants. I don't care if he only pays five ninety-five for dinner. I'll go with him.' Now Saul had an operation, a prostate operation, and she don't want him anymore. . . . That's condo living. And this is all in that man's book!" Violet leans back in the recliner and holds up her hands.

If younger women had told me these stories, I might think them callous and jaded. Since they came from octogenarians, I wonder if they're just realistic. With only one exception, the women I spoke to despaired of love in retirement years. They all disdained women who actively looked for romance, seeing them as feeling inadequate without a man, and willing to be subservient. Their attitudes seemed to come from frustration with the sex roles that may have felt natural in younger days. I got the impression that sexual contact was equated with household drudgery—the appeal of one erased by the unpleasantness of the other. It also seems like health—the ability to go dancing, or to dinner, to "get around beautifully" and not require caretaking—is a major factor in someone's appeal, substituting, almost, for personality, or education, or shared interests.

Violet shows me an old photograph, taken in 1939 on the beach. She is vamping in a wet black suit, curvy and confident, classic cheesecake. She met her husband at the seashore, right before the war. "He used to take me for a walk in the evening and we always ended up at the travel agent's." The two of them traveled all over the world, avoiding only the communist countries. He always dreamed of going to Israel. When they finally went, he got sick in the middle of the trip and died not long after. He's been gone for nine years.

Violet has had a couple of boyfriends since then. But, she says, "No bedroom activities or anything. I made it understood right at the beginning I just wanted to be friends." Since she tells me she was a virgin before she got married, I wonder that she wouldn't be interested in being with a new person after having just one man all her life. "No," she answers. "I had no interest. . . . The women get together and they talk about these things. It's a matter of making sure the laundry is done and making sure that everything is taken care of and making sure that dinner is made, and breakfast, and lunch. This is in the past for me."

"A man is looking for somebody to cook for him, to clean for him," says Diane.

"These guys just want someone to pay half the rent, do the laundry, et cetera," echoes Grandma B.

Many of the women have never had to deal with household finances, automobile maintenance, insurance companies, and so forth. They trade homemaking duties for financial security and an understanding of carburetors. When the husband or boyfriend requires more than the standard amount of care, though, the women will often leave, almost as if the taint of decline were catching. And in a way, with so little time left and so few physical resources to cope with the strain of nursing duties, it is. Marty explains simply and without bitterness the reason she didn't want to marry a third time: "I just didn't want to be a nursemaid anymore."

Health is the dominant concern among Pondside residents. It is anything but trivial. It shapes these people's lives in a way their education, their friendships, and their jobs have not. "I'm just glad that I feel well enough to do the things that I do," says one woman thankfully. So many of her peers do not feel well enough at all, or find their daily activities circumscribed by poor health, their own or that of those they love. Ira, the shy candy man who almost dropped dead of surprise when Diane sat in his lap on their second date, is succumbing to Alzheimer's in the sixty-third year of their marriage. Diane would like to travel, to spend some of the savings they worked to put aside for so many years. Although Ira's bodily health does not prevent him, his disease makes him anxious about money and he doesn't want to part with any. "He's like a three-year-old all of a sudden."

Diane's mother was in a nursing home until she died two years ago, and Diane visited every day. Aunt Maudie required nearly as much care: "She had a lung problem, she was wearing a pacemaker, her stomach was not good. I had her to seven of the finest doctors here in Florida and nobody could help her. But she was one that was so feisty. She would never say she can't go. Wanna go? Go. The bunions on her foot from the gout were so bad she couldn't walk. She had to cut holes out of all her shoes. And they had to match!"

Violet has had two cataract operations, and recently, an unusual kind of calcium deposit on her cornea. Many of her friends then rushed to the eye doctor to see if they had the same problem. None of them did, of course. None of them even had the symptoms that had led Violet to get her eyes checked in the first place. Crazy as that sounds, this is not a community of hypochondriacs. It is a culture in which health is the key to happiness. An ill or aging body can become a prison. A hysterectomy at a young age, a husband's bad heart, a mother's weak frame, a cataract operation, skin cancer: these are the things that structure the rhythms of life at Pondside. They decide sexual and social relationships. Men's shorter life span is the largest determining factor, but the bodily histories these people have carry enormous weight in their personal interactions: Aunt Maudie's broken bones, the oversexed man with Alzheimer's, Joe's wife's waning energy, Violet in the recliner chair. Health determines who floats in the pool and gets the gossip, who plays Friday night canasta, how early dinner is. It determines what people eat, and whom they see. Days are filled with foot doctors, dentists, eye doctors, nursing home visits.

"Years ago," says Diane, "nobody knew from all the sicknesses. You died, you died. You got sick, you got sick. It didn't have a name. Today, it's diabetes, and it's cancer, and it's osteoporosis, and it's high blood pressure or low blood pressure or you got gout. All of a sudden everything's got a name. . . . Then there's arthritis and you can't move and then you got a disk and your back don't work so good and your kidneys don't work so good. You don't think of any of this when you're young."

I am back from Florida, now. I have a tan. Soaking up the light, basking in warmth, my senses tell me that the sun is good for me. My whole body cries it out. I feel it. I cannot believe I am killing myself with cancer, though everyone tells me so. The wagging finger of the medical world is rebuking me. The threat of melanoma is lurking behind a beach chair.

I do not know whom to trust: my senses, or my doctors. Is this decline masquerading as nourishment? What exactly am I supposed to fear? I suspect that even if skin cancer didn't exist, the fact that we equate wrinkles with decay and illness would make people tell me I shouldn't lie out—eschewing the sun, they would tell me, "prevents aging," and denying my body the pleasure of a sun bath will help forestall bodily rebellion. Possibly. Later on, they tell me, I'll be thankful. I compromise by wearing sunblock. But I also lie to those who love me about how much I'm wearing and how often I use it. And I wonder what this vice will bring upon me.

My skin, in the mirror, looks glorious: golden brown, with a glow of pink on my nose and cheeks. Up close, though, it is strange. It shrivels along the folds of my abdomen when I lean forward, like the edge of a half-cooked steak. It erupts in tiny, blistering bubbles along my shoulders; it has contracted across the backs of my knees and is beginning to flake and peel on my hipbones.

Eating the early bird suppers and strolling gingerly through the shopping malls and bingo parlors of Grandma B.'s retirement, I have kissed face after face mapped through with wrinkles. Soft cheeks are criss-crossed with furrows. The skin is not leathery, but more like crumpled linen, warm from the dryer. "I got these wrinkles because I earned them!" Diane tells me. "They wouldn't give them to me for nothing!" She's got a pride in her age that accompanies her frustration with the illnesses that plague her friends and family. Her body is slowly rebelling—refusing to keep up the pace, refusing to keep up the appearance of youth—but even as she resents its rebellion, Diane can embrace it, for her body reflects her mind, and her history.

My own young flesh shows unearned wrinkles, products of my idle hours by the Pondside pool. Its tightness ever so slightly restricts my movement, preventing my usual fluid stretch of limbs. The invisible scarring caused by the sun reminds me of its presence with a persistent itch. Here is a taste of the physical changes that will come with age. My tan is telling me the future.

bibliography

Below is a selected list of the printed sources I used to research *Tongue First*. Most I quote from or discuss directly, but a few simply served as inspiration or starting points for thinking about certain issues. I have not listed web sites, e-mail lists, newsgroups, pamphlets, CD-ROMs, films, performances, or personal interviews, although I relied on such sources as well.

Abramsky, Sasha, and Kristan Schiller. "Decent Exposure." *Time Out New York,* April 10, 1996, pp. 6–9.

American Sunbathing Association. *Bare With Us: Nudist Park Guide.* Orlando, FL: ASA, 1975.

Anand, Margo. *The Art of Sexual Ecstasy: The Path of Sacred Sexuality for Western Lovers.* New York: Putnam, 1989.

———. *The Art of Sexual Magic.* New York: Putnam, 1995.

Anson, Briah. *Rolfing: Stories of Personal Empowerment.* Kansas City, MO: Heartland Personal Growth Press, 1991.

Arbus, Diane. *Untitled.* New York: Aperture, 1995.

Baker, Roger. *Drag: A History of Female Impersonation in the Performing Arts.* London: Cassell, 1994.

Bakos, Susan Crain. *Kink: The Hidden Sex Lives of Americans.* New York: St. Martin's Press, 1995.

Bogdan, Robert. *Freak Show: Presenting Human Oddities for Amusement and Profit.* Chicago: University of Chicago Press, 1988.

Bordo, Susan. *Unbearable Weight: Feminism, Western Culture and the Body.* Berkeley, CA: University of California Press, 1993.

Brain, Robert. *The Decorated Body.* New York: Harper & Row, 1979.

Bright, Susie. *Sexwise.* Pittsburgh, PA: Cleis, 1995.

Cahn, Susan. *Coming On Strong: Gender and Sexuality in Twentieth-Century Women's Sport.* New York: Free Press, 1994.

Califia, Pat. *Public Sex: The Culture of Radical Sex.* Pittsburgh, PA: Cleis, 1994.

Carskadon, Mary A., ed. *The Encyclopedia of Sleep and Dreaming.* New York: Macmillan, 1993.

Chang, Stephen Thomas. *The Complete Book of Acupuncture.* Berkeley, CA: Celestial Arts, 1976.

Chermayeff, Catherine, Jonathan David, and Nan Richardson. *Drag Diaries.* San Francisco, CA: Chronicle Books, 1995.

Coleridge, Samuel Taylor. "The Rime of the Ancient Mariner," in *The Norton Anthology of English Literature,* vol. 2, ed. M. H. Abrams. New York: Norton, 1979.

Comfort, Alex. *The New Joy of Sex. A Gourmet Guide for Love-making in the Nineties.* New York: Pocket Books, 1991.

Conrad, Barnaby. *The Martini.* San Francisco, CA: Chronicle Books, 1995.

Cotton, Leo, ed. *Old Mr. Boston DeLuxe Official Bartender's Guide.* Boston, MA: Mr. Boston, 1935.

DeMello, Margaret. "The Carnivalesque Body: Women and Tattoos," *Pierced Hearts and True Love: A Century of Drawings for Tattoos.* New York and Honolulu: The Drawing Center and Hardy Marks, 1995, pp. 73–79.

De Quincey, Thomas. *Confessions of an English Opium-Eater.* 1822. Reprint, London: Penguin, 1971.

DeVoto, Bernard. *The Hour.* Cambridge, MA: Riverside, 1951.

Doyle, Arthur Conan. *Sherlock Holmes: The Complete Novels and Stories.* New York: Bantam, 1986.

Feitis, Rosemary, ed. *Ida Rolf Talks About Rolfing and Physical Reality.* Boulder, CO: Rolf Institute, 1978.

Fleisher, Julian. *The Drag Queens of New York: An Illustrated Field Guide.* New York: Riverhead Books, 1996.

Foster, Patricia, ed. *Minding the Body: Women Writers on Body and Soul.* New York: Anchor/Doubleday, 1994.

Friday, Nancy. *My Secret Garden: Women's Sexual Fantasies.* New York: Trident, 1973.

Fussell, Samuel Wilson. *Muscle: Confessions of an Unlikely Bodybuilder.* New York: Avon, 1991.

Garber, Marjorie. *Vested Interests: Cross Dressing and Cultural Anxiety.* New York: Harper Perennial, 1993.

Gimmy, Arthur, and Brian B. Woodworth. *Fitness, Racquet Sports and Spa Projects.* Chicago: American Institute of Real Estate Appraisers, 1989.

Gray, John. *I Love Mom: An Irreverent History of the Tattoo.* Toronto: Key Porter, 1994.

Green, Harvey. *Fit For America.* New York: Pantheon Books, 1986.

Handler, Evan. *Time on Fire: My Comedy of Terrors.* New York: Henry Holt, 1996.

Heimel, Cynthia. *Sex Tips for Girls.* New York: Simon & Schuster/Fireside, 1983.

Hite, Shere. *The Hite Report. A Nationwide Study on Female Sexuality.* New York: Macmillan, 1976.

Janus, Samuel S., and Cynthia L. Janus. *The Janus Report on Sexual Behavior.* New York: John Wiley & Sons, 1993.

Johnson, Dirk. "Gym Students Still Sweat, They Just Don't Shower," *The New York Times,* April 22, 1996, p. 1.

Kaptchuk, Ted J. *The Web That Has No Weaver: Understanding Chinese Medicine.* Chicago: Congdon and Weed, 1983.

Klein, Alan M. *Little Big Men: Bodybuilding Subculture and Gender Construction*. Albany, NY: State University of New York Press, 1993.

Lasch, Christopher. *The Culture of Narcissism: American Life in an Age of Diminishing Expectations*. New York: Norton, 1978.

Levenson, Randal. *In Search of the Monkey Girl*. Millertown, NY: Aperture, 1982.

Lifson, Robert. *Enter the Sideshow*. Bala Cynwyd, England: Mason, 1983.

Lilly, John C. *The Center of the Cyclone: An Autobiography of Inner Space*. New York: Julian, 1972.

Macy, Marianne. *Working Sex: An Odyssey into Our Cultural Underworld*. New York: Carroll & Graf, 1996.

Mayle, Peter. *Acquired Tastes*. New York: Bantam, 1992.

Nelson, Mariah Burton. *The Stronger Women Get, The More Men Love Football: Sexism and the American Culture of Sports*. New York: Harcourt Brace, 1994.

Polhemus, Ted. *Body Styles*. Luton: Lennard, 1988.

Pollari, Pat. *Garbage Time*. New York: Bantam, 1996.

———. *The Great Puke-off*. New York: Bantam, 1996.

Rand, Erica. *Barbie's Queer Accessories*. Durham, NC: Duke University Press, 1995.

Rice, Anne (writing as A. N. Roquelaure). *Beauty's Punishment*. New York: Plume/Penguin, 1984.

Rolf, Ida P. *Rolfing: Reestablishing the Natural Alignment and Structural Integration of the Human Body for Vitality and Well-Being*. Rochester, VT: Healing Arts, 1977.

Rose, Jim. *Freak Like Me: Inside the Jim Rose Circus Sideshow*. New York: Dell, 1995.

RuPaul. *Lettin' It All Hang Out: An Autobiography*. New York: Hyperion, 1995.

Rusid, Max. *Sideshow: Photo Album of Human Oddities*. New York: Amijon, 1975.

Sanders, Clinton R. *Customizing the Body: The Art and Culture of Tattooing.* Philadelphia, PA: Temple University Press, 1989.

Schumann, Charles. *American Bar: The Artistry of Mixing Drinks.* New York: Abbeville Press, 1995.

Schwartz, Hillel. *Never Satisfied: A Cultural History of Diets, Fantasies and Fat.* New York: Free Press, 1986.

Sedaris, David. *Naked.* New York: Little, Brown, 1997.

Siman, Ken. *The Beauty Trip.* New York: Pocket Books, 1995.

Smith, Dinita. "Step Right Up! See the Bearded Person!" *The New York Times,* June 9, 1995, p. C1.

Solomon, Philip, et al., eds. *Sensory Deprivation: A Symposium Held at Harvard Medical School.* Cambridge, MA: Harvard University Press, 1961.

Steele, Valerie. *Fetish: Fashion, Sex and Power.* New York: Oxford University Press, 1996.

Suedfeld, Peter. *Restricted Environmental Stimulation: Research and Clinical Applications.* New York: John Wiley & Sons, 1980.

Tennyson, Alfred. "The Lady of Shalott," in *The Norton Anthology of English Literature,* vol. 2, ed. M. H. Abrams. New York: Norton, 1979.

Thevoz, Michel. *The Painted Body.* New York: Rizzoli, 1984.

Thomson, Rosemarie Garland, ed. *Freakery: Cultural Spectacles of the Extraordinary Body.* New York: New York University Press, 1996.

Thorpy, Michael J., and Jan Yager. *The Encyclopedia of Sleep and Sleep Disorders.* New York: Facts on File, 1991.

Tierra, Michael. *The Way of Herbs.* New York: Pocket Books, 1990.

Tisdale, Sallie. *Talk Dirty To Me: An Intimate Philosophy of Sex.* New York: Anchor, 1994.

Vale, V., and Andrea Juno, eds. *Modern Primitives.* San Francisco, CA: Re/Search, 1989.

Vallack, Phil. *Nude As a Newt: A Sideways Look into Naturism.* Self-published. Hastings, England, 1991.

Vernon, Jack A. *Inside the Black Room*. New York: Clarkson N. Potter, 1963.

Westheimer, Ruth. *Dr. Ruth's Guide to Good Sex*. New York: Warner Books, 1983.

————. *Dr. Ruth's Guide for Married Lovers*. New York: Warner Books, 1986.

Wilde, Oscar. *The Portable Oscar Wilde,* ed. Richard Aldington and Stanley Weintraub. Middlesex, England: Penguin, 1946.

Wolf, Naomi. *The Beauty Myth: How Images of Beauty Are Used Against Women*. New York: Anchor, 1991.

Wroblewski, Chris. *Tattooed Women*. London: Virgin, 1992.